Practice Test and Review Manual

Scott A. Bailey
TEXAS LUTHERAN UNIVERSITY

THIRD EDITION

Stephen F. Davis
EMPORIA STATE UNIVERSITY

Joseph J. Palladino
UNIVERSITY OF SOUTHERN INDIANA

Prentice Hall, Upper Saddle River, New Jersey 07458

© 2000 by PRENTICE-HALL, INC.
Pearson Education
Upper Saddle River, New Jersey 07458

0-13-022320-4
Printed in the United States of America

CONTENTS

P R E F A C E

HOW TO USE THIS *PRACTICE TEST AND REVIEW MANUAL*

This manual was created especially for you. The format of the manual conforms exactly to your textbook, *Psychology*, Third Edition, by Drs. Steve Davis and Joe Palladino.

Use this manual when you study your textbook and when you prepare for exams and quizzes. The two resources go hand-in-hand. Each chapter of the manual contains a skeletal outline that was taken exactly from the corresponding chapter in the textbook. To get the most from each resource and from your psychology class, find a place to study where you can spread out all your material for the course.

Here are the elements that you will find in the chapters of this manual:

1. **Chapter Overview.** The first page of each chapter of the manual has the artwork and brief outline from the beginning of each respective chapter of the text.

2. **Outline.** The second page of each chapter begins a formal outline of the corresponding chapter from the textbook. Space has been provided so that you may jot down notes or questions that occur to you as you study the text.

   a. **Key Words.** The key words from the text have been italicized and incorporated into the outline in the manual. Use this space to record a definition for each term as you work your way through the chapter.

   b. **Maximize Use of the Text.** The *Tip* section at the end of Chapter 6 of this manual, *Getting the Most from Your Textbook,* presents several ideas that help make the process of studying text material an active one.

3. **Learning Objectives.** At the end of each chapter outline is a list of questions and statements that relate to the content from the chapter. Having studied the chapter, you should be able to address each of these.

4. **Naming Exercises.** Exercises to test your knowledge of key names, terms, and anatomical structures are presented following the learning objectives in each chapter. The correct answers to these items are presented immediately following the practice tests. Naming exercises take one of two forms:

   a. **Labeling Exercises.** In Chapters 2 and 3, you will find figures that represent brain and neuron anatomy and the organs responsible for sensory awareness.

   b. **Key Word Exercises.** For every chapter except Chapters 2 and 3, you will find fill-in-the-blank exercises to test your knowledge of key words.

5. **Practice Tests.** Each chapter has a multiple-choice practice test. Take each of these after you have studied all the material from the relevant chapter. Answers and explanations are presented following the answers for the naming exercises.

6. **Key Vocabulary Term Cards.** After the answers to the practice tests you will find several pages of "cards" that contain the vocabulary terms from the respective chapters. They have the terms on one side and the textbook definition on the other, and can be cut out.

The pages of this manual are perforated to make them easy to remove. When you are preparing for a test, you may find it easier to carry only the pages that correspond to the chapters for which you are responsible. Another suggestion would be to remove and combine the naming exercises and practice tests relevant to the material for the coming test. You could take the tests for all of the chapters at once rather than doing them as you go. Finally, the perforated pages will make it easy to remove and cut up the key vocabulary terms cards.

The manual has been three-hole punched so that you can easily remove and insert the pages into your binder for the class. You will find that organizing your class notes, practice tests, and materials distributed by your professor (including assignments, quizzes, and tests) will be helpful when you need to refer to them in the future. So that you do not lose the vocabulary cards, you may want to purchase some plastic zip-closing sleeves to insert into your binder as well. Consider paper-clipping or rubber-banding the cards together by chapter or by exam unit so that you will know how to find them in the future.

Tips for Success **Topics.** In addition to the chapter-related material, a dozen *Tip for Success* sections are included in this manual. The *Tips* are presented, one per chapter, at the end of the first 12 chapters. Start with the ones that will be of most use to you. The ambitious student will skip ahead and examine each tip within the first few days of the semester. Others will review them throughout the semester. They cover a range of topics (see list below), and represent ideas and techniques that can help you to be your best.

Please Send Your Comments. This *Practice Test and Review Manual* should help you master the content of your psychology course. If you have suggestions for changes to the manual, ideas for exercises that would make learning the material easier, or would be willing to share any other feedback, please send it to:

Scott A. Bailey, Ph.D.
Department of Psychology
Texas Lutheran University
1000 West Court Street
Seguin, Texas 78155
Email: SBailey

CHAPTER 1

Psychology, Research, and You

Use the space provided in this outline to record notes from the textbook as well as from class lectures and discussion. Questions related to the *Psychological Detective* sections in the text have been presented in the outline; use the associated space to respond to the questions and to record your own comments about the issues. *Keywords and terms* from the text have been italicized and inserted into the outline so you can practice writing their definitions. The pages in this study guide are perforated and can be removed for use as study sheets for quizzes and exams.

I. Becoming a Psychological Detective

psychology—

A. Arthur Conan Doyle's Belief in Fairies

1. It may be useful to question statements made by credible people.

2. Bias may unintentionally influence objective thinking.

bias—

B. Mentalism Revealed

 Why are mentalists, such as Kreskin, not so amazing after all?

1. It is important to be clear about claims people make.

2. Given two or more competing explanations, adopt the one that makes the fewest assumptions.

law of parsimony—

C. Guidelines for the Psychological Detective

1. What is the statement or claim and who is making it?

2. Is the statement or claim based on scientific observations?

3. What do statistics reveal?

4. Are there plausible alternatives to the statement or claim?

   placebo effect—

II. Research Methods in Psychology

   scientific method—

   theory—

   hypothesis—

A. The Case Study

   case study—

B. Naturalistic Observation

   naturalistic observation—

C. Correlational Research

   scatterplot—

   correlation coefficient—

List several factors that could be responsible for an association between SAT scores and grade-point averages.

D. Survey Research

survey method—

How might survey questions influence the kind of information produced in response to them?

representative sample—

E. The Experimental Method

experimental method—

independent variable (IV)—

dependent variable (DV)—

operational definition—

experimental group—

control group—

Why is it important to manipulate only one independent variable at a time in an experiment?

extraneous variables—

random assignment—

F. Statistics and Psychologists

🔍 How do statistics help summarize research data for clearer presentation of experimental results?

    statistics—

    descriptive statistics—

🔍 How do measures of central tendency and measures of variability for a given data set help make individual data from the set more meaningful?

    inferential statistics—

1. Descriptive Statistics

    measures of central tendency—

    measures of variability—

2. Inferential Statistics

G. Research Ethics

1. Protection from Harm

2. Confidentiality

3. Voluntary Participation

   informed consent—

4. Deception and Intimidation

   debriefing—

5. The Ethics of Research with Animals

III. The Origins of Modern Psychology

   A. Wundt and Structuralism
      structuralism—

      introspection—

      cognitive psychology—

   B. Functionalism
      functionalism—

   C. Gestalt Psychology
      Gestalt psychology—

   D. The Behavioral Perspective
      behavioral perspective—

   E. Sigmund Freud and the Psychodynamic Perspective
      psychodynamic perspective—

psychoanalytic therapy—

F.   The Humanistic Perspective

     humanistic perspective—

G.   The Physiological Perspective

     physiological perspective—

H.   The Cognitive Perspective

     cognitive perspective—

I.   The Cultural and Diversity Perspective

IV. Present-Day Psychology

     eclectic approach—

V.   Psychological Specialties

A.   Clinical and Counseling Psychology

     clinical psychology—

     psychiatrist—

     counseling psychology—

B.   Other Specialties

     research psychologist—

     ethnocentrism—

cross-cultural psychology—

 List several ways that cultural issues can affect the development and conduct of psychological research.

school psychologist—

industrial and organizational (I/O) psychologist—

consumer psychology—

health psychology—

C. Emerging Specialties

forensic psychologist—

sport psychologist—

neuropsychologist—

After you have studied the chapter, you should be able to respond to the following statements and questions to convey your understanding of the material.

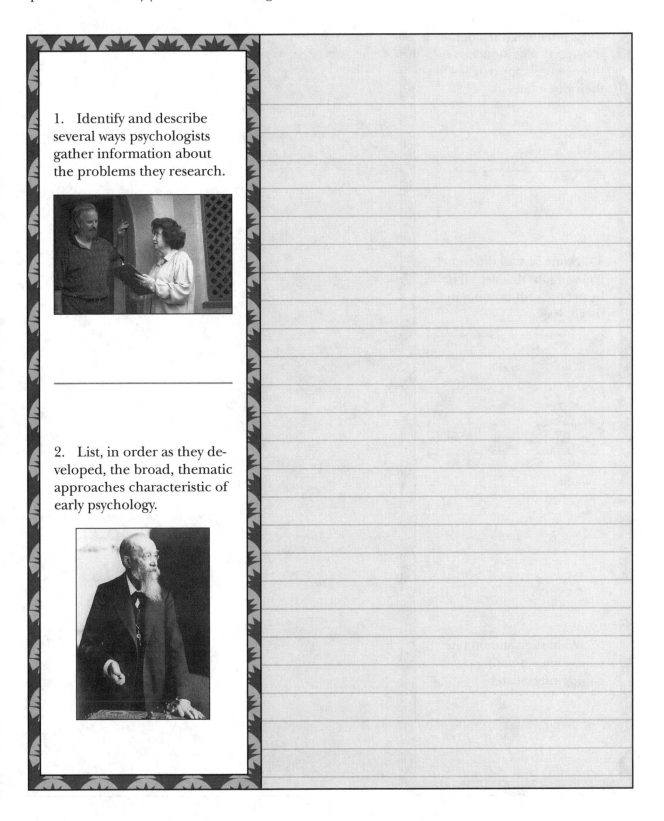

1. Identify and describe several ways psychologists gather information about the problems they research.

2. List, in order as they developed, the broad, thematic approaches characteristic of early psychology.

3. How do the perspectives (e.g., physiological, cognitive) psychologists adopt influence their approaches to their discipline?

4. Name several different types of jobs that are all held by people with training in psychology.

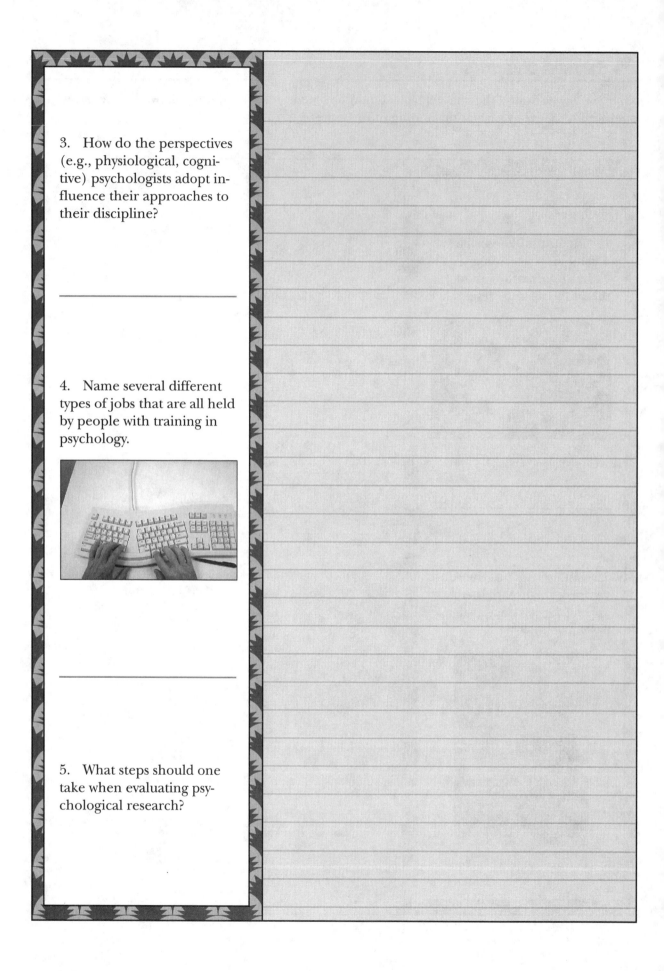

5. What steps should one take when evaluating psychological research?

Fill in the blanks in the following statements with key words and terms from the textbook. Answer as many as you can without referring to your notes or to the book. If you have blanks after thinking about each item, try using your book. The answers are presented after the practice test.

1. Psychologists strive to design experiments that are void of _____ that may unintentionally influence the data they gather.

2. When describing research results, psychologists opt for the most _____ explanations, as they are the ones that rely on the fewest assumptions.

3. A _____ control group is one that illustrates the influence of having taken *any* medication in a drug experiment, even when the medication does not contain an active ingredient.

4. A Sesame Street definition of *hypothesis* is: an educated guess. More specifically, hypotheses are testable ideas that are carefully derived out of organized general principles called _____.

5. Correlations are relationships between sets of two variables in which changes in the level of one variable are associated with changes in the level of the other. The degree of relationship is expressed both in terms of the statistic r, and graphically with a _____.

6. _____ _____ was noted for emphasizing that perception of a whole differs from that of individual stimuli.

7. In spite of efforts to control extraneous variables, researchers are challenged by the fact that these unwanted influences on experimental data will persist. One way to reduce their impact is to distribute them among all the groups in an experiment. However, as they are typically unknown, one must use _____ _____, a technique that is employed in many experimental designs.

8. The _____ _____ was started by Pavlov and continued by Watson as an attempt to get psychologists to focus only on that which is overtly observable.

9. Though Harvard University refused to grant her a Ph.D. because of her gender, _____ _____ _____ was still elected as the 14th president of the APA.

10. The _____ _____ to psychology is one that many psychologists adopt because they use several approaches in their work.

PRACTICE TEST

Circle the letter that corresponds to the *best* alternative for each of the following items. Read each alternative carefully. The answers are presented at the end of this study guide chapter. Be sure to learn *why* each correct alternative is better than the others.

1. Proverbs are examples of:
    a. folk wisdom.
    b. falsifiable hypotheses.
    c. positive action words; their complements are converbs.
    d. universally applicable theories derived from cross-cultural research.

2. As discussed in the text passage on Arthur Conan Doyle's belief in fairies, *mediums* are:
   a. only slightly larger than smalls.
   b. the shirt sizes Doyle's Sherlock Holmes wore.
   c. descriptive statistics that share characteristics with both the mean and the mode.
   d. people who claim they can contact the spirit world and communicate with the dead during a séance.

3. *Bias* can unintentionally:
   a. cloud our observations.
   b. influence the questions we ask.
   c. influence the methods we use and the ways we interpret data.
   d. all of the above are true.

4. Which of the following statements is most parsimonious?
   a. Well-rested participants were more accurate than sleep-deprived participants.
   b. Accuracy of responding is impaired as a function of hormone cycle variations in sleep-deprived participants.
   c. Sleep-deprived participants were too fatigued to concentrate and consequently performed poorly in comparison to well-rested participants.
   d. Hormone cycle shifts, combined with the impact of overall fatigue, impaired the accuracy of functioning in sleep-deprived participants when they were compared to well-rested participants.

5. The experimental method is a preferred means of gathering information because it:
   a. is easy to use in most research contexts.
   b. can provide the basis for cause-and-effect statements.
   c. has a name that conveys credibility, and credibility is the primary goal of psychological research.
   d. is a fairly inexpensive technique when compared with other approaches (e.g., naturalistic observation).

6. Marie's research project indicated, with statistically significant data, that among first year college students, those who took introductory psychology scored higher on a problem-solving test than did a comparable group of students who did not enroll in introductory psychology. According to this statement:
   a. students should take psychology if they get the chance.
   b. psychology students are smarter than non-psychology students.
   c. even though the psychology students did statistically better, they did not perform absolutely better.
   d. psychology students out-performed non-psychology students at a level greater than would be predicted by chance alone.

7. A third-variable problem occurs when people attribute a causal link between:
   a. the second and fourth variables.
   b. experiments, but not within experiments.
   c. two variables that share a relation with another variable.
   d. administrations of the independent and dependent variables.

8. Which of the following was **not** offered in the textbook as a guideline for evaluating a claim?
   a. What do statistics reveal?
   b. In what language are the data in question published?
   c. Is the statement or claim based on scientific observations?
   d. Are there plausible alternative explanations for the statement of claim?

9. Like all scientists, psychologists employ the scientific method to investigate phenomena. The scientific method always involves:
   a. microscopes, beakers, and the like.
   b. summarizing findings into widely applicable laws of behavior.
   c. using theories to derive hypotheses which may be tested experimentally.
   d. challenging daily the claims made by popular press information sources.

10. Which of the following statements is true about the relationship between the case study and naturalistic observation?
    a. Data from both generalize well to other contexts.
    b. Both have limitation but are useful in developing research ideas.
    c. With both, participants are never aware they are being studied.
    d. Naturalistic observation involves essentially several concurrent case studies.

11. Which of the following values is indicative of the strongest degree of relationship between two variables?
    a. $r = -0.8$
    b. $r = -0.2$
    c. $r = +0.1$
    d. $r = +0.75$

12. When conducting survey research, it is important to use a representative sample of the population of interest. In other words,
    a. it is important to survey everyone in the population.
    b. one must gather a population of participants that mirrors the population of actual interest.
    c. contacting state or national governmental representatives should yield an accurate reflection of the population.
    d. the participants should reflect the gender, cultural, and other significant attributes of the population of interest.

13. Within the context of the experimental method, the independent variable is to the dependent variable as ___ is to ___.
    a. measure; manipulate
    b. manipulate; measure
    c. experimental; control
    d. control; experimental

14. If an experiment has a comparison group that does not receive the effect of the independent variable, it may be said that the experiment has a(n):
    a. control group.
    b. extraneous variable.
    c. operational definition.
    d. representative sample.

15. A significant advantage of the experimental method over other techniques for gathering information is that the experimental method can provide the basis for making cause-and-effect statements. This is because when using the experimental method, one manipulates ___ variables, controls for ___ variables, and measures ___ variables
    a. dependent; independent; extraneous
    b. extraneous; dependent; independent
    c. independent; extraneous; dependent
    d. dependent; extraneous; independent

16. Using the random assignment procedure is one way:
    a. to ensure a proper control group.
    b. to control for extraneous variability.
    c. to really mess up an experiment; all assignments should be non-random.
    d. to scramble the independent and dependent variables and to help guard against bias.

17. In Bandura's study of the effects of modeling on aggression, the dependent variable was:
    a. the population of nursery school children.
    b. whether participants were in the experimental group or not.
    c. the number of hits delivered by participants to the Bobo doll.
    d. systematic exposure to either the aggressive model or the non-aggressive model.

18. Descriptive statistics are to inferential statistics as ___ is to ___.
    a. summarize; analyze
    b. analyze; summarize
    c. central tendency; variability
    d. variability; central tendency

19. The ethical guidelines that all experiments must meet concern all but which of the following issues?
    a. protection of subjects from harm
    b. the quality of the experimental design
    c. confidentiality of participants' names and identities
    d. whether subjects are debriefed after participating in an experiment involving deception

20. Much of what we understand about behavior has been learned from experiments involving animal subjects. Partially to address concerns about the use of animal subjects in medical and psychological research, the American Psychological Association has:
    a. promoted the animal rights movement.
    b. come out strongly in favor of experiments involving animals.
    c. adopted a set of principles to consider when designing an experiment.
    d. formed a task force called the Committee on Animals in Medicine and Psychology (CAMP).

21. Modern psychology represents a sort of blending of early philosophy and physiology. The first psychology laboratory did not exist until it was established by Wilhelm Wundt in 1879. Wundt was trained as a physician, but his mission in establishing the laboratory was to:
    a. describe the contents of the mind.
    b. study the purposes of consciousness.
    c. focus the study of behavior on that which was overtly observable.
    d. challenge the notion that conscious experience could be broken down into elements.

22. Sigmund Freud had a profound influence on psychology, although it is important to note that his contributions to the field have been highly controversial. It is interesting to note that Freud's background was:
    a. in neurology.
    b. greater than the sum of its parts.
    c. in the early school of thought in psychology: behaviorism.
    d. characterized by numerous unconscious sexual urges which led him to study psychology.

23. Early psychology was characterized by schools of thought such as Structuralism, Functionalism, Gestalt Psychology, and Behaviorism. Today, psychology:
    a. is in a school of thought known as the Cognitive Movement.
    b. is comprised of two major components: the Basic Movement and the Applied Movement.
    c. bears little resemblance to its earlier forms as its focus has shifted from behavior to consciousness.
    d. is a diversified field that is made up of several specialties, a growing number of which involve providing services to clients.

24. Clinical psychologist is to ___ as psychiatrist is to ___.
    a. Ph.D.; M.D.
    b. M.D.; Ph.D.
    c. less serious problems; serious problems
    d. serious problems; less serious problems

ANSWERS TO KEYWORD EXERCISES

1. biases
2. parsimonious
3. placebo
4. theories

5. scatterplot
6. Gestalt Psychology
7. random assignment

8. behavioral perspective
9. Mary Whiton Calkins
10. eclectic approach

PRACTICE TEST ANSWERS AND EXPLANATIONS

1. a. Proverbs are forms of folk wisdom—a category of information that can provide explanations for every conceivable event, but can never be proved wrong.

2. d. Mediums are people who profess special abilities to communicate with those who have passed.

3. d. Bias, or preconceptions, can unintentionally influence the behaviors of researchers and participants.

4. a. Parsimonious statements (see law of parsimony) are simple explanations that rely on few or no assumptions.

5. b. Scientists prefer the experimental method because by systematically manipulating independent variables in experiments, while also using appropriate control conditions, it becomes possible to infer causal relationships from experimental results.

6. d. Statistically significant data are those that are sufficiently different than one would predict based on chance factors alone.

7. c. Changes in the levels of two different variables often co-occur because both share a link with a third variable, and it is the third variable that is responsible for the correlation. An additional example would be the changes that occur in language acquisition and shoe size as a function of changes in level of maturation. Maturation is responsible for the changes, rather than one of the other two causing changes in the other.

8. b. While it is important to consider the source of information one receives, the textbook focused on critiquing the claim rather than the source for its communication.

9. c. The scientific method is a cyclical process that involves ever adjusting the specificity of theories by way of testing the they hypotheses generate.

10. b. Both are useful in helping develop research questions that may be addressed with the experimental method, but both also have shortcomings with respect to the validity and generalizability of the results they generate.

11. a. The correlation coefficient, r, may potentially assume any value between −1.0 and +1.0, inclusive. The *strength of association* is expressed by the value's proximity to a non-zero integer (+/-1); the *direction of the relationship* is indicated by the value's sign (+ or -).

12. d. Participants that comprise the *sample* in a survey project should reflect the diversity of the larger population that researchers are interested in studying.

13. b. Researchers manipulate independent variables, and measure dependent variables.

14. a. A control group is essentially an experimental group that does not receive the effect of the independent variable. Experimental and control groups are treated similarly in all other ways.

15. c. See explanation to #13, above. Note also that experimenters attempt to control, or hold constant, unwanted, or extraneous, variability.

16. b. One way to control for extraneous variability is to assign participants to groups randomly; this assures that each group is equally likely to have participants with any given characteristic.

17. c. The dependent variable is that which is *measured* in an experiment; Bandura measured hits.

18. a. Descriptive statistics summarize data sets; inferential statistics are analytic in nature.

19. b. Institutional review boards review proposals to determine that the potential participants will be treated ethically; IRBs are not organized to provide feedback on experimental designs.

20. c. The APA is concerned that animals be used in experimentation only after consideration of the seven principles that are presented on page 26 in your textbook.

21. b. Wundt's interest in establishing a laboratory was to describe the contents of the conscious mind.

22. a. Freud was trained as a neurologist. His training facilitated his recognition that the symptoms of one of his patients were neurologically impossible, and that the patient must have had a psychological rather than a neurological disorder.

23. d. Present-day psychology is a diverse field that is comprised of many specialties.

24. a. One must have a Ph.D. to be a clinical psychologist; psychiatrists are medical doctors who specialize in the medical treatment of illnesses.

Key Vocabulary Terms

Cut out and use as study cards; terms appear on one side and definitions are on the other.

psychology

bias

law of parsimony

placebo effect

scientific method

theory

hypothesis

case study

Key Vocabulary Terms

Cut out and use as study cards; terms appear on one side and definitions are on the other.

Beliefs that interfere with objectivity	Science of behavior and mental processes
In drug research, positive effects associated with a person's beliefs and attitudes about the drug, even when it contains no active ingredients	Principle that simple explanations of phenomena are preferred to complex explanations
Explanation for a phenomenon based on careful and precise observations	System involving careful observations of a phenomenon, proposal of theories to explain it, hypotheses about future behaviors, and tests of hypotheses through more research
In-depth study of a single person that can often provide suggestions for further research	Prediction about future behaviors that is derived from observation and theories

naturalistic observation	scatterplot
correlation coefficient	survey method
representative sample	experimental method
independent variable (IV)	dependent variable (DV)
operational definition	experimental group

Figure that illustrates a relationship between two variables

Study of behavior in its typical setting, with no attempt to alter it

Research method that involves collecting information from a selected group of people who are representative of a larger group

Number ranging between +1.00 and −1.00 that represents the degree and direction of relationship between two variables

Research method that involves manipulating independent variables to determine how they affect dependent variables

Sample selected so that it reflects the characteristics of a population of interest to the researcher

Variable that shows the outcome of an experiment by revealing the effects of an independent variable

Variable manipulated by a researcher to determine its effects on a dependent variable

The group in an experiment that receives the effect of the independent variable being manipulated

A careful and precise definition that allows other researchers to repeat an experiment

control group	extraneous variables
random assignment	statistics
descriptive statistics	inferential statistics
measures of central tendency	measures of variability
informed consent	debriefing

Variable, other than the independent variable, that can influence the outcome of an experiment

A comparison group in an experiment that does not receive the effect of the independent variable being manipulated

Branch of mathematics that involves collection, analysis, and interpretation of data

Assignment of experimental participants to two or more groups on the basis of chance

Procedures used to analyze data after an experiment is completed; used to determine if the independent variable has a significant effect

Procedures used to summarize any set of data

Descriptive measures that tell us about the amount of variability or spread in a set of data

Descriptive measures of a set of data that tell us about a typical score

Procedure during which a complete explanation of research that has involved deception is provided to a participant

Written document in which a person who might be involved in a research study agrees to participate after receiving information about the researcher's specific procedures

structuralism	introspection
cognitive psychology	functionalism
Gestalt psychology	behavioral perspective
psychodynamic perspective	psychoanalytic therapy
humanistic perspective	physiological perspective

Structural psychologists' major method, in which participants reported the contents of their conscious experience

Earliest approach in modern psychology; founded by Wilhelm Wundt; its goal was to analyze the basic elements of conscious experience

Approach to psychology that focused on the functions of consciousness

Study of higher mental processes, such as thinking, knowing, and deciding

Perspective that focuses on observable behavior and emphasizes the learned nature of behavior

Approach to psychology most noted for emphasizing that our perception of a whole is different from our perception of the individual stimuli

Treatment for maladaptive behavior developed by Sigmund Freud; its goal is to bring unconscious causes of behavior to the conscious level

View taken by Sigmund Freud and his followers suggesting that normal and abnormal behaviors are determined primarily by unconscious forces

View that behaviors and mental processes can be understood and explained by studying the underlying physiology

Approach to psychology associated with Abraham Maslow and Carl Rogers; emphasizes free will and individuals' control of their behavior

cognitive perspective	eclectic approach
clinical psychology	psychiatrist
counseling psychology	research psychologist
ethnocentrism	cross-cultural psychology
school psychologist	industrial and organizational (I/O) psychologist

View of psychology that combines several different approaches	View that focuses on the study of how thought occurs, how our memories work, and how information is organized and stored
Medical doctor with specialized training in the medical treatment of mental and emotional disorders	Specialty of psychology that involves the diagnosis and treatment of psychological disorders
Psychologist whose primary activity is to conduct and report the results of experiments	Specialty of psychology that deals with less serious problems than those treated by clinical psychologists
Branch of psychology whose goal is to determine if research results can be applied to other cultures	The view that other cultures are viewed as an extension of one's own
Psychologist who applies psychology to problems of business and other organizations	Psychologist whose specialty encompasses diagnosing and treating learning disabilities and providing consultation on other problems of school-aged children

consumer psychology	health psychology
forensic psychologist	sport psychologist
neuropsychologist	

Subfield of psychology that is concerned with how psychological and social variables affect health and illness

Specialty of psychology that studies consumers and the choices they make

Psychologist who supplies services to athletes and coaches based on psychological principles

Psychologist who applies psychology to law and legal proceedings

Psychologist trained in the diagnosis and rehabilitation of brain disorders

So What is a Goal, Exactly?

Webster's dictionary defines *goal* as aim or purpose. When put in those terms, it is difficult to imagine not having goals, for to not have goals would be to have no aim or purpose. In a broader sense, a goal is anything you could do, have, or be. Goal setting helps people to live meaningful lives and to attain the careers they wish to have. Let us try breaking these ideas of what goals are into three categories: those that should be accomplished within the next few days, those that should be accomplished within the next several months, and those that you hope to accomplish in some years to come.

Note that the language associated with the first two categories indicated that the goal should be accomplished *within* some allotted time frame. Depending on the specific circumstances surrounding certain goals, you may need to be more precise with respect to when the goal will be met. Other goals, however, fall into a category of things that may be done within a range of times. Added precision regarding when the goal will be accomplished may be helpful in ensuring that the goal is, in fact, met. The third category, on the other hand, was described with a fairly undetermined, indefinite range of time in mind. These goals are nearly always more abstract and therefore it is more difficult to schedule target completion dates for them.

In short, a goal is anything you could do, have, or be, and it may be done according to one of three time frames. For ease of reference, those time frames will be referred to as immediate, short-term, and long-term goals. Some people prefer to add another category, intermediate-term, that facilitates greater specificity for the more not-so-far-off long-range objectives. You should organize your goals in a way that is most meaningful for you.

Whose Goals?

First off, it is important that the goals you set are *your own goals*. If someone else imposes them on you, you may not have the sense of ownership you will need to proceed in striving to meet them. This issue is related to the concepts of intrinsic and extrinsic rewards. Intrinsic rewards come from within you—the positive feelings you get for doing a job well, meeting the expectations you set for yourself, and so on. Extrinsic rewards come from outside. Money and material items, praise from others, and various forms of entertainment are all forms of extrinsic rewards.

It is worth noting that behaviors that are intrinsically rewarding are far more persistent than those that rely on reward and recognition from outside. The very act of achieving a goal you set out to meet is intrinsically rewarding. On the other hand, if others set your goals for you, you will likely depend on others to reward you when you meet them. If that reward is not forthcoming, your productivity will trail off predictably. Set your own goals and take pride in meeting them.

A Healthy Attitude Goes a Long Way

In addition to understanding *why* you should set goals, it will be helpful to consider *how* you will go about attaining your goals. A key to meeting goals is embodied in the attributes of a positive attitude. No doubt, your life experiences to date have helped you to understand that keeping your chin up, so to speak, is exceedingly helpful when you fall short of a mark. People who are able to persist in spite of their shortcomings are simply more successful at meeting their goals than those who get down on themselves when they do not succeed. The old adage, "can't do it never did anything," really fits here. Attitude may not be everything, but without a good attitude it is hard to do anything.

Sometimes you will fail. Setting goals that keep you working your hardest is the best way to ensure a high degree of productivity. If you fall short of your mark, take stock of what happened, re-evaluate the goals you are striving to meet, and proceed with the knowledge you gained from the experience.

Why Are Goals So Important Anyway?

Learning to set appropriate goals and to attain them is one of the most important things you can do, both in terms of making the most of your college experience and in terms of living a fulfilling life beyond your college years. However, it is not an easy task to set appropriate goals; and meeting the challenges you set for yourself can be difficult at times. In the end, though, the process of setting goals and striving to meet them is well worth doing and will put you in charge of using your time in ways that are rewarding and meaningful. Before describing some important things to consider when defining goals, it will be useful to discuss why goals are helpful.

Perhaps the most important reason to set goals is that they provide a focus for your attention and energy. If you know what you want to achieve, determining what to do at any given time is easy. On the other hand, if you lack the focus gained by setting goals, it can be hard to decide how to use available time. Unfortunately, when people have a hard time deciding how to use time, they often waste it. Eventually those wasted minutes and hours return to haunt us when we find ourselves pressed to accomplish something, such as studying for a test or writing a paper. One of the most disconcerting feelings people can have is the sense they get when they realize they are unable to produce their very best work because they did not plan appropriately. Setting goals and monitoring progress toward them is an excellent way to guard against this problem.

Another reason for setting goals has to do with the mixed blessing of independent living. Many college students find it exciting to begin living without having to report on their whereabouts to others. They feel liberated being able to come and go as they please, set their own hours, perform tasks and duties when they want to rather than as instructed by someone else. With freedom, though, comes responsibility. You will find it to be rewarding to determine, more or less, when you will do these things. You will discover also that it will be up to you to monitor your own progress and decision making. By learning to set and achieve goals, you will meet your responsibilities and be able to appreciate your freedom.

What are two good reasons for setting goals?

Greater Opportunities through Goal Setting

A word of clarification is appropriate here. The notion of setting goals for the reason of meeting responsibilities is only part of why you should embrace goal-setting as a way of organizing your activity. The other reason, which has been implied in the previous paragraphs, is that as you meet more goals you will gain greater opportunities. Those opportunities are extensions of the freedom you get for living responsibly—that is, for responsibly setting and meeting your goals. As a student, greater opportunities will enrich your experience and expand your choices for employment or for graduate or professional training following receipt of your bachelor's degree. Enhanced opportunities in the workplace typically mean more meaningful work and better pay. People who do not set and achieve goals simply do not have the same opportunities as those who do.

Some Specific Examples: Which Goals Go Where?

Let us illustrate these categories with more detailed descriptions of the categories. Immediate goals are those that you should list each evening for the following day. This exercise will make your mornings a little less hectic, and your memory of items from the list will allow you to begin planning for each day as you retire the preceding evening, and again as you get around the next morning. These goals constitute essentially a "to-do list." Be as specific as you can with these items; think in terms of filling 15-minute intervals. If you can learn to make use of the small chunks of time in your days, you will be more productive, and will have more discretionary time in your schedule. A failure to take advantage of the small chunks of time will likely lead to a sense of frustration with your schedule, and conflicts between your need to do academic work and your desire to engage in social activity.

Identify some Immediate Goals in the spaces below:

1. _____
2. _____
3. _____
4. _____

Can you assign priorities to the items in your list?

The short-term goals you set for yourself will probably center on spending a certain amount of time preparing for classes, including writing drafts of papers and organizing notes to study for quizzes and exams. Additionally, you will want to include objectives dealing with proper rest, exercise, and opportunities to pursue extra-curricular interests. It is worth noting that your college experience will be most memorable and meaningful if you can keep up with your academic responsibilities *and* participate in the life of your community, be it a residential campus, a church community, or your neighborhood. Interaction with others during your college years will constitute a significant percentage of your opportunities to grow and develop. However, be certain to keep track of the academic goals you set for yourself in this category. It is a tremendous feeling to be able to relax and go to bed early on the eve of an exam because you have prepared well along the way. By stark contrast, it is miserable and counterproductive to cram the night before an exam because you procrastinated.

What are 4 short-term goals you have set for yourself?

1. _____
2. _____
3. _____
4. _____

Did you list your short-term goals in order of priority?

The long-term goals you set for yourself will, in part, determine the short-term and immediate goals of days to come. If you select a given academic discipline as your major, for example, it is a long-term goal to meet the criteria for that major. That goal will influence the courses you choose, and the assignments, quizzes, and exams for the courses will in turn influence your immediate range goals. As you progress through your academic career, your long-term goals may well change. That is all right. It is common for students to change their majors once or twice during the course of their academic careers. Just keep updating your goals and measuring progress toward them and you will be able to mark progress in your development as a scholar and as a responsible person living a meaningful life.

Identify 3 long-term goals:

1. _____
2. _____
3. _____

Do these reflect your range of interests?

Make Your Goals Challenging

If you have ever competed with someone who is just slightly better than you most of the time, you know how that interaction can really cause you to work your hardest and do your best. Think about how much you improve your debate, musical, athletic and other skills when you are challenged. The same principles apply to goal setting and attainment. If you set goals you can easily reach, you are bound to be bored. Set appropriately challenging goals, and you will experience significant growth and development.

Take Baby Steps

One of the most prized experiences humans have is attaining a goal. On the other hand, if you were to sit down to try to attain a long-term goal in an afternoon, say becoming a financially independent person with a meaningful career, you would throw your arms in the air before you were to get started. The real value of long term goals is to provide focus. If you can measure the steps necessary to reach a long term goal, and then work on each of them, one at a time, you will be less daunted about how to begin.

Starting Over

Maslow's hierarchy of needs, which is discussed in chapter four of your textbook, suggests that after meeting needs from basic levels, humans strive for increasingly abstract goals. These include belongingness, esteem needs, and self-actualization needs. Self-actualization refers to the need to develop one's full potential. If you are to reach your potential, it will be important for you to constantly monitor your progress on goals, adding new ones when appropriate. It is not enough to set a long-term goal—say completing graduate or professional school and establishing a career-you will need to renew your goals to help maintain your focus.

Make Your Goals Measurable

In order to make the most of the goal-setting process, you should strive to set goals that you can measure. This is easier for some categories of activity than it is for others. For example, it is easier to assess whether you achieved a goal or a particular mark on an exam or paper than it is to determine whether you improved your attitude toward your roommate. However, if you are creative, you can come up with ways to determine whether you are making desirable progress toward a given goal.

Try using an end-of-the-day log for charting progress toward goals. Such a log might include responses to the following questions:

1. What goals did I accomplish today?

   _____

2. Which short- and long-term goals did I make progress on today?

   _____

3. Which immediate goals did I not attain today?

   _____

4. How should I change my goals lists based on what I accomplished and did not accomplish today?

   _____

Use Feedback

If the techniques you have developed for measuring progress toward your goals indicate that you are doing what you set out to do, you will surely enjoy the satisfaction of meeting your aims. If you determine that something is not going as you had hoped, this is useful too. Provided you are regularly evaluating your progress, you will be worlds ahead of where you would be if you did not attach measurable goals to your activity. Use the feedback you obtain to establish a fresh plan of action—whether that means to bear down and work harder, to punt, or to change horses.

More Remarks about Goal-Setting

Goal-setting is a critical component of leading a productive, satisfying life. However, it is not enough to merely set goals; you must implement activities that are targeted at meeting the goals, review whether the goals were in fact met, and constantly revise your goals in order to make the most of the process. A critical step in this process involves being able to locate the goals you set for yourself. Some people record their goals in daily organizers or calendars that they carry with them at all times. Benjamin Franklin is noted for having done this and being rather successful because of it. Others prefer to keep a notebook or computer file that can be accessed easily for regular monitoring of their progress toward their goals. Do what ever works best for you. It is probably worth experimenting with a few different systems until you find a good fit for your style.

Consider the Following Goal-Related Questions

1. Why did you go to college?
2. Why did you enroll in a psychology course?
3. What about the other courses you are taking?
4. What career goal(s) have you established for yourself?
5. What kind of preparation will you need to meet your career goal?
6. What resources are available to help you answer these questions?

These questions should provide fodder for a good deal of thought. If you cannot answer each of them readily, relax and schedule some time to think about them. Make it a goal to answer these and other questions regarding your life as a student. Doing so will keep you on track to becoming the best student you can be. This is the key to gaining the most from your college experience.

Commit It To Writing

While it is helpful to simply think about goal setting, it is best to record your goals in writing. So get busy. Identify goals according to each of the timelines listed above and write them down. Tape the list to your bathroom mirror or put it on your dresser. Keep your goals list current and read it often.

CHAPTER 2

Biological Foundations of Psychology

Use the space provided in this outline to record notes from the textbook as well as from class lectures and discussion. Questions related to the *Psychological Detective* sections in the text have been presented in the outline; use the associated space to respond to the questions and to record your own comments about the issues. *Keywords and terms* from the text have been italicized and inserted in the outline so you can practice writing their definitions. The pages in this study guide are perforated and can be removed for use as study sheets for quizzes and exams.

I. **Biopsychology, Neuroscience, and the Evolutionary Perspective**

   evolutionary perspective—

   natural selection—

II. **Sensing, Processing, and Responding**

   stimulus—

   receptors—

III. **The Nervous System**

   central nervous system—

   peripheral nervous system—

   neurons—

   A. The Peripheral Nervous System
   1. The Somatic Division

   somatic division—

   afferent (sensory) nerves—

   efferent (motor) nerves—

2. The Autonomic Division

autonomic division—

a. The Sympathetic Division

sympathetic division—

Take a few minutes to study the components of the autonomic nervous system that are activated by the sympathetic system. How do they compare with those that are activated by the parasympathetic system? Be sure to examine the way each organ is innervated. Can you explain why some organs are stimulated by one branch of the autonomic system, and others by the opposing branch?

b. The Parasympathetic Division

parasympathetic division—

homeostasis—

B. The Central Nervous System
1. The Spinal Cord

reflex—

2. The Brain

a. The Hind Brain

hindbrain—

medulla—

pons—

cerebellum—

cranial nerves—

b. The Midbrain

midbrain—

reticular formation—

c. The Forebrain

forebrain—

corpus callosum—

subcortical structures—

cerebral cortex (cerebrum)—

limbic system—

thalamus—

Why does it matter if a researcher damages cortical tissue when manipulating subcortical structures in an experiment?

3. Studying the Functions of the Brain

a. Early Surgical Approaches

b. The Case Study Method

c. Brain Damage

   stroke—

d. Stereotaxic Surgery

   stereotaxic instrument—

e. The Electroencephalograph

   electroencephalograph (EEG)—

f. Computerized Brain Imaging

   positron emission tomography (PET)—

   computerized axial tomography (CT/CAT)—

   magnetic resonance imaging (MRI)—

   functional MRI (fMRI)—

 Write down the purpose(s) for using each of the imaging techniques you just defined.

IV. Neurons: The Cells of the Nervous System

A. Components of the Neuron
   1. The Cell Membrane

2. Dendrites

   dendrites—

3. The Soma (Cell Body)

   soma—

4. The Axon

   axon—

5. Terminal Buttons

   terminal buttons—

6. The Myelin Sheath

   myelin sheath—

   glia cells—

   nodes of Ranvier—

What does the myelin sheath contribute to a neuron's functioning? What happens when the myelin for a cell degenerates?

   multiple sclerosis—

   ataxia—

B. The Synapse and Neurotransmitters

   1. The Synapse

      Synapse—

   2. Neurotransmitters

      neurotransmitters—

      synaptic vesicles—

   3. Clearing the Synapse

      reuptake—

   4. Neurotransmitters and Drug Action

      a. Agonists

         agonist—

      b. Antagonists

         antagonist—

      c. Neuromodulators

         neuromodulators—

         opioid peptides—

         substance P—

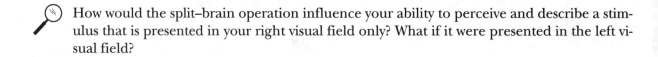

Why is it important that we be able to experience pain?

C. The Nature of the Neural Signal

ions—

resting state—

depolarization—

hyperpolarization—

1. Depolarization and Excitatory Synapses

action potential—

refractory period—

2. Hyperpolarization and Excitatory Synapses

V. **The Split–Brain Operation and Neuropsychology**

A. The Split–Brain Operation

How would the split–brain operation influence your ability to perceive and describe a stimulus that is presented in your right visual field only? What if it were presented in the left visual field?

B. Brain Asymmetries

brain asymmetries—

1. Aphasias

aphasia—

2. Apraxias

    apraxia—

C. Neuropsychology

What experiments could be used to test whether Dr. P could process non–visual sensory information appropriately?

VI. The Endocrine System

   endocrine system—

   hormones—

A. Major Endocrine Glands

   1. The Pituitary Gland

      pituitary gland—

   2. The Thyroid Gland

   3. The Pancreas

   4. The Gonads

   5. The Adrenal Glands

   6. The Liver

After you have studied the chapter, you should be able to respond to the following statements and questions to convey your understanding of the material.

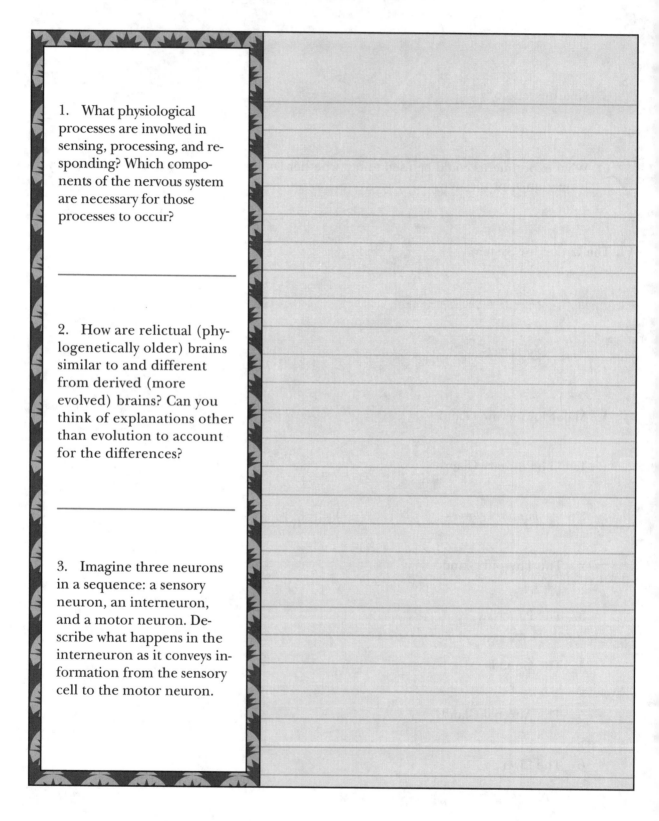

1. What physiological processes are involved in sensing, processing, and responding? Which components of the nervous system are necessary for those processes to occur?

2. How are relictual (phylogenetically older) brains similar to and different from derived (more evolved) brains? Can you think of explanations other than evolution to account for the differences?

3. Imagine three neurons in a sequence: a sensory neuron, an interneuron, and a motor neuron. Describe what happens in the interneuron as it conveys information from the sensory cell to the motor neuron.

It is helpful when learning the information from this chapter to study the how some of the terms are used in the contexts of figures and tables. Having studied the chapter you should be able to fill in the missing information. The answers are given at the end of the chapter.

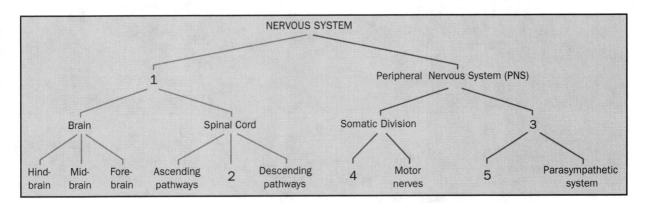

1. _____   4. _____

2. _____   5. _____

3. _____

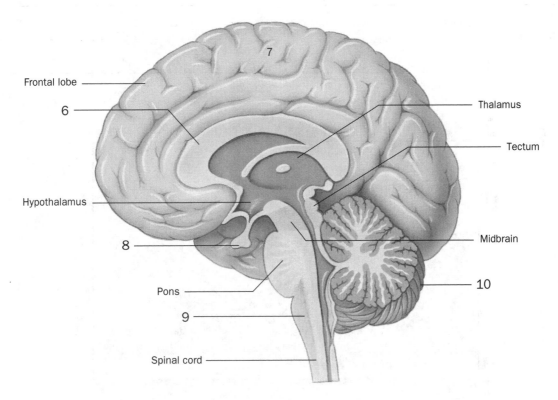

6. _____   9. _____

7. _____   10. _____

8. _____

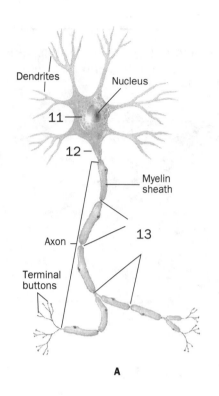

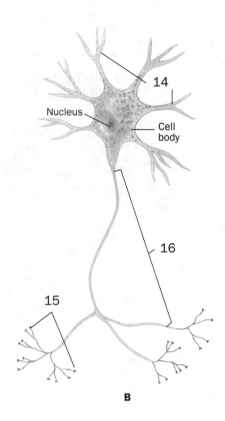

A

B

11. _____   14. _____

12. _____   15. _____

13. _____   16. _____

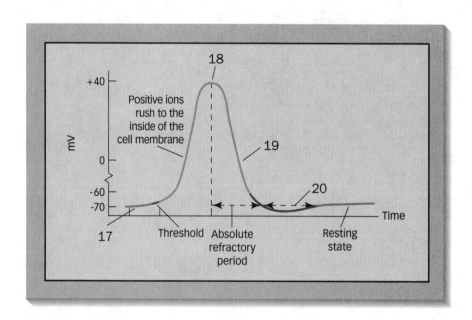

17. _____   19. _____

18. _____   20. _____

Circle the letter that corresponds to the *best* alternative for each of the following items. Read each alternative carefully. The answers are presented at the end of this study guide chapter. Be sure to learn *why* each correct alternative is better than the others

1. A common question asked by psychologists who adopt an evolutionary perspective is:
   a. How will I survive over generations?
   b. Why does a given behavior survive over generations?
   c. Which physiological and/or biological structures developed over generations?
   d. What role does a given structure or behavior play in survival and adaptation?

2. Environmental feature is to specialized cell as ___ is to ___.
   a. vision; audition
   b. space suit; toxin
   c. stimulus; receptor
   d. atmosphere; ambiance

3. An important step between the sensing of raw stimulus information and responding to it is:
   a. positioning limbs for responding.
   b. processing the information for meaning.
   c. ignoring other raw stimulus information.
   d. focusing on the raw stimulus information.

4. Quite literally, the central nervous system (CNS) is that portion of the larger nervous system that is located in the center of your body. The peripheral nervous system (PNS) constitutes the remainder of the larger system. The two major divisions of the PNS are:
   a. the brain and the spinal cord.
   b. the somatic and the autonomic.
   c. the forebrain and the hindbrain.
   d. the autonomic and the parasympathetic.

5. The autonomic nervous system may be considered as operating on a continuum as its components are antagonistic. That is, one component of the autonomic nervous system opposes the other for each function the system serves. These components are known as:
   a. extremes.
   b. neurons and glands, respectively.
   c. the left—hand, and right—hand systems.
   d. the sympathetic and parasympathetic systems.

6. Interneurons are cells:
   a. situated in the spinal cord between sensory and motor cells.
   b. that support the brain, and are technically not neurons at all.
   c. that enter neurons in order to promote more efficient activity.
   d. that die off after helping the brain turn over new cells during adolescence.

7. The hindbrain is, from an evolutionary perspective, the oldest portion of the brain. It makes sense, then, that this portion of the brain includes the structure that controls breathing, swallowing, and blood circulation. The structure that serves these functions is called the:
   a. pons.
   b. tectum.
   c. medulla.
   d. hippocampus.

8. If you accidentally drift, while driving a car, into the center section of a road or onto the shoulder of the road, you will likely be startled by the sound of your tires rolling on a different texture and making a lot of noise. The ___ is responsible for the startle response bringing you to full attention.
   a. sound of the road
   b. reticular formation
   c. ventromedial hypothalamus
   d. formation of the surface of the road

9. The limbic system regulates:
   a. the arms and legs.
   b. several branches of the PNS.
   c. heartbeat, respiration, and other vital activities.
   d. emotions and motivated behaviors including hunger, thirst, and aggression.

10. The thalamus is sometimes called a sensory switchboard because it:
    a. integrates and relays incoming information.
    b. resembles the appearance of an old time phone station.
    c. contains cells that convert raw stimulus information into neural signals.
    d. switches off and on, to conserve metabolic energy, rather than working constantly.

11. Contemporary human brains are ___ than prehistoric brains.
    a. larger, in absolute terms.
    b. smaller, in absolute terms.
    c. the same size, in relative terms.
    d. more wrinkled and crumpled on the surface.

12. By selectively destroying or stimulating the tissue in living brains, researchers have:
    a. developed maps of the cortex.
    b. determined which parts we actually need.
    c. effectively discovered everything there is to know about the brain.
    d. None of the above. You cannot gain access to brain tissue without killing it.

13. The stories of "Tan" and Phineas Gage are:
    a. too poorly documented to be of lasting value.
    b. examples of the case study method for gathering information.
    c. entertaining ways of remembering some of the complex information on the brain.
    d. mere myths, but have nevertheless served to stimulate interest in brain functioning.

14. Brain structure is to brain activity as ___ is to ___.
    a. MRI; PET
    b. fMRI; MRI
    c. fMRI; CT/CAT
    d. EEG; CT/CAT

15. Charles Scott Sherrington's discovery that a dog's reflex took too long:
    a. confirmed what cat lovers knew all along.
    b. was instrumental in learning about neural impulses.
    c. was exaggerated by the fact that his stopwatch was broken.
    d. occurred in the context of a brain stimulation experiment in the mid–1800s.

16. In general, signals are received by ___ and sent out by ___.
    a. axons; cell bodies.
    b. nodes of Ranvier; myelin.
    c. dendrites; terminal buttons.
    d. dendrites; nodes of Ranvier.

17. Glia cells comprise the myelin associated with about 50 percent of nerve cells. An interesting characteristic of the myelin sheath is that it has gaps, or ___, that break up the fatty covering of the axon.
    a. skips.
    b. dendrites.
    c. glia gaps.
    d. nodes of Ranvier.

18. Presynaptic cells are able to communicate with postsynaptic cells because of ___ that cross(es) the microscopic cleft that separates them.
    a. ions
    b. myelin
    c. anions
    d. neurotransmitters

19. After a signal crosses a synapse, it is important to clear the gap immediately to prepare for the next signal. This occurs in one of two ways:
    a. slashing and burning.
    b. flushing and rushing.
    c. breakdown and reuptake.
    d. all of the above are ways in which residual transmitter material is removed from the cleft.

20. Psychoactive drugs are those that impact the cells in the central nervous system. These drugs fall into two main categories: ___, that enhance the operation of a given transmitter, and ___ that block the action of a given transmitter.
    a. agonists; antagonists
    b. antagonists; agonists
    c. promoters; blockers
    d. helpers; blockers

21. Neurotransmitter is to neuromodulator as ___ is to ___.
    a. fast; local
    b. local; long
    c. widespread; fast
    d. long; widespread

22. When it is at its resting state, a nerve cell:
    a. has no charge.
    b. has a slight positive charge.
    c. has a relatively strong negative charge.
    d. None of the above; cells do not have charges, batteries do.

23. Depolarizing is to ___ as hyperpolarizing is to ___.
    a. negative; positive
    b. positive; negative
    c. less negative; more negative
    d. more negative; less negative

24. During the absolute refractory period, a nerve cell is:
    a. hyperpolarized.
    b. merely depolarizing.
    c. not involved in ion exchange.
    d. at the peak in the course of its action potential.

25. The split brain operation:
    a. was used to treat Phineas Gage after his accident.
    b. is a common procedure for treating migraine headaches.
    c. produces baffling results because brains continue to work normally in spite of tissue damage.
    d. affects dramatically the capacity for the two cerebral hemispheres to communicate with each other.

26. Which of the following is an example of functional asymmetry?
    a. Mean cell densities differ between hemispheres.
    b. The left hemisphere is more involved in speech, the right in spatial abilities.
    c. The surface anatomies of the left and right cerebral hemispheres are different.
    d. The motor strip of each respective hemisphere controls the behavior of the opposite side.

27. Aphasia is to ___ as apraxia is to ___.
    a. vertebrate; invertebrate
    b. communication; nonverbal skills
    c. central nervous system; peripheral nervous system
    d. treatable with psychoactive drugs; incurable deficit of the brain

28. Neuropsychologists differ from physiological psychologists and comparative psychologists, in that their primary interest is:
    a. in mapping the nervous system.
    b. to relate and compare the behaviors of different species.
    c. to discover the functional contributions of each brain structure.
    d. in testing individuals with brain injuries to determine the nature of damage and its effects.

29. Psychologists are interested in the endocrine system because it impacts the nervous system. In some ways, its chemicals, ___, are analogous to neurotransmitters in that they are released from one location and influence another.
    a. hormones
    b. pheromones
    c. neuropeptides
    d. neuromodulators

30. An interesting difference between Southeast Asians and people from many other cultures is:
    a. the capacity to convert alcohol into a harmless substance.
    b. the shape of the brain part that processes mathematical concepts.
    c. the number and variety of neurotransmitters used for an average function.
    d. all of the above are noteworthy differences between many Southeast Asians and others.

ANSWERS TO LABELING EXERCISES

1. Central Nervous System (CNS)
2. Interneurons
3. Autonomic Division
4. Sensory Nerves
5. Sympathetic System
6. Corpus Callosum
7. Cerebral Cortex

8. Pituitary Gland
9. Medulla
10. Cerebellum
11. Cell Body
12. Axon Hillock
13. Nodes of Ranvier
14. Dendrites

15. Terminal Buttons
16. Axon
17. Resting State
18. Action Potential
19. Positive Ions Being Pumped Out
20. Relative Refractory Period

PRACTICE TEST ANSWERS AND EXPLANATIONS

1. d. Psychologists are interested in behavior. Those who adopt the evolutionary perspective consider behavior as a function of the brain and biological structures that give rise to it.

2. c. The sensing process involves receiving stimulus information from the environment through receptors that have evolved to receive specific information—e.g., taste, touch.

3. b. Before any activity can transpire in response to a sensory experience, the information has to be processed.

4. b. the PNS may be further divided into the somatic and autonomic nervous systems.

5. d. The autonomic nervous system is comprised of the sympathetic and parasympathetic nervous systems.

6. a. Interneurons are located in the gray matter of the spinal cord and transfer signaling from sensory fibers to motor fibers or up the spinal cord to the brain.

7. c. The medulla regulates these. Also it monitors blood chemistry and other survival promoting functions.

8. b. Before you have a chance to appraise what has happened your reticular formation activates your brain.

9. d. The limbic system is a network of subcortical brain structures that regulates a variety of emotions and behaviors.

10. a. The thalamus receives incoming information and directs it to the cerebral cortex.

11. d. The wrinkled and crumpled appearance is the result of *convolutions* in the cortical layer of the brain. Effectively, the convolutions permit more cerebral mass to be contained within the skull. By analogy, you can put more notebook paper in a water glass if you wad it up.

12. a. The early surgical approaches to studying the brain were effective in mapping its functions.

13. b. These case study examples are both key components to psychology's prehistory.

14. a. The standard MRI is used to gain structural information about the brain; PET tells researchers about the functional activity of the brain.

15. b. Sherrington's discovery expanded on Ramón y Cajal's discovery of neurons being discrete units by adding that signals had to be transmitted from one cell to another for an impulse to travel through the nervous system.

16. c. Usually nerve signals are received by dendrites, processed in the cell body, and sent out through the terminal buttons.

17. d. The gaps between the glia cells that make up the myelin sheath are called nodes of Ranvier.

18. d. Neurotransmitters bridge the synaptic gaps that adjoin two neurons.

19. c. Depending on their type, neurotransmitters are either broken down or taken back into the presynaptic cells through a process called reuptake.

20. a. Agonists enhance the operation of a given transmitter, while antagonists block the action of a given transmitter.

21. b. Neurotransmitters are local, fast acting chemicals. Neuromodulators are longer–lasting and cover more widespread regions.

22. c. At resting most nerve cells have net negative charges of approximately -70 millivolts.

23. c. As a cell depolarizes (becomes less polarized), it loses its negative charge. When a cell is hyperpolarized (hyper–is a prefix that means *more* or *excessive*) it has a stronger negative charge than it has when it is at its resting state.

24. a. During the relative refractory period, when it is difficult to get the neuron to fire, the cell's charge has dipped below its normal resting potential.

25. d. The split brain operation involves the severing of the corpus callosum, a bundle of fibers that connects the left and right cerebral hemispheres.

26. c. Functional asymmetry refers to differences based on what the two sides *do*. The left hemisphere is more involved in speech, the right in spatial abilities.

27. b. Aphasias are deficits in communication, while apraxias are nonverbal deficits.

28. d. Neuropsychologists work primarily in human clinical settings and are trained to determine the characteristics of brain injuries and their resulting effects on adaptive behavior.

29. a. Hormones are the chemicals of communication within the endocrine system.

30. a. Many people from Southeast Asia are unable to metabolize acetaldehyde into acetic acid.

Key Vocabulary Terms

Cut out and use as study cards; terms appear on
one side and definitions are on the other.

evolutionary
perspective

natural selection

stimulus

receptors

central nervous
system

peripheral
nervous system

neurons

somatic division

Key Vocabulary Terms

Cut out and use as study cards; terms appear on one side and definitions are on the other.

The principle that the strongest or most fit organisms are the ones that adapt best to their environment

Interest in the role a physiological structure or behavior plays in helping an organism adapt to its environment

Specialized cells that are sensitive to specific types of stimulus energy

Environmental feature that provokes a response

Division of the nervous system that consists of neural fibers lying outside the brain and spinal cord

Division of the nervous system that consists of the brain and spinal cord

Division of the peripheral nervous system that consists of nerves coming from the receptors to the brain and spinal cord, as well as nerves that go from the brain and spinal cord to the muscles

Basic cells of the nervous system

afferent (sensory) nerves	efferent (motor) nerves
autonomic division	sympathetic division
parasympathetic division	homeostasis
reflex	hindbrain
medulla	pons

Nerves that carry information from the brain and spinal cord to the muscles

Nerves that carry information from the receptors to the spinal cord and brain

Subdivision of the autonomic nervous system that is responsible for mobilizing the body in times of stress, and preparing for fight or flight

Division of the peripheral nervous system involved in the control of bodily functioning through organs and glands

Tendency of the body to maintain a balanced state; characterized by the functioning of an optimal range of physiological processes

Subdivision of the autonomic nervous system that is responsible for returning the body to a resting or balanced state

Oldest of the three main divisions of the brain; its major structures are the medulla, pons, and cerebellum

Automatic behavior in response to a specific stimulus

Structure of the hindbrain that connects the two halves of the brain; has nuclei that are important for sleep and arousal

Structure located in the hindbrain that regulates automatic responses such as breathing, swallowing, and blood circulation

cerebellum	cranial nerves
midbrain	reticular formation
forebrain	corpus callosum
subcortical structures	cerebral cortex (cerebrum)
limbic system	thalamus

The twelve pairs of nerves that control the sensory and motor information from the skin and muscles of the head and internal organs

Structure of the hindbrain that coordinates muscular movements

Nerve fibers passing through the midbrain that control arousal

Major division of the brain that contains fibers known as the reticular formation

Wide band of neural fibers that connects the two hemispheres of the brain

Major division of the brain that consists of subcortical structures and the cerebral cortex

The convoluted (wrinkled) outer layer of the brain

Structures of the forebrain, such as the amygdala, hypothalamus, and thalamus, that are located beneath the cerebral cortex

Subcortical structure that relays incoming sensory information to the cerebral cortex and other parts of the brain

System of interconnected subcortical structures that regulates a variety of emotions and motivated behaviors, such as hunger, thirst, aggression, and sexual behavior

stroke	stereotaxic instrument
electroencephalograph (EEG)	positron emission tomography (PET)
computerized axial tomography (CT or CAT)	magnetic resonance imaging (MRI)
functional magnetic resonance imaging (fMRI)	dendrite
soma	axon

Instrument that holds the head in a fixed position to allow precise surgery on subcortical structures

Temporary loss of blood flow to the brain; also known as a cerebrovascular accident

Imaging technique that involves monitoring the metabolic activity of the brain

Device that monitors and records electrical activity of the brain

Imaging technique that involves the use of radio waves and a strong magnetic field to produce a signal that can be interpreted by a computer

Imaging technique that involves the production of a large number of X–rays interpreted by a computer

Short, branchlike structures of a neuron that receive information from receptors and other neurons

A modification of the standard MRI procedure that allows both structural and temporal images to be gathered

Part of a neuron that transmits information to other neurons and to muscles and glands

Cell body of a neuron

terminal buttons	myelin sheath
glia cell	nodes of Ranvier
multiple sclerosis	ataxia
synapse	neuro-transmitters
synaptic vesicles	reuptake

Fatty protein substance that covers some axons, increasing speed of transmission

Structures located at the ends of the axon in which neurotransmitters are stored before release

Regularly spaced gaps in the myelin sheath

Special type of cell found in the nervous system that forms the myelin sheath

Loss of motor coordination

Disease caused by degeneration of myelin in the central nervous system

Chemical substances, stored in the terminal buttons, that facilitate the transmission of information from one neuron to another

Site where two or more neurons interact but do not touch

Method of clearing a neurotransmitter from the synaptic cleft, in which the neurotransmitter is taken back into the terminal buttons

Small pockets or sacs located in the terminal buttons that contain a neurotransmitter

agonist	antagonist
neuromodulators	opioid peptides
substance P	ions
resting state	depolarization
hyperpolarization	action potential

Drug that blocks the operation of a neurotransmitter

Drug that enhances the operation of a neurotransmitter

Painkillers that are produced by the body

Chemicals that may have a widespread or general effect on the release of neurotransmitters

Electrically charged particles

Neurotransmitter involved in sensing pain

Process in which the electrical charge of the neuron becomes less negative

Electrical charge (-70 mV) of a neuron when it is not firing

Reversal in electrical charge of a neuron that occurs when the neuron fires

Process in which the electrical charge of the neuron becomes more negative

refractory period	brain asymmetries
aphasia	apraxia
endocrine system	hormones
pituitary gland	

Differences between the two hemispheres of the brain

Brief period following an action potential when the neuron is returning to the resting state and cannot be fired

Deficits in nonverbal skills

Loss of the ability to speak or understand written or spoken language

Chemicals produced by the glands of the endocrine system that are carried by the bloodstream to other organs

System of glands that produce and secrete chemicals

Gland located below the thalamus and hypothalamus; called the master gland because its secretions control many other glands

The Road Is Paved with Good Intentions

Goal setting was the topic in the first Tip for Success section. Another topic that is central to being successful is time management. Time management and goal setting go hand-in-hand. You may have noticed that the concept of time was mentioned in the section on goal setting. That was because it is not enough to have good intentions. If you want to be successful, you have to use your time to work toward achieving those intentions. Similarly, making yourself aware of time with clocks and calendars is of little value if you do not have goals. This section will focus on ways you can make the most of *your time*.

There Is Plenty of Time

That is right, there is plenty of time. Take a few moments to do the following thought exercise. Pick a task you wanted to do, but then used time as an excuse for not having done it. Now, imagine you are back in the setting for completing that task and assign a value to the task. Depending on the task, you may have to increase the value. Try setting the value at: $5...$50...$1,000...$1 Million...your life! A familiar saying goes, where there is a will, there is a way. If you want to do something badly enough, you can find the time just as you can find the resources.

The issue, then, is assigning priorities to the things you do, bearing in mind that you will need time to accomplish each of your goals, and using your time to work on your goals. You have probably heard someone say, "time is money." Consider this: there are 168 hours in a week. It does not matter which side of town people grow up on, how ambitious or lazy they are, who does their hair, or what kind of car they drive, everyone gets the same allocation of this priceless commodity. It is how people invest the commodity that determines their success.

If you require eight hours of sleep per night, then your 168 hours are down to 112. If you need more than eight hours, or like to sleep in on weekends, reduce the number accordingly. Next, subtract the number of hours you need to spend in school, preparing for classes (plan 2-4 hours outside of class for every hour spent in class), at work, eating, and so forth. How much time do you need to travel from one place to the next throughout the course of the week? Next, factor in time for exercising, reading, quiet reflection, attending to personal needs, doing laundry... The remainder is all you get for everything else you like to do: social commitments, hobbies, shopping, hanging out, or whatever. How you use *your time* is directly related to how successful you are at meeting the goals you set for yourself. Successful goal attainment will make you healthier, happier, and more likely to get exciting opportunities in the future.

Know Your Priorities

Being a student is costly. If you divide the cost of tuition at your school by the number of hours you are taking, you may be surprised at what it costs per hour for you to be enrolled. Given the costs, plus the fact that your education will determine, in part, how satisfying your life will be, it makes sense to make the most of your investment. Do not schedule appointments during your classes. If you do, you are telling yourself and others that other things are more important to you than planning with your future in mind. Using appointments and other excuses for missing class is a pet peeve for most professors.

Even though the hours you designate for studying are somewhat flexible, they deserve the same priority as your classes. Can you make the most of your investment in a class if you do not prepare for it? Do not allow a part-time job, your roommate's sudden need for a ride to the airport, or whatever, to prevent you from making the most of the academic component of your education.

Forget About Time

Have you ever noticed what happens when you got a chance to talk with an old friend, were engrossed in a good book or movie, or got caught up in a game or working on a hobby? *Time flies.* How about the last half-hour before you get off work, when you are waiting for a call, or when you are stuck in traffic? *Time stands still.* How can both of these pearls of folk wisdom be right? The answer lies in what one focuses on. Time races away or stalls endlessly depending on what you are doing, and it is almost always at the wrong pace, right? Wrong. Time knows only one pace, no matter how you measure it. Worrying about time will merely serve to distract you from progress toward your goals. Focus on your goals; time will take care of itself. Now, it is usually helpful to work in designated units of time, so do not trade your watch for a sundial. But do not be a slave to your watch either.

Put Yourself Under a Time Microscope

It is important to study the ways you use your time. In academia there are regular opportunities to reorganize your schedule and use of time. In addition to taking advantage of the obvious opportunities at the beginning and end of each term, try to examine your efficiency at the middle and end of the term. You already have the resources you need to determine whether you are using your time effectively and efficiently. The table at the end of this section may be photocopied to do the exercise that is described below.

Photocopy the table at the end of this section, or make your own table. You will need enough copies to cover one week. Each cell corresponds to a 15-minute period in the day. Next, carry each day's chart with you and fill it out as accurately as possible. Write enough information in the cells that you will know how to figure out what you did at a given time. If you continue doing something through more than one block of time, simply draw an arrow to indicate continuation of the last activity. Do this for a week, then study the things you did and compare them with what you wish you had done. Assuming there is room for improvement, reread your list of goals and use your notes to plan a schedule for the next week. Carry each day's schedule with you, attending to whether the times you designated are appropriate for meeting your goals. Adjust your schedule as necessary to ensure that you are allowing for all the things you need and want to do.

If you are already fairly organized, challenge yourself by estimating how you will spend each block of time in the coming week. If you get close, congratulations! You are already aware of the advantages of keeping a schedule. If you do not get as close as you had hoped to, this exercise may help you find your schedule stumbling blocks. Repeat this process as often as it is helpful in getting you on track toward meeting your goals.

Threats to *Your Time*

It is important to always remember that the time you spend is yours. Sure, you have obligations, unexpected things come up, and there are occasions when you will not feel like you are in charge of how you are spending your time. Sometimes it is necessary to realize that even though you may not enjoy what you are doing, the activity may still be linked to goal attainment. Your time should always be spent in ways that are consistent with your goals, be they academic- or leisure-related. If you wonder whether you should be engaging in a given behavior, ask yourself whether you will be glad to have spent your time that way the next day...next month...in five years. It is surprising that we sometimes do things that seem really important at the moment, but thoughtful reflection would tell us to do something different.

The following list provides suggestions for combating common threats to effective use of *your time*. You may have different challenges to your schedule, or different solutions to the problems. What is important is that you give thought to making the most of every moment you get. Another adage, *time marches on,* reflects the importance of spending time wisely, for once a moment has passed, you cannot have it again.

1. **Know When You Are at Your Best.** Timing matters. Do you think more clearly after a good night's rest, or after you have been awake all day? If you are able to concentrate better in the morning, that is when you should study. If it takes 3 hours for your brain to begin working each day, you may be better off setting aside study time in the early afternoon. It is not always possible to study or work when your mind is operating at peak efficiency. However, if you choose to study at times when you are better able to concentrate, your learning will be both more efficient and longer lasting.

2. **Save the Best for Last.** The Premack Principle, discovered by psychologist David Premack, suggests that more rewarding activities may be used to reinforce less rewarding activities. Most people are familiar with that concept, even if they have never heard of the principle. For example, have you ever been told you can do something you want to do badly only *after* you do a household chore? It was effective, wasn't it? Use the principle on yourself for most everything you do. If you have a long list of things to study, start with the homework you are *least* excited about. If you need some incentive to make it through a set of responsibilities, establish a reward structure for yourself that will encourage you to work.

3. **Use Idle Time.** At any moment you may have to wait on someone or something for an undetermined amount of time. Waiting to meet with someone for an appointment, when your transportation plans are unexpectedly delayed, at a busy restaurant or cafeteria, or in a number of other circumstances is annoying. What is more, it chips away at your precious time. Take charge of how you use time by having something to do at any given moment. You will want to prepare according to how far from home base you will be. Bring a book (or more) with you when you travel in case your travel arrangements are altered. If you are headed to meet with an advisor, or your dentist, bring something that you can start and stop working on easily. The flash cards in this study guide were designed for just these kinds of occasions.

4. **Just Say No.** This is much easier said than done. However, if you consider each decision you make in terms of the goals you are striving to meet, it should be clear whether it is in your best interest to do something someone else asks of you. While they may be disappointed, most people will respect your need to protect your time for the goals you are already working on. The more clearly defined your goals are, the better able you will be to help others understand why you cannot always take on additional responsibilities.

5. **Be Clear about How You Use Your Time.** Sometimes the most respectful people will accidentally interrupt your activity because they do not realize *when* you are busy. Good communication can go a long way toward helping protect your time against disruptions, even if those disruptions are things that you would welcome at other times. Let people know when you are studying, whether by telling them which times are off limits, by hanging a "do not disturb" sign on your door, or by donning a hat or jacket that acts as a signal.

6. **Monitor Your Effectiveness.** Sometimes in spite of good planning, you are unable to be as productive as you need to be. Sometimes you are plenty able to be productive, but allow yourself to get lazy. What would pay yourself for the efforts you are exerting? Can you remember what you just read a few minutes ago? If the answer is no, you may want to refer to your goals list for something else you can do more effectively until you are better focused.

7. **Monitor Your Efficiency.** Perhaps you are plenty effective, but are not working as efficiently as you could be. Are you taking shortcuts where and when you should? Are you bogging yourself down by focusing too much on the details? In addition to asking yourself these few questions periodically, try this idea. Time yourself when reading a page from your textbook. As you read subsequent pages, check every once in a while to make sure you are not slowing down.

8. **Take One More Step.** Often when you are finishing a work session you have the necessary focus and additional energy to do a little more. Just as making one extra payment annually on a home loan will greatly reduce the cost of the mortgage, so too will taking one more step toward your goals when you have reached a targeted stopping point.

9. **Keep Your Word.** Some very important deals are sealed with nothing other than a handshake and a promise. Promises should be taken seriously, and should not be violated. Make promises to yourself and others as appropriate, and keep them. Do not let yourself or others down by failing to keep your word. If you adopt this attitude when *making* promises, they will serve as powerful motivators for striving toward your goals.

10. **Don't Take Any Excuses.** It is bad enough when someone else makes a promise and then fails to keep her or his word. If there is anything that is worse, it is when one lets oneself down. If you stick to your schedule as if it were a promise, you will surely be more productive and feel good about it.

Not a Paradox

It may seem contradictory that filling your schedule is the key to having enough time for relaxing, or whatever else you like to do. Many people find at the end of an evening, long weekend, or semester break, that somehow they failed to do all the work they had intended to do *and* they did not do the all the other activities they had planned either. The fact is that if we do not have our time scheduled, it is easy to put off getting started on anything. As a result, too many hours get whiled away. By scheduling in everything that is important to you, you can be sure to have time for doing it. Whether its writing two pages on a term paper, playing tennis, listening to music, or propping your feet up in front of the TV, scheduling time for it and sticking to your schedule is the only way you will get it done.

Poor Time Management Is Linked To Stress

When we run out of time for completing responsibilities, we experience stress. While some stress may be helpful in motivating activity, too much stress can inhibit your ability to perform your very best. Often the sources of stress are linked to poor time management. It is clear to see that if you do not manage time effectively and experience stress as a result, it will become increasingly difficult to meet your goals, which, in turn, will create more stress. This cycle can negatively impact your attitude, behavior and physical wellness. It is remarkable that poor time management can have such profound effects on these central issues in your life. If you desire to be happy, productive, and healthy, you will want to learn to take control of your time.

You Are Not Alone

Survey a group of successful people about the keys to their successes. Whether they are leaders in the student body, college professors, local business people, clergy, or others you may define as successful, each of them will identify the need to manage time wisely. Issues surrounding the ways that people use time are pervasive in our society. The company we keep and the people we look up to will influence us. Songs, books and plays, special seminars for business employees, and sections in bookstores are a few examples of places and ways we are exposed to comments on the usage of time.

Model your lifestyle after those who fit your definition of success. If you aspire to be a leader, but are acting like someone who is destined for a minimum wage career, something is awry. Do whatever it takes to learn to make the most of your time.

Time Microscope

Day:
Date:

AM	PM
Midnight	**Noon**
12:15	12:15
12:30	12:30
12:45	12:45
1:00	1:00
1:15	1:15
1:30	1:30
1:45	1:45
2:00	2:00
2:15	2:15
2:30	2:30
2:45	2:45
3:00	3:00
3:15	3:15
3:30	3:30
3:45	3:45
4:00	4:00
4:15	4:15
4:30	4:30
4:45	4:45
5:00	5:00
5:15	5:15
5:30	5:30
5:45	5:45
6:00	6:00
6:15	6:15
6:30	6:30
6:45	6:45
7:00	7:00
7:15	7:15
7:30	7:30
7:45	7:45
8:00	8:00
8:15	8:15
8:30	8:30
8:45	8:45
9:00	9:00
9:15	9:15
9:30	9:30
9:45	9:45
10:00	10:00
10:15	10:15
10:30	10:30
10:45	10:45
11:00	11:00
11:15	11:15
11:30	11:30
11:45	11:45

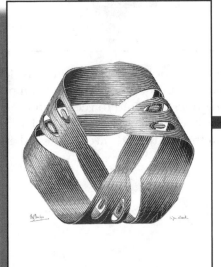

CHAPTER 3

Sensation and Perception

Use the space provided in this outline to record notes from the textbook as well as from class lectures and discussion. Questions related to the *Psychological Detective* sections in the text have been presented in the outline; use the associated space to respond to the questions and to record your own comments about the issues. *Keywords and terms* from the text have been italicized and inserted in the outline so you can practice writing their definitions. The pages in this study guide are perforated and can be removed for use as study sheets for quizzes and exams.

I. Sensation, Perception, and Psychophysics

    A. Sensation and Perception

        sensation—

        perception—

        transduction—

        adaptation—

    B. Psychophysics

        Weber's law—

        just noticeable difference (jnd)—

    C. Thresholds

        absolute threshold—

        differential threshold—

        signal detection theory—

II. Sensory Systems

A. Vision

wavelength—

amplitude—

saturation—

radiant light—

reflected light—

Why is a 'red' rose everything but red?

1. How We See: The Visual System

accommodation—

conjunctive eye movements—

vergence eye movements—

retina—

bipolar cells—

ganglion cells—

blind spot—

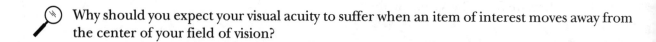

Why are people not constantly distracted by the flashing on and off of their visual worlds when they blink?

2. The Visual Pathway

   optic chiasm—

3. The Visual Receptors

   rods—

   cones—

   fovea—

Why should you expect your visual acuity to suffer when an item of interest moves away from the center of your field of vision?

4. Theories of Color Vision

   trichromatic theory—

   opponent-process theory—

   color afterimage—

How could you determine whether an animal can differentiate colors?

4. Color Deficiencies

   monochromat—

dichromat—

anomalous trichromat—

B. Audition (Hearing)

    audition—

  1. What We Hear: The Auditory Stimulus

    hertz (Hz)—

    decibel (db)—

  2. How We Hear: The Auditory System

    ossicles—

    oval window—

    basilar membrane—

    organ of Corti—

    tectorial membrane—

How, given that hair cells in the ear transduce acoustic information by bending, are we able to differentiate among sounds of varying frequencies?

    place theory—

    frequency theory—

3. Hearing Disorders

   conduction deafness—

   sensorineural deafness—

   central deafness—

   American Sign Language—

C. The Chemical Senses: Taste and Smell
   1. Taste (Gustation)

      gustation—

      a. What We Taste: The Gustatory Stimulus

      b. How We Taste: The Gustatory System

         taste buds—

         papillae—

         microvilli—

How, using only four basic tastes, can we explain the wide variety of tastes we are able to experience?

   2. Smell (Olfaction)

olfaction—

    a. What We Smell: The Olfactory Stimulus

    b. How We Smell: The Olfactory System

  3. The Interaction of Smell and Taste

D. Other Sensory Systems
  1. Vestibular Sense

    vestibular sense—

    semicircular canals—

    utricle—

  2. Kinesthetic Sense

    kinesthetic sense—

  3. Somatosensory Processing

  4. Pain

    gate control theory—

    endorphins—

    somatosensory receptors—

III. Perception

A. Motivation and Attention

   1. Motivational Influences

   2. Attention

     divided attention—

B. Basic Perceptual Abilities: Patterns and Constancies

   1. Pattern Perception

     pattern perception—

     feature analysis theory—

   2. Perceptual Constancies

     perceptual constancy—

     a. Shape Constancy

      shape constancy—

     b. Size Constancy

      size constancy—

     c. Depth Perception

      depth perception—

binocular cues—

monocular cues—

    d. Binocular Cues

binocular disparity—

    e. Monocular Cues

C. Gestalt Principles of Perceptual Organization
    1. Figure and Ground

figure-ground relationship—

    2. Principles of Grouping

proximity—

similarity—

good continuation and direction—

inclusiveness—

closure—

D. Perception of Movement
    apparent motion—

E. Perceptual Hypotheses and Illusions

perceptual hypothesis—

perceptual illusions—

 Explain why the grass really appears greener on the other side of the fence.

F. Contemporary Issues and Findings in Perception Research
  1. Parallel Processing, Visual Search, and the Application of Basic Perceptual Research

  visual search—

  2. Perception is Affected by Social Context

 What do contextual stimuli contribute to our perceptual experiences?

IV. **Paranormal Phenomena**

extrasensory perception (ESP)—

A. Skeptical Scientists

B. A Believing Public
  1. A Final Word

![star icon] **LEARNING OBJECTIVES**

After you have studied the chapter, you should be able to respond to the following statements and questions to convey your understanding of the material.

1. Describe the systems that receive sensory information about vision, hearing, taste, smell, body position, and movement. What do these systems have in common? How are they different?

2. How are the processes of sensation and perception related? What does each process contribute to one's ability to interact with the world?

3. How is perception affected by influences such as motivation and attention?

4. What roles do coincidences and chance occurrences play in beliefs about the paranormal?

It is helpful when learning the information from this chapter to study the how some of the terms are used in the contexts of figures and tables. Having studied the chapter you should be able to fill in the missing information. The answers are given at the end of the chapter.

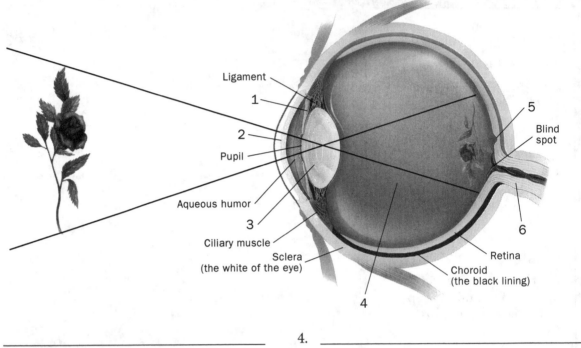

1. _____ 4. _____

2. _____ 5. _____

3. _____ 6. _____

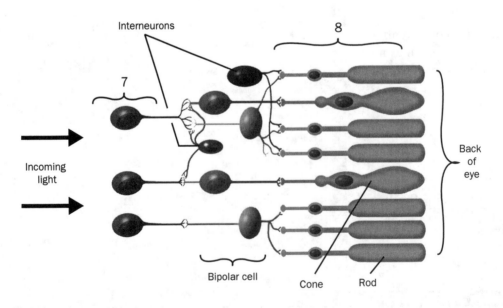

7. _____ 8. _____

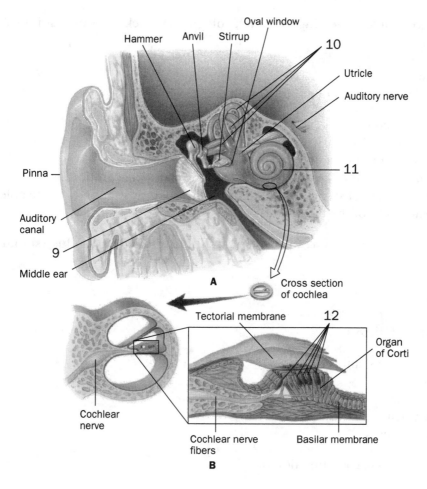

9. _____   11. _____

10. _____   12. _____

Circle the letter that corresponds to the **best** alternative for each of the following items. Read each alternative carefully. The answers are presented at the end of this study guide chapter. Be sure to learn *why* each correct alternative is better than the others

1. Sensation is to perception as ___ is to ___.
    a. left brain; right brain
    b. right brain; left brain
    c. seeing something red; identifying something as an apple
    d. identifying something as an apple; seeing something red

2. A common feature of the basic sensory processes is that they:
    a. involve transduction.
    b. all work the same way.
    c. were each evolved from a common process.
    d. are all involved in sensing stimuli at a distance.

3. Frank is unaware that he is wearing too much cologne. His lack of awareness is probably due to:
   a. adaptation.
   b. transduction.
   c. Weber's law.
   d. the just noticeable difference (jnd) for olfaction.

4. An absolute threshold is:
   a. a dangerous level of sensory stimulation.
   b. the largest amount of stimulation a person can perceive.
   c. the minimum amount of energy required for conscious recognition.
   d. the smallest amount of stimulation that must be added or subtracted to be able to notice the difference 50% of the time.

5. ___ suggests that the threshold varies with the nature of the stimulus (signal) and background stimulation.
   a. Weber
   b. The jnd
   c. Experience
   d. Signal detection theory

6. Wavelength is to ___ as amplitude is to ___.
   a. brightness; color
   b. color; brightness
   c. saturation; purity
   d. brightness; intensity

7. The color of a car occurs as a function of:
   a. amplitude
   b. saturation
   c. radiant light
   d. reflected light

8. Chris is a theater technician. Her job involves manipulating the gels that go between light bulbs and the objects they illuminate on stage. A psychologist might say her job is:
   a. boring.
   b. dangerous.
   c. to manipulate radiant light.
   d. to attend to sources of reflected light.

9. When you mix primary paints together you yield a dark, yucky color. Mixing light primaries, however, produces white light. The processes underlying these differences are called ___ and ___, respectively.
   a. additive; subtractive
   b. subtractive; additive
   c. visual art; performing art
   d. performing art; visual art

10. Conjunctive eye movements are to vergence eye movements as ___ is to ___.
    a. same; different
    b. different; same
    c. up; down
    d. in; out

11. The photoreceptor cells, rods and cones, are:
    a. distributed equally throughout the retina.
    b. disproportionately located outside the retina.
    c. in the back of the retina, pointing away from the cornea.
    d. in the front of the retinal layer, positioned to receive light as it comes though the lens.

12. Color afterimages, such as seeing blue dots for awhile after someone takes your picture with a camera and a flash, are (were) explained well by:
    a. the fovea.
    b. the trichromatic theory.
    c. the opponent-process theory.
    d. Gestalt psychologists in the 1920s.

13. Which of the following was NOT mentioned in the text as a variety of color deficiency?
    a. dichromat
    b. achromatosis
    c. monochromat
    d. anomalous trichromat

14. In vision, the wave characteristic, *complexity,* corresponds to the saturation level of the hue. What does complexity correspond to in audition?
    a. hertz (Hz)
    b. decibels (db)
    c. timbre
    d. none of the above

15. In order to hear frequencies at the extremes of our range of sensitivity (20-20,000 Hz), the amplitude of the wave needs to be:
    a. higher.
    b. significantly lower.
    c. proportional to the wave's length.
    d. executed in the following sequence: elbow, elbow, wrist, wrist

16. In audition, changes in air pressure (sound waves) are translated into fluid waves when the *stirrup* causes movement of the:
    a. ossicles.
    b. basilar membrane.
    c. tectorial membrane.
    d. oval window of the cochlea.

17. Rock concert is to ear wax as ___ is to ___.
    a. gross; great
    b. soft; loud
    c. central deafness; sensorineural deafness
    d. sensorineural deafness; conduction deafness

18. Microvilli are:
    a. hairs that project from taste receptors.
    b. small clusters of houses in rural areas.
    c. the name for the hair cells on the basilar membrane.
    d. the small gaps between myelin cells on the auditory nerve.

19. When we smell, airborne particles come in contact with our ___, which, in turn, send signals into the CNS.
    a. nasal mucus
    b. olfactory bulbs
    c. thalamic nuclei
    d. olfactory epithelium

20. Inner ear is to muscles and joints as ___ is to ___.
    a. audition; kinesthesia
    b. aching; hearing
    c. kinesthetic sense; vestibular sense
    d. vestibular sense; kinesthetic sense

21. The ability to process more than one source of stimulation at the same time is called:
    a. synesthesia.
    b. schizophrenia.
    c. divided attention.
    d. paranormal perception.

22. ___ is the phenomenon that permits you to recognize a door as a door, even when you see it from its edge.
    a. Feature detection
    b. Shape constancy
    c. Binocular disparity
    d. Good continuation and direction

23. Depth perception, or the ability to see our world three-dimensionally, involves ALL BUT which of the following:
    a. binocular cues.
    b. monocular cues.
    c. binocular disparity.
    d. retino-depth detectors.

24. Which of the following grouping principles is responsible for your ability to fill in gaps in your visual world?
    a. closure
    b. proximity
    c. inclusiveness
    d. good continuation and direction

25. What do flashing road construction sign arrows and cartoons have in common?
    a. nothing
    b. reliance on apparent motion
    c. that only a small minority pays attention to them
    d. all of the above

26. The magnitude of the Ebbinghaus illusion is greatest when:
    a. it is presented by Ebbinghaus himself.
    b. it is presented against a blue background.
    c. the target stimulus is surrounded by identical stimuli.
    d. the target stimulus is surrounded by different stimuli.

27. Clairvoyance, telepathy, precognition, and psychokinesis are all examples of:
    a. ESP.
    b. horse puckey.
    c. experimentally demonstrable phenomena.
    d. anomalistic psychological (or parapsychological) phenomena.

28. Which of the following, according to your textbook, is partially responsible for the fact that people commonly believe in psychic phenomena?
    a. influence by the media
    b. underestimating chance occurrences and coincidences
    c. many have had psychic experiences, or interpret their experiences as having been psychic
    d. all of the above

 ## ANSWERS TO LABELING EXERCISES

1. Iris	5. Fovea	9. Eardrum
2. Cornea	6. Optic Nerve	10. Semicircular canals
3. Lens	7. Ganglion Cell Layer	11. Cochlea
4. Vitreous Humor	8. Photoreceptor Layer	12. Hair cells

 ## PRACTICE TEST ANSWERS AND EXPLANATIONS

1. c. Sensation is the act of receiving stimuli from the environment; perception involves organizing and making sense of the information.

2. a. Transduction is the process of receiving stimuli and translating them into forms that can be used by the nervous system.

3. a. Adaptation is a loss of sensitivity to a stimulus by the receptors as a result of continued presentation of that stimulus.

4. c. The absolute threshold is the minimum amount of energy required for conscious detection of a stimulus 50 percent of the time.

5. d. The question in item 5 is the definition of signal detection theory.

6. b. Changes in perceived hue (or color) result from changes in wavelength whereas manipulating wave height results in shifts in intensity (or brightness).

7. d. Objects that do not emit light are sources of reflected light

8. c. Radiant sources of light include light bulbs and the sun. By placing gels in front of a source of radiant light, one manipulates (selectively filters) the wavelength qualities of the light.

9. b. Mixing pigments is a subtractive process whereas mixing lights is additive. Note that the primaries for these processes are different.

10. a. Conjunctive eye movements involve moving the eyes in the same direction (e.g., left or right when watching a bird fly). Vergence eye movements are movements of the eyes in opposite directions, such as when focusing on an object that is getting nearer or farther away.

11. c. Interestingly, the photoreceptors point away from the front of the eye, rather than toward it.

12. c. The opponent-process theory explains the phenomenon of color afterimages.

13. b. The three types of color-deficient people are monochromats, dichromats, and anomalous trichromats.

14. c. Timbre is the acoustic property that has to do with purity of a sound wave. It is what is responsible for the difference in sound generated by two different musical instruments playing the same note.

15. a. In order to hear higher frequency waves, we need them to be of greater amplitude (i.e., louder).

16. d. As the ossicles move, the stirrup (the third middle-ear bone) causes movement of the oval window, which, in turn, sets fluid inside the cochlea into motion.

17. d. Rock concerts can cause sensorineural deafness; ear wax can cause conduction deafness.

18. a. Microvilli are the hairs that project from taste receptors.

19. d. The olfactory epithelium receives airborne molecules and transmits information to the olfactory bulbs.

20. d. The vestibular sense results from activity in the inner ear, whereas the kinesthetic sense stems from receptors in the muscles and joints.

21. c. Divided attention is the ability to process two or more sources of sensory stimulation.

22. b. *Shape constancy* permits the perception of an object's shape as constant despite changes in its retinal image.

23. d. Retino-depth detectors do not exist.

24. a. *Closure* helps us perceive incomplete visual stimuli as complete.

25. b. The illusion of movement in a stationary object is called apparent. Both examples rely on this.

26. c. The Ebbinghaus illusion is strongest when target stimuli are surrounded by identical stimuli.

27. d. Clairvoyance, telepathy, precognition, and psychokinesis are all examples of anomalistic psychological (or parapsychological) phenomena.

28. d. The reasons why people believe in psychic phenomena vary across individuals.

Key Vocabulary Terms

Cut out and use as study cards; terms appear on
one side and definitions are on the other.

sensation	perception
transduction	adaptation
Weber's law	just noticeable difference (jnd)
absolute threshold	differential threshold

Key Vocabulary Terms

Cut out and use as study cards; terms appear on
one side and definitions are on the other.

The process of organizing and making sense of sensory information

Activation of receptors by stimuli in the environment

Loss of sensitivity to a stimulus by the receptors as a result of continued presentation of that stimulus

Conversion of stimuli received by the receptors into a form (patterns of neural impulses) that can be used by the nervous system

Smallest difference between two stimuli that is noticeable 50 percent of the time by participants

The observation that the amount of stimulus increase or decrease required to notice a change, divided by the original stimulation, is a constant

Smallest amount of stimulation that must be added to or subtracted from an existing stimulus for a person to be able to detect a change 50 percent of the time (see jnd)

Minimum amount of energy required for conscious detection of a stimulus 50 percent of the time by participants

signal detection theory	wavelength
amplitude	saturation
radiant light	reflected light
accommodation	conjunctive eye movements
vergence eye movements	bipolar cells

Physical length of a light wave measured in nanometers

The contention that the threshold varies with the nature of the stimulus (signal) and background stimulation (noise)

Trueness or accuracy of a color

Strength or intensity of a stimulus (brightness for visual stimuli; loudness for auditory stimuli)

Energy that is reflected by objects

Visible energy emitted by an object

Movements of the eyes in the same direction

In focusing, action of the ciliary muscles to change the shape of the lens

Cells in the retina that connect the receptors to ganglion cells

Movements of the eyes in opposite directions

ganglion cells

blind spot

optic chiasm

rods

cones

fovea

trichromatic
theory

opponent-
process theory

color afterimage

monochromat

Location at which the optic nerve leaves the eyeball; contains no receptors

Cells in the retina whose axons form the optic nerve

Most prevalent visual receptors; have lower threshold and lower acuity than cones and do not detect color

Point at which the optic nerve fibers from each eye join; fibers from the nasal half of the retina cross to the opposite hemisphere of the brain

Indented spot in the center of the retina that contains only cones

Visual receptors that are less prevalent than rods; have a higher threshold and higher acuity and are able to detect color

Color vision theory stressing the pairing of color experiences; activation of one process can inhibit its partner

Color vision theory stating that there are three types of color receptors

Person who sees only shades of gray owing to a rare form of color deficiency

Perception of a color that is not really present; occurs after viewing the opposite or complementary color

dichromat	anomalous trichromat
audition	hertz (Hz)
decibel (db)	ossicles
oval window	basilar membrane
organ of Corti	tectorial membrane

Person with a form of colorblindness in which one of the three primary colors (red, blue, or green) is processed incorrectly

Person who has trouble seeing one of the primary colors (red, blue, or green) owing to a form of color deficiency

Unit of measure (in cycles per second) of the frequency of a sound wave

Sense of hearing

Three bones (hammer, anvil, and stirrup) located in the middle ear that conduct sound from the outer to the inner ear

Unit of measure of the amount of energy producing the vibrations we perceive as sound

Membrane located in the cochlea of the inner ear; movement of cochlear fluid causes it to vibrate

Structure that connects the middle ear with the cochlea of the inner ear; its movement causes fluid in the cochlea to move

Membrane located above the organ of Corti in the inner ear

Structure located on the basilar membrane of the inner ear that contains the auditory receptors

place theory	frequency theory
conduction deafness	sensorineural deafness
central deafness	American Sign Language (ASL)
gustation	taste buds
papillae	microvilli

Theory stating that the basilar membrane vibrates at different rates to create the perception of different pitches

Theory stating that the basilar membrane vibrates at different places to create the perception of different pitches

Deafness caused by damage to the inner ear, especially the hair cells

Deafness owing to problems associated with transmitting sounds through the outer and middle ear

A manual-visual language developed within the American deaf community

Deafness resulting from disease and tumors in the auditory pathways or auditory cortex of the brain

Structures that contain the taste receptors

Sense of taste

Hairs that project from taste receptors

Bumps or protrusions distributed on the tongue and throat that are lined with taste buds

olfaction	vestibular sense
semicircular canals	utricle
kinesthetic sense	gate control theory
endorphins	somatosensory receptors
divided attention	pattern perception

System located in the inner ear that allows us to make adjustments to bodily movements and postures

Sense of smell

Fluid—filled chamber in the inner ear that detects changes in gravity

Fluid-filled passages in the inner ear that detect movement of the head

Theory of pain stating that the release of substance P in the spinal cord produces the sensation of pain

System of receptors located in the muscles and joints that provides information about the location of the extremities

Receptors in the skin that provide sensory information

Opiatelike substances produced by the body that block pain by inhibiting the release of substance P

The ability to discriminate among different figures and shapes

The ability to process more than one source of stimulation at the same time

feature analysis theory	perceptual constancy
shape constancy	size constancy
depth perception	binocular cues
monocular cues	binocular disparity
figure-ground relationship	proximity

The tendency to perceive the size and shape of an object as constant even though its retinal image changes

Theory of pattern perception stating that we perceive basic elements of an object and assemble them mentally to create the complete object

The tendency to perceive the size of an object as constant despite changes in its retinal image

The tendency to perceive the shape of an object as constant despite changes in its retinal image

Cues for depth perception that involve the use of both eyes

The ability to perceive our world three-dimensionally

The difference between the images seen by the two eyes

Cues for depth perception that involve the use of only one eye

Gestalt principle stating that perceptual elements that are close together are seen as a group

Organization of perceptual elements into a figure (the focus of attention) and a background

similarity	good continuation and direction
inclusiveness	closure
apparent motion	perceptual hypothesis
perceptual illusions	visual search
extrasensory perception (ESP)	

Gestalt principle stating that smooth, flowing lines are more readily perceived than choppy, broken lines

Gestalt principle stating that perceptual elements that are similar are seen as a group

Gestalt principle stating that organizing perceptions into whole objects is easier than perceiving separate parts independently

Gestalt principle stating that the identity of a smaller figure may be lost within a larger, more complex figure

Inference about the nature of stimuli received from the environment

Illusion of movement in a stationary object

identifying the presence of a target stimulus among a group of other, distractor items

Misperceptions or interpretations of stimuli that do not correspond to the sensations received

Behaviors or experiences that cannot be explained by information received by the senses

The Right Place at the Right Time

Think of *where* you would expect to go for each of the following services:

1. to get a manicure
2. to invest a large sum of money
3. to get a paint job on a valuable automobile
4. to get advice on native plants for landscaping
5. to have a delicate surgical procedure performed on you

The people who provide these services have very diverse backgrounds, but they all share at least one thing in common. Their work is done in environments that supports their occupations. That is, they work in places that have conditions and resources that permit them to do their very best. Could you imagine: getting your nails done in a dark place without tables and chairs; handing your hard-earned money to someone on the street; getting your car painted outside on a windy day; going to a grocery store to determine which plants would be best for your yard; or having surgery performed on you in an old warehouse? While things might work out all right in each of those scenarios, the conditions are clearly not conducive to the services.

The principles that apply to professional services share things in common with those for establishing an effective study environment. You need the appropriate environment, tools, and access to the resources you may need if you are to make the most of your time for studying. Anyone would agree that beauticians, stockbrokers, autobody painters, horticulturists, and surgeons need to work in the contexts we usually associate with them. For some reason, though, perhaps because books are fairly portable, it is not uncommon to see students 'studying' in the darndest places. It is curious that students will walk right past the library en route to the busiest building on campus to study. If your goal is to socialize, why not leave the books at home?

List the last four places you where you studied:

_____

_____

List four places you think would be ideal for studying:

_____

_____

Did you notice any differences? Why or why not?

_____

The Student Union Is a Great Place to Meet People

But it is a poor place to study, for exactly the same reasons. Because of schedule differences, different people pass through there at different times of the day: the environment is ever changing. Think about how goofy it would be if the professionals mentioned above were to do their same work, but to trade working places for a day. It would be more than disconcerting to hear the horticulturist talking about dirt and microorganisms in the surgery wing of a hospital. Or, what if the surgeon were on the floor of a stock exchange building, with her bright lights, instruments, and hair net, carving away on somebody? It is hard to imagine the brokers in the room attending to the changing of decimal points on the electronic tickertape.

The point is simple. Now that you have established goals, and have organized a schedule that will permit you to make the best use of your time, you need to focus on the places where you work at your most attention-demanding activity: studying. Do not be tempted to think that the portability of books means they are equally useful anywhere you might take them. The books may work equally well in a variety of places, but all they have to do is sit there. You will not work equally well in a variety of environments; find one or two places that will help you maximize learning efficiency. If you work when you should be working, and play when you should be playing, you will be much happier about both activities.

How can studying in a dedicated place help meet your academic and your leisure-time goals?

_____

_____

So Where *Should* I Study?

This may come as a shock: the library is probably the best building on your campus for studying. Think about it. It has the best collection of resources, such as books in every academic field, dictionaries, and probably even computers that can be used to find resources both on and off campus. But, you might say, I do not need those things if I am merely reading novels for my literature class or working math problems. It is hard to imagine anyone, your professors included, reading a book without a dictionary available. All too often people read right past words that are brand new to them, or that are somewhat familiar but are being used in an unusual way. The best way to get the most from what you read, and to expand your vocabulary, is to use a dictionary to study the meanings of words as you see them used in text passages.

Libraries are outstanding learning environments for other reasons, too. What comes to mind when you think of the library? Unless you have visited some mighty strange libraries, you probably think of a building that is fairly quiet, in which people work diligently and independently. There is little question concerning whether students who study in libraries are there to do homework. What about the student who sets up camp in the student union?

Perhaps your library is different though. Or for some unexplainable reason, maybe you are not able to focus there. There are plenty of other places on your campus or in your community. What is important is that you identify a place or two that you can use to give your undivided attention (recall the passage in Chapter 3 that discussed the need to focus attention, at times such as when driving in busy traffic).

List two or three places that might be good for studying that you have not yet tried.

_____

_____

Characteristics of the Designated Space

When you begin looking for a few places you can use for studying, adopt the criteria for evaluating good libraries. When you enter the context it should be immediately clear to you that you are preparing to concentrate. The place you choose should be quiet. You should have at your disposal, or bring with you, any resources necessary to make the most of your dedicated study time. The place you choose should also be well lit, and heated or cooled appropriately for your comfort needs. In short, aside from having the necessary resources, you need a place that anybody could go to and recognize as a good place to study.

The following are examples to help you get started thinking about where to study.

1. **Empty Classrooms.** Perhaps the best ones are those that you have regular class meetings in when they are not in use, but any empty classroom should be fine.

2. **Study Carrels.** These are distributed throughout the library, and perhaps in other designated spaces on campus. Study carrels can be great places to work because they limit your ability to be distracted and often provide shelving to organize your things.

3. **A Local Community Library.** If, with any regularity, your friends take you away from your studies, you no longer have a situation that is conducive to learning. Find a new one. Local libraries have many of the same characteristics as university libraries and can be great places to study.

4. **Bookstores, Coffee Shops, and Galleries.** These kinds of places are presently very trendy. If it is a business that sells drinks and snacks, but is also good for studying, the cost of a cup of coffee or a bagel is cheap in exchange for the opportunity to work there. Some businesspeople try to attract students and to maintain good study places.

Regardless of where you go, make sure it is away from distractions, including telephones and friends who do not take their homework as seriously as you do. If you have a cellular phone or pager, TURN IT OFF. You cannot possibly give your undivided attention to your academic goals if you are preoccupied with the phone (or email). If someone needs to get in touch with you, they will. If you have a cellular phone or a pager, you probably also have an answering machine that will take messages for you. Let it do what it is supposed to do.

What three things are most likely to distract you during study time?

_____

_____

_____

Psychologists Study Environments

Classical conditioning (see Chapter 6) helps make an environment more or less effective for a given activity. As an environment becomes familiar, your perceptual systems begin to influence your brain in response to the environmental cues. Have you ever become suddenly hungry when you saw a restaurant advertisement or noticed the time (even though you were not hungry until then)? Environmental cues can influence behavior in powerful ways.

Use your knowledge of classical conditioning to your advantage. If a given context is most strongly associated, for you, with a behavior that is incompatible with focused attention on homework, avoid studying there. For example, the lounge may have many of the characteristics that are appropriate for a good study place, but you may feel compelled to turn on the TV or participate in some other distraction whenever you are there. Avoid tempting yourself. Likewise, your bedroom is designated as a place for resting; trying to study in bed will surely make you tired! Do not allow yourself to be lured into the bed with intentions of learning anything from a textbook.

The real value of identifying one or two places where you will do most of your studying has precisely to do with classical conditioning. Recall the attributes that make libraries effective for studying. That list is the result of conditioning; you have learned that libraries have certain characteristics. Your study places should serve to help you recognize immediately when you should be focusing your attention on homework.

What are some effective cues for letting you know you are in a place that is good for studying?

_____

_____

_____

When One Is Not Enough

It is a good idea to identify two or three places where you can study. Imagine that you have scheduled time to work on your academic goals at your peak time for devoting attention, and that you have found your way to 'your' study carrel in the library. What will you do when someone else is there? What if the library is closed or exceptionally busy? Getting frustrated will only drain your energy and divert your attention from your studies. Smile and head for a quieter place.

Another good reason to have two or more designated study places is to provide some variation on long study days. You may find that you like studying in one place early in the day, but at another in the afternoon or evening. If you prefer to study in a business (e.g., coffee shop), you may need to find another location that has hours that permit you to start working earlier, or to continue later.

List Three Places Where You Could Study Effectively And Their Hours Of Availability

Location: Time Available to You:

_____

_____

_____

Be Mindful of Others

The previous chapter included a comment on good communication. People who are interested in doing things with you need to know when you will be available, and when you are busy. By making it clear that you will not be available until you finish your homework, people will be less inclined to interrupt you. This is especially important if you have a designated space in your room, or are known to be at a certain place when you are studying. An added bonus to communicating when you will be busy studying is that others will help protect your time.

Be aware that the best places for studying are effective because people respect them as places for quiet reflection. If you get restless, or get the urge to make a lot of noise, be courteous and leave before you ruin the environment for others. Also, avoid taking a project group from one of your classes to discuss the material in a place where people are usually quiet. You may be studying, but if your activity affects others, you are not being respectful.

CHAPTER 4

Motivation and Emotion

Use the space provided in this outline to record notes from the textbook as well as from class lectures and discussion. Questions related to the *Psychological Detective* sections in the text have been presented in the outline; use the associated space to respond to the questions and to record your own comments about the issues. *Keywords and terms* from the text have been italicized and inserted in the outline so you can practice writing their definitions. The pages in this study guide are perforated and can be removed for use as study sheets for quizzes and exams.

I.   **What is Motivation?**

      motivation—

II. **Theories of Motivation**

    A. Biological Theories

        instincts—

        1. Ethology

        2. Sociobiology

            sociobiology—

        3. Internal Drive States, Drives, and Drive Reduction

            drive—

            homeostasis—

            drive-reduction model—

        4. Optimum-Level Theories

🔍 Why might changes in stimulation be desirable?

       optimum-level theory—

B. Cognitive Theories

      cognitive theories of motivation—

    1. Cognitive-Consistency Theories

        a. Cognitive Dissonance

        cognitive dissonance—

🔍 List examples of when you have, in your mind, raised the value of an item by reducing the value of another.

    2. Incentive Theories

        incentive theory—

C. Maslow's Hierarchy of Needs

      hierarchy of needs—

      self-actualization—

D. The Role of Learning

learned motives—

learned goals (or learned incentives)—

III. Dealing with Multiple Motives

1. Basic Conflicts

2. Multiple Approach-Avoidance: Several Goals With Good And Bad Features

IV. Specific Motives

A. Hunger

set point—

B. Sex

1. External Factors

pheromones—

2. Hormones

3. Brain Mechanisms

4. The Sexual Response

C. Achievement

achievement—

D. Affiliation

   affiliation—

V. **The What and the Why of Emotion**

   emotion—

A. Relating Emotions and Behavior

VI. **The Physiological Components of Emotions**

A. The First Theories

   1. The James-Lange Theory

       James-Lange theory—

       commonsense view of emotions—

   2. The Cannon-Bard Theory

       Cannon-Bard Theory—

B. Physiological Differences among Emotions

C. The Role of the Brain

What value, if any, is there to having more than one way for information to get to the brain?

   1. The Brain's Hemispheres and Emotions

2. Lack of Emotion

3. The Opponent-Process Theory

   opponent-process theory—

D. Evaluating the Lie Detector

   polygraph—

 How might the anxiety associated with taking a lie detector test increase or decrease the likelihood of the machine detecting a lie when you tell the truth?

VII. **The Expressive Components of Emotions**

A. Universal Elements in the Facial Expression of Emotion

   1. How Many Emotions Are There?

   2. The Facial Feedback Hypothesis

      facial feedback hypothesis—

 How does your ability to smile or frown influence your emotionality?

      display rules—

3. Smiling

Is a sincere smile different from an insincere one? If so, how?

B. Nonverbal Communication

nonverbal communication—

1. Body Language

2. Paralanguage

paralanguage—

C. Gender Effects

VIII. The Cognitive Components of Emotions

A. The Language of Emotion

1. The Schacter and Singer Appraisal Model

2. Other Appraisal Theories of Emotion

B. The Development of Emotion

1. Emotional Intelligence

After you have studied the chapter, you should be able to respond to the following statements and questions to convey your understanding of the material.

1. Differentiate between biological and cognitive theories of emotion.

2. Identify the four basic categories of motives that were outlined in your book. How are they similar and how are they different?

3. How is the brain involved in the regulation of emotions?

4. What elements of emotions are universal?

5. How is cognition related to emotion?

Fill in the blanks in the following statements with key words and terms from the textbook. Answer as many as you can without referring to your notes or to the book. If you have blanks after thinking about each item, try using your book. The answers are presented after the practice test.

1. _____ _____ are triggered or released by specific environmental events called *releasing stimuli.*

2. _____ _____ of motivation suggest behavior is motivated by the goal the organism seeks to attain.

3. Deciding whether to study for a quiz instead of going out with friends or to go out with friends and risk failing an exam is an example of an _____-_____ _____.

4. When considering making a purchase, you may find yourself attracted to and repulsed by a variety of goals. The term for this circumstance is: _____ _____ _____ _____.

5. The menstrual synchrony found among lesbian couples has supported speculation about the role of _____ in controlling some aspects of human behavior.

6. During the resolution phase of the sexual response cycle, physiological changes associated with sexual arousal gradually _____.

7. The _____ _____ theory of emotion can be used to explain why people participate in anxiety-provoking activities such as skydiving.

8. Research on the universality of emotions has demonstrated that there are at least _____ emotions that are recognized everywhere.

9. _____ _____ are cultural norms that tell us to laugh when someone (particularly one's boss) tells a joke.

10. _____ _____ includes such abilities as motivating oneself, persisting in the face of frustrations, and controlling impulses, as well as being aware of the emotions one is experiencing.

PRACTICE TEST

Circle the letter that corresponds to the *best* alternative for each of the following items. Be sure to read each alternative carefully and to learn why each correct alternative is better than the others. The answers are presented at the end of this study guide chapter.

1. The study of motivation has three aspects. Which of the following is not one of these?
   a. the goal(s) toward which the behavior was directed
   b. the factor or motivational state prompting the behavior
   c. the reasons for differences in the intensity of the behavior
   d. all of the above are aspects associated with the study of emotions

2. Instincts are:
   a. essentially reflexes.
   b. smells that come from within.
   c. the building blocks for motivation.
   d. unlearned behaviors that are more complex than reflexes.

3. The red spots on the bellies of male stickleback fish:
   a. are releasing stimuli for other males.
   b. occur because the fish swim to close to the ground.
   c. develop as the fish mature and become large enough to mate.
   d. fade to gray when the fish are no longer interested in mating.

4. A compelling feature of the sociobiology theory is that it:
   a. is interdisciplinary in nature.
   b. can explain altruistic behavior.
   c. successfully predicted homelessness would be a problem.
   d. explains human and animal behavior without presuming motives.

5. Homeostasis is the tendency of the body to maintain balance. Drive reduction theory suggests physiological needs known as ___ motivate activity that will restore balance.
   a. drives
   b. homeostats
   c. psychophysical wants
   d. the 'basics' (for humans these include the need to shop, for example)

6. Which theories of motivation stress the processing and understanding of information?
   a. ethology
   b. sociobiology
   c. optimum-level theory
   d. cognitive theories of emotion

7. When a person has inconsistent or incompatible thoughts or cognitions, this is called:
   a. hysteria.
   b. mass confusion.
   c. cognitive dissonance.
   d. feeling wishy-washy.

8. Drive-reduction theories are to incentive theories as ___ is to ___.
   a. go; stop
   b. push; pull
   c. accelerate; brake
   d. slow down; speed up

9. Maslow's hierarchy of needs has five categories of motivated behavior that can be ordered in hierarchical fashion along which dimension(s)?
   a. the *type* of motivation
   b. the *strength* of motivation
   c. both a. and b.
   d. neither a. nor b.

10. Self-actualization:
    a.   is met concurrently with basic needs.
    b.   is reached by most people by the time they are 30.
    c.   comes from developing one's unique potential to develop fully.
    d.   takes a lifetime to accomplish; since most people do not live that long it is rare.

11. Money, diamonds, gold, and concert tickets are examples of:
    a.   rare commodities.
    b.   intrinsic motivators.
    c.   valued natural resources.
    d.   learned goals or incentives

12. Which category of conflict is characterized as having only one goal?
    a.   approach-approach
    b.   approach-avoidance
    c.   avoidance-avoidance
    d.   multiple approach-avoidance

13. Which category of specific motives is hardest to define precisely?
    a.   sex
    b.   hunger
    c.   affiliation
    d.   achievement

14. The concept of *set point* has to do with which category of motive?
    a.   sex
    b.   hunger
    c.   affiliation
    d.   achievement

15. Human sexual behavior is a function of an interplay between all but which of the following?
    a.   genetic factors
    b.   prenatal factors
    c.   environmental factors
    d.   all the above factors are involved

16. The James-Lange theory of emotions, and the commonsense view of emotions:
    a.   are opposite.
    b.   are very similar.
    c.   were developed simultaneously.
    d.   both implicate physiological arousal as the cause of emotion.

17. In some respects, the Cannon-Bard theory is:
    a.   a reaction to the James-Lange theory.
    b.   a variation of the commonsense view.
    c.   a compromise between the commonsense view and the James-Lange theory.
    d.   the most significant theory in psychology's short history as it is right on the mark.

18. Experiments that measured autonomic nervous system arousal as the dependent variable demonstrated which of the following with respect to emotional expressions?
    a. Categorically different emotions produce different levels of autonomic arousal.
    b. Autonomic arousal changes as a function of emotional intensity, irrespective of the category.
    c. Though they may 'feel' different, all the emotions are very similar in terms of autonomic arousal.
    d. None of the above are true.

19. The ___ is a component of the limbic system and is essential in evaluating the emotional meaning of stimuli.
    a. amygdala
    b. hippocampus
    c. hypothalamus
    d. cerebral cortex

20. The opponent-process theory of emotion is:
    a. based on homeostatic mechanisms.
    b. supported by research using the polygraph.
    c. an interesting model, but holds little scientific value.
    d. based on the need for cognitive appraisal of an emotion's hedonic value.

21. Eckman's research that involved showing pictures (of people expressing a variety of emotions) to people from the world over revealed:
    a. that there are 4 basic emotions.
    b. while emotions may be common, their expression varies widely.
    c. that the number of emotions one may experience varies with cultural exposure.
    d. that there is a high degree of agreement across cultures in recognizing basic emotions.

22. According to the facial feedback hypothesis, holding your face in a frown:
    a. is metabolically expensive.
    b. will cause it to get stuck that way.
    c. provides feedback that will influence your emotionality.
    d. None of the above; the text mentions no such hypothesis.

23. Display rules are:
    a. more for children.
    b. examples of cultural norms.
    c. really more like guidelines than rules.
    d. directions for confederates in emotion research experiments.

24. The meanings of gestures (also called emblems):
    a. are fairly universal.
    b. are difficult to discern unless you are part of the in-group.
    c. are determined by the emotional experience of the communicator.
    d. vary from culture to culture, though sometimes the meanings are shared.

25. The German term *schadenfreude*, and the Japanese term *ijirashii* refer to:
    a. the same things.
    b. the opposite things.
    c. emotions for which the English language has no labels.
    d. emotions that are basically positive, but are unlike anything experienced by an American.

ANSWERS TO KEY WORD EXERCISE

1. Instinctive (or innate) behaviors
2. incentive theories
3. avoidance-avoidance conflict
4. multiple approach-avoidance conflict
5. pheromones
6. decline
7. opponent-process
8. six: anger, disgust, fear, happiness, sadness, and surprise
9. Display rules
10. Emotional intelligence

PRACTICE TEST ANSWERS AND EXPLANATIONS

1. d. Answers a. - c. represent the range of aspects addressed in the study of emotion.

2. d. Instincts are unlearned behaviors that play roles in determining motivation. That is, they are native (innate) to the species of interest.

3. a. The red spots serve to identify that the territory an intruder is entering is already occupied.

4. b. Sociobiological theory posits that individuals act in unselfish ways to perpetuate their genes. According to the theory, sometimes this means giving one's life so that (genetic) relatives live.

5. a. Drive reduction theory, as the name implies, suggests that drives motivate behavior.

6. d. Cognitive theories stress the active processing of information.

7. c. Cognitive dissonance is an aversive state that occurs when thoughts are incompatible.

8. b. Drive-reduction theories say drives push us toward goals (thirst causes us to engage in seeking something to drink); incentive theories suggest that we are pulled by the goal (money might encourage your behavior).

9. c. Maslow's hierarchy uses both dimensions: type and strength of motivation.

10. c. Self-actualization, according to Maslow's theory, is the need to develop one's fullest potential.

11. d. These are examples of learned goals or learned incentives. Each can act as a powerful motivator.

12. b. An approach-avoidance conflict has one goal that has good and bad aspects associated with it.

13. d. Achievement is difficult to define, but usually involves behaviors directed toward attainment of a goal or avoiding an aversive event. The abstract nature of what goals or events influence achievement motivation makes it hard to define.

14. b. One's *set point* is a range of weight that the body usually maintains.

15. d. Factors a. - c. all interact to influence human sexual behavior.

16. a. The two are opposite with respect to perspective on when bodily changes occur.

17. c. Although it has its shortcomings, the Cannon-Bard theory, which is a bit of a compromise between the commonsense view and the James-Lange theory, was a good idea for its time.

18. a. Different categories of emotion are associated with different patterns of autonomic activity.

19. a. The amygdala is important for processing emotional information.

20. a. The opponent-process theory of emotions assumes a need for emotional homeostasis and posits opposing processes to account for the range of experiences we have.

21. d. There is a high degree of agreement among people of widely varying cultures about what expressions convey.

22. c. The facial feedback hypothesis suggests that making a certain expression will produce the corresponding emotion.

23. b. Display rules are examples of cultural norms, and concern which emotions to display, to whom, and under which circumstances.

24. d. Gestures' meanings vary from culture to culture. The meaning of a given gesture may be in stark contrast to what people think they are communicating when using gestures.

25. c. These terms refer to experiences that English-speaking people understand, but for which they have not developed specific words.

Key Vocabulary Terms

Cut out and use as study cards; terms appear on one side and definitions are on the other.

motivation	instinct
sociobiology	drive
homeostasis	drive-reduction model
optimum-level theory	cognitive theories of motivation

Key Vocabulary Terms

Cut out and use as study cards; terms appear on one side and definitions are on the other.

Unlearned behavior that is more complex than a reflex	Physiological and psychological factors that account for the arousal, direction, and persistence of behavior
Internal motivational state created by a physiological need	The study of the genetic and evolutionary basis of social behavior
Theory that views motivated behavior as directed toward the reduction of a physiological need	Tendency of the body to maintain an optimum, balanced range of physiological processes
Theories that stress the active processing of information	Theory that the body functions best at a specific level of arousal, which varies from one individual to another

cognitive dissonance	incentive theory
hierarchy of needs	self-actualization
learned motives	learned goals (or learned incentives)
set point	pheromones
affiliation	emotion

Theory that views behavior as motivated by the goal the organism seeks to attain

Aversive state produced when an individual holds two incompatible thoughts or cognitions

Need to develop one's full potential

Maslow's view that basic needs must be satisfied before higher-level needs can be satisfied

Goals or incentives that are learned

Motives that are learned or acquired

Chemical odors emitted by some animals that appear to influence the behavior of members of the same species

A range of weight that the body seems to maintain under most circumstances

Physiological changes and conscious feelings of pleasantness or unpleasantness, aroused by external and internal stimuli, that lead to behavioral reactions

The need to be with others and avoid being alone

James-Lange theory	commonsense view of emotions
Cannon-Bard theory	opponent-process theory
polygraph	facial feedback hypothesis
display rules	nonverbal communication
paralanguage	

View that emotions precede and cause bodily changes

Theory that physiological changes precede and cause emotions

Theory that following an emotional response, the brain initiates the opposite reaction in an attempt to achieve homeostasis

Theory that the thalamus relays information simultaneously to the cortex and to the sympathetic nervous system, causing emotional feelings and physiological changes to occur at the same time

Hypothesis that making a certain facial expression will produce the corresponding emotion

An electronic device (often called a lie detector) that senses and records changes in several physiological indices including blood pressure, heart rate, respiration, and galvanic skin response

Communication that involves movements, gestures, and facial expressions

Culturally specific rules for which emotions to display, to whom, and when they can be displayed

Communication that involves aspects of speech such as rate of talking and tone of voice, but not the words used

Thus far in the *Tips for Success* sections we have examined essential issues concerning habits and practices that will help you make the most of your college years and beyond. By learning to set goals and monitor progress, to use your time wisely, and to locate environments that are conducive to effective studying, you will make significant strides toward reaching your potential for each of your endeavors. In addition to these skills, you will want to minimize distractions from your attention.

You Are Already Much of the Way There

If you acted on the suggestions from the *Tips* section on creating an effective study environment, you have already done much of what you need to do to avoid distractions. However, you will find that in spite of your having designated good locales for studying, you can still be distracted from your efforts. In turn, this will marginalize the time you have allocated for working on your goals. Thus, the balance of your schedule will be impacted, as may be your ability to attain your goals. This section was prepared to help you learn to concentrate and communicate, and to avoid the negative impact brought on by distractions.

On Concentration

Things that can serve to distract your concentration fall into two broad categories: those that you can control, and those that you cannot control. The following list identifies a few common issues related to distractions you can control to some extent:

1. **Knowing What to Do.** One of the biggest distractions people face is wondering where to begin, or how to proceed on a given task or set of tasks. This concern with what to do usually results from not having set adequate goals, or from having goals that are too vague. Breaking your goals down into discrete steps will make it easier to know what to do next.

2. **Reducing Stress.** The anxiety that comes from an approaching deadline, having a full schedule, or from any number of personal issues can be very distracting. Whenever possible begin working on projects early. Writing term papers and preparing for exams becomes increasingly stressful as deadlines approach. Controlling stressors when you *can* makes it everything easier.

3. **Be Healthy.** If you feel well, get adequate sleep, exercise regularly, and have a balanced diet, you will find it much easier to concentrate. Alternatively, if you are not generally healthy, concerns about modifying your lifestyle will sometimes preoccupy your mind and distract you from doing your best work. Being healthy benefits you several-fold; it will make you feel energetic, you will work more efficiently, and you will not be preoccupied with your health.

4. **Know When to Say "When".** Your capacity to concentrate is directly related to your productivity. Active studying is time-intensive, fatiguing work. You will benefit the most if you work under peak concentration conditions, and take breaks when you notice you are not processing information as efficiently. Depending on the material you study and issues such as those mentioned above, you should probably plan to work in 20-30 minute blocks. A five to ten minute break should serve to help you regain good concentration. If you cannot remember something you just read, it is time for a break.

Identify four distractors that have made it difficult for you to concentrate. What will you do to guard against each of these in the future?

	Distractor	Your Plan to Guard against the Distraction in the Future
1.		
2.		
3.		
4.		

On Communication

Sometimes you will do everything right—identifying a goal or set of goals to work on, scheduling your time, finding a good place to work—but circumstances beyond your control will divert you as you do your work. Many distractions stem from other people who want your time and attention. Letting others know how you use your time will reduce the likelihood of having them distract you. Because people will contact you when you are working for several different reasons, you will need several different plans for responding to protect your time. The following list addresses some common reasons people may contact you, and suggestions about how you might respond.

1. **Roommates and Living Mates.** Those with whom you live are perhaps the most likely to distract you, even though they may want you to do your very best. If you study in a place that is also used for other activities, it is a good idea to have another study place that can serve as a back-up. Establishing a plan or schedule for how and when the space will be used will help. Consider taking advantage of times when those you live with are asleep or away to do your homework. The first few hours of each day are usually the quietest. Those who live in residence halls or apartments have slightly different issues than those who live at home.

    a. **Residence Hall and Apartment Roommates.** Whether you picked your roommate or had one assigned to you, it will be important to develop ground rules for when the environment needs to be quiet for studying, and when it is ok to have friends over, or to listen to the radio, or to watch TV. Try posting one or more copies of a "quiet hours" schedule where others can see it.

    b. **Family Members.** If you live at home, your family members will probably be receptive of your requests for quiet time to study. Younger siblings and children, however, have more difficulty understanding the need for uninterrupted time. In addition to setting "quiet hours" for your living quarters, consider signaling others that you are studying by hanging a sign on your door that you can take down when you are not studying.

2. **People Who Stop by Unexpectedly.** You may have friends or family members who periodically stop by unannounced. While sometimes the timing may be perfect and you will welcome a visitor, other times it will disrupt you. Occasionally the lure of a friend who wants to do something with you may even cause you to leave your studies behind before you meet your goal. It is in your long-term best interest to establish a policy whereby people call ahead rather than just stop by. It is much easier to say "no" when you are on the phone than when you are talking face to face. Also, it is easier to keep a phone conversation short than it is to make a personal visit brief.

3. **The Telephone.** When used properly, the telephone can be a great time saving tool. Use it to call ahead for appointments, to check on where something you are looking for may be found, or to make arrangements with others. Unfortunately, the telephone can distract your concentration and lead to wasted time as well. When you study, try doing so in an environment that has no phone, or turn the ringer off on your phone. Sometimes, however the ringing of the phone will disrupt you. Consider these suggestions for each of the following kinds of phone calls:

    a. **Telemarketers.** You can usually identify that someone is trying to sell you something within a few seconds after picking up the phone. Whoever called interrupted you. It is ok to interrupt the caller to state firmly that you do not do business over the phone. Repeat as necessary. Or, try telling her or him to give you *their personal phone number* so *you can call them* back at a time that is more convenient for you. That usually gets the point across!

b. **Friends.** If appropriate, state that you are busy but will return the call when you get to a stopping point in your work. This may feel awkward, but bear in mind that you were distracted. If you call back as promised, your friends will not get too upset. To reinforce the need to respect one another's time, and to acknowledge that the phone can be distracting, begin conversations that you initiate by asking whether you called at a bad time. If your friends adopt that habit by following your example, it will be easy to avoid having long conversations at inappropriate times.

c. **Sometimes It Is Better to Take the Call.** You may decide to talk on the phone in spite of the timing of a call. When possible, try to keep a list of tasks on hand or in your mind that you can work on while you talk. It will probably be important to have them be tasks that do not demand too much attention. Try putting away dishes or laundry, watering plants, etc. while you talk. Doing this will make help you make the most of the distraction.

4. **Televisions, Stereos, and Other Noisy Things.** Most people concentrate best when the environment is completely quiet. Others, however, find that having something to mask the sounds of neighbors, traffic, and other irregular noises is helpful. It is important not to be distracted, however, by anything that you turn on (e.g., the radio) while you are studying. If you prefer to have music playing while you study, play music that has no lyrics so you are not tempted to sing along. Some people actually turn the radio or TV to a frequency that is in between stations. This produces *white noise,* or a sound that is comprised of all frequencies. Provided that it is not too loud, white noise can be an effective way of masking other noise.

Identify five things you can do to help reduce the distractions given the environment in which you live:

1. _____
2. _____
3. _____
4. _____
5. _____

If you can learn to communicate effectively about your availability, you will become more productive. Pay attention to the things that divert you from your homework and identify some steps for preventing the problem in the future.

C H A P T E R   5

States of Consciousness

Use the space provided in this outline to record notes from the textbook as well as from class lectures and discussion. Questions related to the *Psychological Detective* sections in the text have been presented in the outline; use the associated space to respond to the questions and to record your own comments about the issues. *Keywords and terms* from the text have been italicized and inserted in the outline so you can practice writing their definitions. The pages in this study guide are perforated and can be removed for use as study sheets for quizzes and exams.

I. What Is Consciousness?

consciousness—

daydreaming—

altered state of consciousness—

II. The Rhythms of Life

A. Circadian Rhythms

circadian rhythm—

1. The Sleep-Wake Cycle

How is the 25-hour internal clock related to the fatigue one feels after a weekend?

2. Body Temperature

B. Problems with Circadian Rhythms

1. Jet Lag

jet lag—

With respect to internal rhythms and long-distance travel, is it easier to travel from east to west, or from west to east? Why?

2. Shift Work

    a. Improving Shift Work

III. The Study of Sleep

A. A Night in a Sleep Lab
    polysomnograph—

B. The Stages of Sleep
    1. NREM Sleep

        non-REM (NREM) sleep—

        slow-wave sleep—

    2. REM Sleep

        rapid eye movement (REM) sleep—

        sleep cycle—

C. Differences in Individual Sleep Patterns

D. Sleep Deprivation

E. The Functions of Sleep
    REM rebound—

F. Sleep Problems

   1. Insomnia

       insomnia—

   2. Hypersomnias

       hypersomnias—

     a. Narcolepsy

       narcolepsy—

How are the characteristics of REM sleep related to the attacks of muscle weakness that are characteristic of narcolepsy and cataplexy?

     b. Sleep Apnea

       sleep apnea—

   3. Parasomnias

       parasomnias—

     a. Sleepwalking

       sleepwalking—

Is sleepwalking merely the acting out of one's dreams?

   b. Enuresis

      enuresis—

   c. Sleep Terrors

      sleep terror—

      nightmare—

 How do NREM sleep disorders differ from REM sleep disorders with respect to *when* they occur during a night's sleep?

  3. SIDS

     sudden infant death syndrome (SIDS)—

G. Dreams: Nighttime Theater

    dream—

  1. Why We Forget Our Dreams

  2. Interpreting Dreams

     manifest content—

latent content—

activation-synthesis hypothesis—

IV. Hypnosis

A. The History of Hypnosis

B. Hypnotic Induction

    hypnosis—

C. Hypnotic Phenomena

    1. Pain Reduction and Medical Treatment

 How might the components of hypnosis be useful in reducing pain or alleviating some medical problems?

    2. Memory Effects

    3. Perception

    4 Age Regression

 Given that hypnosis is a state of heightened susceptibility to suggestions, what concerns should one have when designing an experiment to test whether hypnosis is effective for age regression?

D. Explanations of Hypnosis

How would you behave if you were hypnotized? What role would your expectations of your behavior play in determining what you would do?

dissociation—

V. Altering Consciousness with Drugs

psychoactive substances—

substance abuse—

substance dependence—

tolerance—

withdrawal—

A. Depressants

depressants—

alcohol—

1. Alcohol

    a. Effects of Alcohol

    b. Factors that Influence Alcohol Use

2. Barbiturates

   barbiturates—

B. Stimulants

   stimulants—

   amphetamines—

C. Opioids

   opioids—

D. Hallucinogens

   hallucinogens—

   lysergic acid diethylamide (LSD)—

   phencyclidine piperidine (PCP)—

   marijuana—

After you have studied the chapter, you should be able to respond to the following statements and questions to convey your understanding of the material.

1. How do biological rhythms influence one's ability to sense or perceive stimuli?

2. What variations in awareness can be caused by using psychoactive drugs? How do the changes brought about by drug use compare with changes that one experiences when under hypnosis?

3. Discuss evidence that social factors can influence awareness.

4. What is dreaming? Discuss varying theories about the content of dreams.

5. Describe the characteristics and functions of sleep. What do problems with sleep contribute to our understanding of sleep and consciousness?

Fill in the blanks in the following statements with key words and terms from the textbook. Answer as many as you can without referring to your notes or to the book. If you have blanks after thinking about each item, try using your book. The answers are presented after the practice test.

1. _____ _____ are internal biological changes that occur on a daily schedule.

2. A sleep researcher would use a _____ to measure and record physiological changes during sleep.

3. _____ is more a symptom than a disorder, and involves difficulty falling asleep, frequent awakenings, or poor-quality sleep.

4. *Narcolepsy* and *sleep apnea* are examples from a category of sleep disorders called _____.

5. _____ is the name psychologists use for "bedwetting" , a problem that affects about 5 million children in the United States.

6. What is known as *hypnosis* today was once called _____, a treatment that was championed by 18th century physician Franz Mesmer.

7. _____ _____ are chemicals that affect consciousness, perception, mood, and behavior.

8. One is said to have developed _____ when increasing dosages of a drug are needed to achieve the same effect as earlier doses.

9. Most states have adopted 0.10% as the _____ _____ _____ that is the legal definition of intoxication.

10. _____ is a colorless, odorless, and tasteless drug that is derived from the ergot fungus that grows on rye.

Circle the letter that corresponds to the *best* alternative for each of the following items. Read each alternative carefully. The answers are presented at the end of this study guide chapter. Be sure to learn *why* each correct alternative is better than the others.

1. Daydreaming may be called an altered form of consciousness because it is:
   a. usually the result of psychoactive drug use.
   b. different from normal waking consciousness.
   c. the same as dreaming that occurs during normal sleep.
   d. rarely recalled accurately by the daydreamer following an episode.

2. ___ rhythms are to ___ rhythms as shorter than 24 hours is to longer than 24 hours.
   a. Ultradian; infradian
   b. Infradian; circadian
   c. Circadian; ultradian
   d. Infradian; ultradian

3. The internal clock for humans is accurate to within a few minutes for most people. However, it tends to run on a 25-hour clock, and therefore must be reset each day. The brain region that is responsible for resetting the internal clock is the:
   a. fornix.
   b. hippocampus.
   c. suprachiasmatic nucleus.
   d. reticular activating system.

4. Which relationship between circadian rhythm and body temperature is accurate for a person who sleeps in the night and is awake during the day?
   a. Body temperature is lowest during the night.
   b. Body temperature is highest during the night.
   c. Body temperature is stable throughout the day for people who are physically well.
   d. There is no relationship between one's body temperature and time of day or presence/absence of daylight.

5. Whether one is a morning person (lark) or evening person (owl) appears to be influenced by:
   a. genetic factors.
   b. the company one keeps.
   c. the time of day of one's birth.
   d. an interaction between one's gender and age.

6. With respect to internal rhythms and long-distance travel, it is easier to travel:
   a. from west to east.
   b. from east to west.
   c. from north to south.
   d. from south to north.

7. According to sleep researchers interested in problems associated with shift work, the common *phase advance* cycle is like working successive weeks in ___, ___, and ___.
   a. light; dark; light
   b. east; central; west
   c. planes; trains; cars.
   d. Denver; Paris; Tokyo

8. Non-REM (NREM) stages 1 & 2 are to ___ as NREM stages 3 & 4 are to ___.
   a. dreams; nightmares
   b. disorders; datorders
   c. slow-wave sleep; sleepwalking
   d. later in the night; early in the night

9. Sleep spindles and K complexes are to ___ as eye movements are to ___.
   a. stage 1; stage 2
   b. stage 2; REM sleep
   c. REM sleep; stages 3 & 4
   d. all NREM stages; all REM stages

10. During the course of a night's sleep, the amount of time spent in REM for each successive 90 minute cycle:
    a. gets slightly shorter.
    b. stays about the same.
    c. gets progressively longer.
    d. is impossible to know given today's technology.

11. To sleep like a baby literally is to:
    a. in other words, sleep like a rock.
    b. sleep in a highly efficient fashion.
    c. have several short episodes of sleep.
    d. sleep for a prolonged period of consolidated sleep.

12. REM rebound is:
    a. a term used to describe the bouncing back and forth of the eyes during REM sleep.
    b. a term used to describe the bouncing back down through NREM stages after REM.
    c. a phenomenon that occurs more frequently among those who live nearer to the equator.
    d. an increase in the amount of REM one experiences following reduction in REM sleep due to sleep deprivation or drug use.

13. The best way to deal with *insomnia* is to:
    a. practice good "sleep hygiene".
    b. take prescription sleep medicine.
    c. take over-the-counter sleeping pills.
    d. have a glass of non-alcoholic beer just before bedtime.

14. It is common for victims of *sleep apnea* to:
    a. wake up dead.
    b. awaken hundreds of times each night.
    c. speak aloud during sleepwalking episodes.
    d. be drowsy even though they oversleep regularly.

15. CPAP is a:
    a. treatment for sleep apnea.
    b. treatment for symptoms of insomnia.
    c. sleep disorder that is most common among adults.
    d. sleep disorder that is most common among children.

16. REM Sleep Behavior Disorder (RBD) affects mainly:
    a. adolescent girls.
    b. swing shift workers.
    c. men over 50 years of age.
    d. infants up to 6 months of age.

17. Sleep terrors (a.k.a. night terrors):
    a. are thought to cause SIDS.
    b. is a special class of nightmares.
    c. last up to 45 minutes in adolescents.
    d. are NREM experiences that effect about 5% of children.

18. Cross cultural research on dreaming and dream content has revealed:
    a. little of any substance.
    b. that dreams are universally similar.
    c. that cultural views can influence the probability of dream recall.
    d. multilingual subjects are equally likely to dream in second and subsequent languages as the first.

19. The activation-synthesis hypothesis:
    a. accurately predicted the behaviors of hypnotized subjects.
    b. incorporates both manifest and latent dream content as key influences.
    c. suggests that dreams are the result of cortical activation during normal REM sleep.
    d. suggests that the dream content reported by most people represents 3+ combined dream reports.

20. One's ability to be hypnotized:
    a. is stable over time.
    b. becomes greater with age.
    c. becomes weaker with age.
    d. varies as a function of factors other than one's age.

21. Dissociation is:
    a. a psychological disorder in which one loses one's identity.
    b. a sleep disorder whereby people cannot remember their dreams.
    c. the splitting of conscious awareness that is believed to facilitate pain reduction.
    d. most common among women who have been hypnotized on the witness stand in court.

22. The most commonly used illicit drug(s) is (are):
    a. alcohol.
    b. marijuana.
    c. amphetamines.
    d. lysergic acid diethylamide.

23. ___ has detrimental effects on a person's health and safety and on social and occupational roles.
    a. Tolerance
    b. Withdrawal
    c. Substance abuse
    d. Substance dependence

24. One's liver can metabolize:
    a. up to one drink each day.
    b. approximately 1 drink per hour.
    c. alcohol during withdrawal only if sufficient tolerance has developed.
    d. only one psychoactive drug at a time, which is why using 2+ drugs at once is dangerous.

25. Barbiturates, like most psychoactive drugs, can:
    a. suppress REM and Stage 4 sleep.
    b. cost less on the street than over the counter.
    c. last for up to three days following administration.
    d. be used with little to no risk for health-related circumstances.

26. Opioids:
    a. is a family of drugs that is also called narcotic analgesics.
    b. are extracted from the coca plant that grows in South America.
    c. are chemicals that the body produces to resemble drugs from outside the body.
    d. are far and away the most commonly abused drugs among high school seniors.

27. Relative to tobacco cigarettes, marijuana cigarettes:
    a. contain more tar.
    b. cost about the same.
    c. contain less carbon monoxide.
    d. are easy for teenagers to get at convenience stores.

 ## ANSWERS TO KEY WORD EXERCISE

1. Circadian rhythms
2. polysomnograph
3. Insomnia
4. hypersomnias
5. Enuresis
6. mesmerism
7. Psychoactive substances
8. tolerance
9. blood alcohol
10. LSD (lysergic acid diethylamide) concentration (BAC)

 ## PRACTICE TEST ANSWERS AND EXPLANATIONS

1. b. Daydreaming is different from normal waking consciousness and is therefore considered an altered state.
2. a. Ultradian rhythms are shorter than 24 hours (e.g., heartbeat). Infradian rhythms are longer than 24 hours (e.g., menstrual cycle).
3. c. The suprachiasmatic nucleus (SCN) resets the body's clock each day.
4. a. Body temperature drops at night. This is why you often have to pull covers on in the night even if you were warm when you went to bed. It is also why you become chilled when you stay up late.
5. a. Genetic factors are at least partially responsible for when people are most alert.
6. b. Phase delays that occur during east to west travel extend the sleep-wake cycle to approximate the body's natural 25-hour cycle.
7. d. Phase advances occur when traveling from west to east. Schedules on typical shift rotations are akin to traveling in phase advance. It would be easier for workers to shift in phase delay.
8. e. Stages 3 & 4 predominate NREM early in the night, while 1 & 2 predominate later on.
9. b. Sleep spindles and K complexes are characteristic of stage 2; REM stands for *rapid eye movement*.
10. c. The amount of time spent in REM gets increasingly longer during the course of a night's sleep.
11. c. For up to about 6 months babies sleep in several short episodes each night.
12. d. REM rebound occurs when one has been deprived of the normal amount of REM sleep.

13. a.   Good sleep hygiene includes such practices as maintaining a regular sleep-wake cycle, avoiding drug use, exercising, and so on (see Table 5-1 in your text).

14. b.   Apnea victims awaken hundreds of times each night. Surprisingly, they get used to awakening, and sometimes go many years without getting an adequate night's rest.

15. a.   CPAP (continuous positive airway pressure) is a common treatment that helps prevent airway collapse in apnea victims.

16. c.   RBD is a syndrome of injurious or disruptive behavior that occurs most frequently in men over 50.

17. d.   These NREM experiences are very frightening for both parents and the children who have them.

18. c.   Cultural views can influence the probability of dream recall. Also, dream content may reflect cultural differences.

19. c.   The activation-synthesis hypothesis suggests that dreams are the result of haphazard cortical activity.

20. a.   The ability of one to be hypnotized remains fairly stable over time.

21. c.   According to Ernest Hilgard, dissociation is the splitting of conscious awareness that is believed to facilitate pain reduction.

22. b.   Marijuana is the most commonly used illicit drug.

23. c.   Substance abuse results in detrimental effects on one's health, and on other factors.

24. b.   If one drinks slowly enough, the liver can break down alcohol before it affects you.

25. a.   Most psychoactive drugs suppress the most important components of the sleep cycle.

26. a.   Opioids are derived from the opium poppy. The drug may be processed to produce morphine and codeine.

27. a.   Marijuana contains more tar than tobacco. However, most marijuana smokers use less of the drug than cigarette smokers use tobacco.

Key Vocabulary Terms

Cut out and use as study cards; terms appear on one side and definitions are on the other.

consciousness

daydreaming

jet lag

polysomnograph

non-REM (NREM) sleep

slow-wave sleep

REM rebound

insomnia

Key Vocabulary Terms

Cut out and use as study cards; terms appear on
one side and definitions are on the other.

A form of consciousness involving
fantasies, usually spontaneous, that
occurs while a person is awake

A person's awareness of feelings,
sensations, and thoughts at a
given moment

Instrument that amplifies and
records signals associated with biological changes taken during a
night in the sleep laboratory

Temporary maladjustment that occurs when a change of time zones
causes biological rhythms to be out
of step with local time

Deep sleep of NREM stages 3 and 4,
characterized by delta waves

Sleep stages 1, 2, 3, and 4; NREM
sleep consists primarily of Stages 3
and 4 early in the night and Stage
2 later on

Complaints of difficulty falling
asleep, staying asleep, frequent
awakenings, or poor-quality sleep

An increase in the typical amount
of REM sleep following reduction
of REM sleep owing to sleep deprivation or the use of certain drugs
that reduce REM sleep

hypersomnias	narcolepsy
sleep apnea	parasomnias
sleepwalking	enuresis
sleep terror	nightmare
sudden infant death syndrome (SIDS)	dream

Sleep disorder characterized by excessive daytime sleepiness and attacks of muscle weakness induced by emotion (cataplexy); the symptoms are due to the intrusion of REM sleep into waking time

Sleep disorders characterized by excessive daytime sleepiness

Sleep disorders, other than insomnia and hypersomnia, which occur more frequently in children and often disappear without treatment

Sleep disorder characterized by pauses in breathing during sleep; most prevalent in older, overweight males

Bedwetting, a sleep disorder that occurs primarily in children

A parasomnia that occurs during Stage 4 sleep, most often consists of sitting up in bed

Frightening dream that occurs during REM sleep

Partial awakening from Stage 4 sleep characterized by loud screams and extreme physiological arousal

A succession of visual images experienced during sleep

Unexpected death of an apparently healthy infant up to age 1 that is not explained by autopsy, medical case information, or an investigation of death scene

manifest content	latent content
activation-synthesis hypothesis	hypnosis
dissociation	psychoactive substance
substance abuse	substance dependence
tolerance	withdrawal

According to Freud, the deeper underlying meaning of a dream, connected by symbols to the manifest content

According to Freud, the dream as reported by the dreamer

State of heightened susceptibility to suggestions

Explanation of dreams that suggests that they result when the cortex seeks to explain the high level of neural activity occurring during REM sleep

Chemicals that affect consciousness, perception, mood, and behavior

Splitting of conscious awareness that is believed to play a role in hypnotic pain reduction

More serious pattern of substance use than found in substance abuse; popularly called addiction and often characterized by drug tolerance

Pattern of substance use that has detrimental effects on a person's health and safety and on social and occupational roles

Changes in behavior, cognition, and physiology that occur when stopping or reducing the heavy and prolonged use of a psychoactive substance

Need for increasing dosages of a drug to achieve the same effect as earlier doses

depressants	alcohol
barbiturates	stimulants
amphetamines	opioids
hallucinogens	lysergic acid diethylamide (LSD)
phencyclidine piperidine (PCP)	marijuana

Depressant psychoactive substance, also known as ethyl alcohol or ethanol

Drugs that slow the activity of the central nervous system, including alcohol and barbiturates

Drugs that increase the activity of the central nervous system

Depressant drugs that are used to induce sleep but can be deadly when combined with alcohol

Drugs that reduce pain

Stimulants that are used to treat attention deficit hyperactivity disorder and narcolepsy

Powerful hallucinogen derived from the ergot fungus found on rye

Drugs that can cause changes in thinking, emotion, self-awareness, and perceptions; these changes are often expressed in hallucinations

Substance derived from the Cannabis sativa plant

Powerful hallucinogen that can have unpredictable depressant, stimulant, hallucinogenic, or analgesic effects

The time you spend in class can be very valuable. The classrooms, laboratories, and studios where your classes meet were designed for student learning. The lectures, demonstrations, and discussions you listen to, watch, and participate in were organized by your professors in order to facilitate your understanding of the course material. Your tuition provides you with access to professionals whose interests are the very courses you take, and to facilities that are meant to support your educational experience. What you make of the opportunities you have, however, will depend on how well you are able to extract ideas and information from your classroom experiences. This section offers several suggestions for helping you make the most of your classroom learning opportunities.

Why Notes Are Important

Your notes should represent your perspective on everything that happens in each class you take. Your notes for a given class will represent those elements from the subject that your professor thinks are of importance for students to know. Attend class regularly, pay close attention to the lectures, demonstrations, and discussions, and take thorough notes. The notes you develop as an active, attentive student will be invaluable to you in the future. As you receive assignments, quizzes, and exams back, 3-hole punch them and add them to your notes. Keeping course material organized and together is useful not only as you prepare for exams, but as reference material in subsequent semesters as well. Students are often surprised at how often they use their notes from one class to help them in other classes.

No matter how good your memory is, you will not recall everything from class. If your professor is really good at presenting difficult concepts, you may find it tempting to not write notes. Avoid that temptation. Too often, students find themselves frustrated when they do not recall how a given concept was explained in class. The very act of writing something down will help you remember it later. One thing is sure: if you write it down, you can always refer to your notes if you need to; if you do not write it down, you may realize too late that you do not understand a concept completely.

Be Prepared

When you go to a given class meeting, you should have a mindset that enables you to benefit as much as possible from the relatively brief opportunity. You can make an important investment in your career by simply preparing your mind for each class meeting. Learning how to do this, and making a habit of it, are the most effective ways for you to pursue your academic goals. Commit the following list to memory, and discipline yourself to do each step.

1. **Know the Topic.** Review your syllabus to learn what the topic of each day will be as you progress through the semester. If you have reading or homework assignments, do them. Completing assignments as you go, rather than 'when you get around to it', even if your professor does not check to see if you are caught up, will keep you in touch with the class. At bare minimum you should flip through the pages from your text to review the variety of things you might expect to learn about.

2. **Know the Environment.** By merely showing up several minutes early, you can usually have your pick of chairs in a classroom. Choose a place in the room that will allow you to see and hear the instructor without having to strain. Any energy you have to spend focusing your attention will detract from your ability to think about the topic at hand. Sitting in the front, center portion of the classroom will allow your professor to see that you are committed to getting the most from your experience. Sitting farther away, or near people who chatter a lot, communicates that you do not think what the professor has to offer is of much value.

3. **Have the Right Tools.** Bring the book or books you may be discussing in class. It is rude to read these instead of paying attention, but it is good to be able to refer to your book if it becomes important to do so. Dedicate a 3-ring notebook, or section of a larger binder, to each class, and bring it with you to every meeting. Your notes from each class meeting will be your only reminders of what you did on a given day. By recording them in a well-designated place you will always know where to look when you need information for the class. The 3-ring format will permit you to add handouts from class, exams, and quizzes, etc. Always have *at least* one extra pen or pencil with you.

4. **Develop Your Own Shorthand.** Having a system of abbreviations will help you keep up with comments from class. It is a good idea to keep a reference page in each notebook for the shorthand/abbreviation system you develop. If a word is used regularly in your notes, use a standard abbreviation or devise a symbol that takes less time to write. Truncate words when possible. But, be sure to keep a glossary of abbreviations so you do not lose track of your system. If you consider that the time it takes to learn an abbreviation is far less than the time it will take to keep writing the word(s) in longhand, you will quickly see the value of using symbols and abbreviations.

You will want to translate these into your glossary. Look at the following examples, then record several other abbreviations that will save you time in class. Add to your glossary as you develop new shortcuts.

~ = approximately	+ or & = and	A: = answer	@ = at
b/c = because	B4 = before	Δ = change	$\sqrt{}$ = check
e.g., = for example	etc. = and so forth	4 = for, fore, four	> = greater than
i.e., = in other words	→ = leading to	< = less than	% = percent(age)
Q: = question	ψ = psychology	← = resulting from	Σ = sum
2 = to, too, two	w/ = with	w/o = without	

What are other ways you can simplify your note taking by using abbreviations and symbols?

_____

_____

Be Early, Be Interested, Be Courteous

Being early to and attentive during class shows your commitment. This will give you a few minutes to prepare (e.g., review notes, look through your text) or to discuss the class with your professor or other students. Being late is disruptive and gives the impression that the class is not a priority for you.

Having selected a seat that is front and center in the room, you are well positioned to give your utmost attention. Maintain eye contact with your professor whenever possible. If you are interested in your professor, your professor will be interested in you. Building on this relationship will help you develop and maintain a commitment to studying and doing good work.

To be eligible to teach the class, your professor studied the topic extensively in graduate school. The class you are taking is on a topic that is very important to your professor. If you discover your mind to be wandering, think about what it is that draws people to the discipline. Ask a question that will help your professor convey her or his passion for the subject. Another good way to keep on task is to take notes continuously. It is hard for your mind to wander if you are busy taking notes. Finally, do not close your notebook or put anything away until your professor has closed the class. Often some important point points are made in the last few minutes; you cannot record them if you have already put your things away. What's more, closing your books is distracting to your professor and to other students.

Approaches to Note Taking

Your notes have to be meaningful to you to be of any use. The most appropriate method for taking notes will depend on your style as a student, your professor's teaching style, the nature of the class, and other variables. Regardless of these things, your notes need to be organized. In addition to dedicating a whole notebook, or section of a larger binder, to each class, you will want to assign a piece of paper to each day. Put each day's date in the same place so that later it will be easy to track what happened by date. If you write on two or more pages, simply rewrite the date and number the page (2, 3, etc.), as appropriate.

Two common methods for taking notes are offered below. Experiment until you find a system that works for you. Take the opportunity to inquire with your professors about the methods that will work best for their particular courses.

1. **The Outline Method.** Some of your teachers will give highly structured notes that fit well into an outline. If the notes fit an outline format well, use that format. Some notes on using an outline, and a sample of the common outline format are provided near the end of this section.

2. **The Cornell System.** Another system for recording notes, that works well whether or not the notes follow an outline format, was developed by Walter Pauk at Cornell University. This system involves dividing each page of notes into three parts. See the end of this section for an example of a page. In short, the system uses a large box for notes on the right-hand section of the page, a narrower strip beside the main box for adding detail later on when you study your notes, and a section at the bottom of each page that spans the page's width where summarizing comments about the page can be made.

Things to Be Sure to Include in Your Notes

Learning to take good notes takes time and practice. It is better to write too much than to write too little, but sometimes students work so hard to transcribe the class discussions exactly that they miss out on the main point(s). By developing a personally meaningful shorthand system, you will be able to spend less time scribbling in you notebook, and more time paying attention in class.

If you notice that something is reiterated, if your professor draws a picture or diagram on the board, or if you hear something in your professor's intonation that emphasizes a given point, make sure your notes reflect it. If a word is written on the board, write it in your notes.

If you are not sure what your professor is trying to communicate, ask. The chances are that if you are not following something in the class, others are also confused. Most professors appreciate it when their students ask questions; asking a question is a way of indicating your interest and that you are paying attention. Many times a question that you may ask will help your professor understand more about you and your commitment, and will also win favor with your fellow students.

Sometimes you understand perfectly well what is being said, but do not have time to record it before your professor moves on to the next topic. Raise your hand and ask that he or she repeat the comment. Again, this will underscore your commitment to getting the most from each class period.

Within a day of taking each set of notes, you should review them, filling in missing information, adding references to figures or text passages from your book, etc. You may even find rewriting your notes to be helpful. The sooner after taking a set of notes that you are able to review them, the better able you will be to fill in gaps, make references to the text, etc.

Notes on Using a Formal Outline

1. There should be at least two points for each level of organization (if there is a I, there should be a II, if there is an A, there should be a B, and so on).

2. Note the numbering and lettering system; it is common to most outlines.

3. Use only key words and sentence fragments. The point of the outline it to record the main points; details are added when the outline is used as a basis for writing a paper or delivering a speech.

Sample Outline Format

I. Major topic (write a sentence fragment here that reflects the main point of the topic or section)
   A. 1st important supporting point
   B. 2nd supporting point
      1. Detail to clarify B
      2. 2nd detail relating to B
         a. small point relating to 2nd detail
         b. 2nd small for 2nd detail under B
         c. 3rd detail
            i. minuet piece of information about 3rd detail
            ii. 2nd minuet piece of information

II. Second Topic
   A. 1st point
   B. 2nd point

Example of Layout for the Cornell Method

The table below represents a piece of 8.5" x 11" notebook paper:

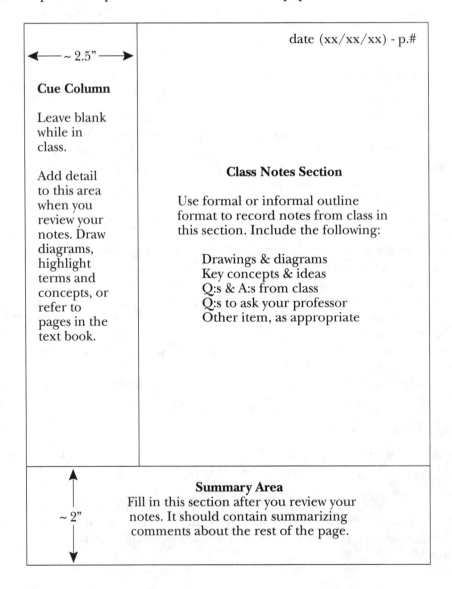

date (xx/xx/xx) - p.#

← ~ 2.5" →

Cue Column

Leave blank while in class.

Add detail to this area when you review your notes. Draw diagrams, highlight terms and concepts, or refer to pages in the text book.

Class Notes Section

Use formal or informal outline format to record notes from class in this section. Include the following:

Drawings & diagrams
Key concepts & ideas
Q:s & A:s from class
Q:s to ask your professor
Other item, as appropriate

~ 2"

Summary Area
Fill in this section after you review your notes. It should contain summarizing comments about the rest of the page.

CHAPTER 6

Basic Principles of Learning

Use the space provided in this outline to record notes from the textbook as well as from class lectures and discussion. Questions related to the *Psychological Detective* sections in the text have been presented in the outline; use the associated space to respond to the questions and to record your own comments about the issues. *Keywords and terms* from the text have been italicized and inserted in the outline so you can practice writing their definitions. The pages in this study guide are perforated and can be removed for use as study sheets for quizzes and exams.

I. **What is Learning?**

  learning—

II. **Classical Conditioning**

  classical conditioning—

  A. Pavlov and the Elements of Classical Conditioning

    neutral stimulus (NS)—

    unconditioned stimulus (US)—

    conditioned stimulus (CS)—

    unconditioned response (UR)—

    conditioned response (CR)—

 Can you determine the stimuli and responses that have contributed to the quality of experience when you hear a favorite song or smell a particular perfume or cologne?

B. Phobias

   phobia—

C. John Watson, Little Albert, and the Ethics of Research

🔍 Under what conditions should parents be able to authorize researchers to study their children? When should they not be able to grant such permission?

D. Pleasant Unconditioned Stimuli

E. Other Aspects of Classical Conditioning

   1. Acquisition

      a. Sequence of CS-US Presentation

      b. Strength of the US

      c. Number of CS-US Pairings

   2. Extinction

      extinction—

   3. Spontaneous Recovery

      spontaneous recovery—

   4. Generalization and Discrimination

      generalization—

discrimination—

How do you anticipate Pavlov's dogs responded when an ellipse, that was associated with the absence of food, was gradually altered to look like a circle (the signal for food)?

F.   Classical Conditioning and Our Motives

      learned motives—

      learned goals (learned incentives)—

G.   Current Trends in Classical Conditioning

   1.   Contingency Theory

   2.   Blocking

      blocking—

   3.   Overshadowing

      overshadowing—

H.   Taste-Aversion Learning and Preparedness

   1.   Taste Aversion

      taste-aversion learning—

   2.   Preparedness

      preparedness—

Diagram an experiment to test whether colors or tastes can be conditioned to an illness US in birds.

III. Operant Conditioning

operant conditioning—

A. Reinforcers

reinforcer—

1. Primary and Secondary Reinforcers

primary reinforcer—

secondary reinforcer—

2. Positive and Negative reinforcers

positive reinforcer—

 What components of an operant conditioning paradigm may be used to explain learning to perform the unethical behavior of cheating?

negative reinforcer—

B. B. F. Skinner and the "Skinner Box"

cumulative record—

schedule of reinforcement—

C. Shaping

   shaping—

Discuss the process of learning to drive an automobile (especially one with a manual transmission) in terms of *shaping*.

D. Schedules of Reinforcement

   1. Continuous Reinforcement

      continuous reinforcement—

   2. Intermittent (Partial) Reinforcement

      intermittent, (or partial), reinforcement—

   3. Ratio Schedules

      ratio schedule—

   4. Interval Schedules

      interval schedule—

E. The Role of Cognition

   1. Insight Learning

      insight learning—

2. Latent Learning

    latent learning—

3. Serial Enumeration

    serial enumeration—

4. Decision-Making Strategies

5. Encoding Visual Stimuli

6. Social Communication of Taste Preferences

F. Punishment: The Opposite of Reinforcement

    punisher—

    law of effect—

    punishment—

Select an undesired behavior and outline a plan for decreasing or eliminating the behavior using punishment. What issues concerning the administration of punishment need to be considered?

IV. Extinction

A. The Partial Reinforcement Effect

    partial reinforcement effect—

B. Operant Conditioning and Stimulus Control

discriminative stimulus—

V. Observational Learning

observational learning (social learning theory)—

vicarious reinforcement—

vicarious punishment—

VI. Behavior Modification

behavior modification—

LEARNING OBJECTIVES

After you have studied the chapter, you should be able to respond to the following statements and questions to convey your understanding of the material.

1. Describe *learning* as an adaptive behavior that supports natural selection.

2. What role do sensory and perceptual processes play in learning?

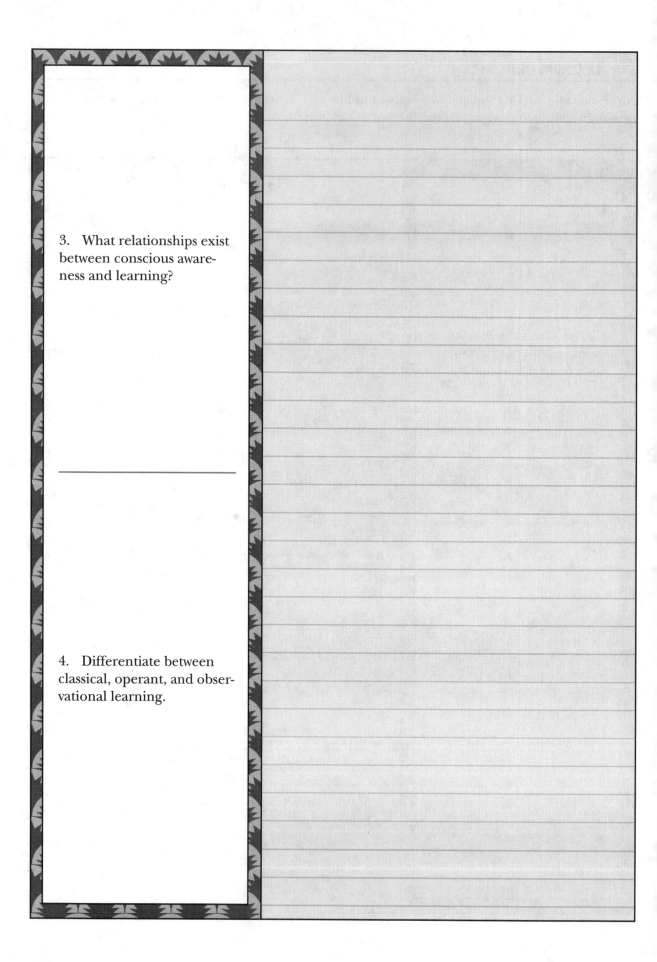

3. What relationships exist between conscious awareness and learning?

4. Differentiate between classical, operant, and observational learning.

Fill in the blanks in the following statements with key words and terms from the textbook. Answer as many as you can without referring to your notes or to the book. If you have blanks after thinking about each item, try using your book. The answers are presented after the practice test.

1. Reactions or reflexes that are elicited automatically when certain stimuli are presented are called _____ _____.

2. _____ is the training stage during which a particular response is learned.

3. When a sprinter has a false start because of hearing a loud noise other than the start gun, _____ is said to have occurred.

4. _____ occurs when a compound stimulus is paired with a US and the more intense (salient) CS elicits a stronger CR.

5. If you have ever become nauseated after eating an unfamiliar food, you probably developed a(n) _____ _____ as a result.

6. A(n) _____ _____ is a stimulus that has innate reinforcing properties.

7. A(n) _____ ___ _____ is a preset pattern of delivering reinforcement.

8. Reinforcement that follows every target response is called _____ _____.

9. Imagine that a child learns the laws regarding when to stop, and when to drive through intersections with traffic lights without ever driving. This would be an example of _____ _____.

10. Experiments have demonstrated that rats can remember a series of events. Thus, rats are capable _____ _____.

✹ PRACTICE TEST

Circle the letter that corresponds to the *best* alternative for each of the following items. Read each alternative carefully. The answers are presented at the end of this study guide chapter. Be sure to learn *why* each correct alternative is better than the others.

1. A critical distinction between learned behaviors and those that become possible through maturation is that learned responses:
   a. are innate, or preprogrammed.
   b. occur as a function of experience(s).
   c. outlast those that are gained through maturation.
   d. are acquired in strictly controlled laboratory conditions.

2. ___ ___ is to ___ ___ as stimulus-stimulus learning is to response-outcome learning.
   a. Classical conditioning; operant conditioning
   b. Operant conditioning; observational learning
   c. Observational learning; classical conditioning
   d. Operant conditioning; instrumental conditioning

3. A conditioned stimulus (CS):
    a. is an automatically produced reaction.
    b. is a stimulus that does not elicit a particular response.
    c. is an event that automatically produces a response without prior training.
    d. starts out neutral, but acquires the ability to elicit a response through training.

4. Unconditioned response (UR) is to conditioned response as ___ is to ___.
    a. sight; sound
    b. pleasure; pain
    c. automatic; learned
    d. none of the above; these terms mean the same thing.

5. The flinching people do when they see a long needle being stuck through a balloon results from learning, and is called:
    a. magic.
    b. extinction.
    c. conditioned excitation.
    d. a conditioned response.

6. Many phobias can be understood in terms of:
    a. operant conditioning.
    b. classical conditioning.
    c. observational learning.
    d. a psychological deficiency.

7. Watson's research with "Little Albert" demonstrated:
    a. what Holmes knew all along.
    b. that white rats can be conditioned to fear children.
    c. that emotional responses may be conditioned in humans.
    d. that children will act violently toward a Bobo doll after watching an adult do the same.

8. Which of the following is not a variable for determining the rate or quality of acquired responding?
    a. the strength of the US
    b. the strength of the CR
    c. the number of CS-US pairings
    d. the sequence of stimulus (CS & US) presentation

9. Spontaneous recovery is:
    a. more common in children than in adults.
    b. a phenomenon that is associated only with lab-based research.
    c. the reappearance of an extinguished CR after the passage of time.
    d. most often associated with patients suffering from mild psychological illnesses.

10. When a musician can recognize a note as "Middle C", rather than another note near "Middle C", this is an example of:
    a. generalization.
    b. discrimination.
    c. dishabituation.
    d. a learned goal (or learned incentive).

11. Contingency theory predicts that the better the CS is able to predict the occurrence of the US, the ___ conditioning will be.
    a. weaker
    b. stronger
    c. longer-lasting
    d. more resistant to extinction

12. ___ is a situation in which the conditionability of a CS is weakened when it is paired with a US that has previously been paired with another CS.
    a. Blocking
    b. Foreshadowing
    c. Overshadowing
    d. Latent Learning

13. An interesting feature of taste-aversion learning is that it:
    a. requires two CSs.
    b. is strong, but often short-lived.
    c. works well with novel and familiar CSs.
    d. occurs when the CS-US interval is lengthy.

14. The fact that some events go together naturally, and are therefore easily learned, is fundamental to the theory of:
    a. preparedness.
    b. easy learning.
    c. relative conditioning.
    d. conditioned associations.

15. A secondary reinforcer:
    a. always follows the CS in classical conditioning.
    b. concerns items of interest after basic needs have been met.
    c. can sometimes go unnoticed by the participant, but is nevertheless powerful.
    d. acquires reinforcing properties by virtue of an association with a primary reinforcer.

16. Hitting the snooze button on your alarm in the morning is:
    a. positively reinforced.
    b. negatively reinforced.
    c. not reinforced if you fall asleep again.
    d. only reinforced if you fall asleep again.

17. Shaping involves:
    a. reinforcement of the target response.
    b. reinforcement of activity other than the target response.
    c. reinforcement that does not follow every target response.
    d. reinforcement of successive approximations of the target response.

18. A cumulative record:
    a. is the peak response rate in a Skinner box..
    b. is a way of displaying results of conditioning trials.
    c. is another name for the acquisition strength of a trial.
    d. is usually released by a band after they have had several hits.

19. The two main types of intermittent schedules of reinforcement are ___ and ___.
    a. interval; ratio
    b. partial; complete
    c. positive; negative
    d. terminal; continuing

20. Conditioning in which we structure perceptual stimuli differently is called ___.
    a. latent learning
    b. insight learning
    c. serial enumeration
    d. perceptual learning

21. Negative punishers are:
    a. painful in nature.
    b. to be avoided at all costs.
    c. the same as positive punishers.
    d. pleasant stimuli that are removed.

22. The partial reinforcement effect:
    a. results from administering only a portion of a reward each time.
    b. is robust with respect to the quality of the reinforcer that is employed.
    c. describes the pattern of responding when one is on an FI schedule and only reacts part of the time.
    d. is reflected when extinction takes longer following intermittent reinforcement than after continuous reinforcement.

23. A stimulus that signals the participant that responding will be reinforced:
    a. is called a discriminative stimulus.
    b. is called a Boojum—as was used in the Snark experiment.
    c. would be Bob Barker yelling, "come on down", for example.
    d. cannot last fewer than 15 seconds, or longer than 1 hour 25 minutes.

24. When older siblings help their younger siblings learn which behaviors will be punished, and which will be reinforced, the younger siblings experience:
    a. behavior modification.
    b. observational learning.
    c. synthesis of vicarious activation.
    d. prolonged extinction trials for acquired responses.

25. Behavior modification:
    a. is more easily done than said.
    b. was once a common treatment for the mentally ill, but is now considered unethical.
    c. has been defined as the application of the results of learning theory and the application of experimental psychology to the problem of altering maladaptive behavior.
    d. involves placing group housed clients in mental institutions in giant Skinner boxes and rewarding them on schedules as has been done previously with pigeons and laboratory rats.

1. unconditioned responses
2. Acquisition
3. generalization
4. Overshadowing

5. taste aversion
6. primary reinforcer
7. schedule of reinforcement

8. continuous reinforcement
9. latent learning
10. serial enumeration

 PRACTICE TEST ANSWERS AND EXPLANATIONS

1. b. Learning results from experience, whereas changes associated with maturation do not require environmental influence.

2. a. Classical conditioning involves learning about the relationships among stimuli. Operant conditioning involves learning response-outcome contingencies.

3. d. CSs start out as neutral stimuli, but take on meaning after being presented in conjunction with USs.

4. c. URs are automatic reactions that occur without training. CRs are expressed as a function of classical conditioning, or learning.

5. d. Flinching in anticipation of a "bang" when a needle passes through a balloon is an example of conditioned responding.

6. b. Phobias often result from classically conditioned cues associated with an unpleasant experience.

7. c. Watson's research, which would not pass today's APA guidelines, showed the ease with which emotional responses can by conditioned.

8. b. The strength of the CR might be used as an index of the degree of conditioning, but does not influence acquisition as it is the product of acquisition.

9. c. Spontaneous recovery takes place after a CR has been extinguished and there has been a break in conditioning and testing trials.

10. b. Discrimination is the occurrence of a response to a specific stimulus.

11. b. Contingency theory predicts stronger conditioning as a function of the CS's value in predicting the US.

12. a. Blocking refers to one CS impairing another's ability to acquire associative strength and value.

13. d. Taste-aversion learning can occur with CS-US intervals that were surprisingly long when the phenomenon was first discovered.

14. a. Preparedness refers to a theory of biological readiness to learn certain associations.

15. d. Secondary reinforcers are stimuli that take on meaning because they are associated with primary reinforcers.

16. b. An example of negative reinforcement is the termination of an alarm by pushing a button.

17. d. Shaping is also known as the method of (reinforcing) successive approximations.

18. b. A cumulative record is used to show the rate of responding in a conditioning trial.

19. a.   Interval and ratio schedules are the two main categories of intermittent reinforcement schedules.

20. b.   Insight learning involves the sudden grasp of a concept (the ah-ha experience) as a result of perceptual restructuring.

21. d.   Negative punishment involves the termination of a satisfier (e.g., losing privileges).

22. d.   The partial reinforcement effect describes the phenomenon of extended responding during extinction of a behavior that was reinforced only some of the time during acquisition.

23. a.   A discriminative stimulus signals the participant that reward contingencies are in place for target behaviors.

24. b.   Observational, or vicarious learning, occurs when one models learning for another (either purposely or otherwise).

25. c.   Behavior modification uses learning principles to decrease undesirable behaviors and increase desired ones. See discussion at the end of Chapter 6 in your textbook for more on behavior modification.

Key Vocabulary Terms

Cut out and use as study cards; terms appear on
one side and definitions are on the other.

learning	classical conditioning
neutral stimulus (NS)	unconditioned stimulus (US)
conditioned stimulus (CS)	unconditioned response (UR)
conditioned response (CR)	phobia

Key Vocabulary Terms

Cut out and use as study cards; terms appear on one side and definitions are on the other.

A relatively permanent change in behavior or the potential to make a response that occurs as a result of experience

Learning that occurs when two stimuli—a conditioned stimulus and an unconditioned stimulus—are paired and become associated with each other

Stimulus that, before conditioning, does not elicit a particular response

Event that automatically produces a response without any previous training

Neutral stimulus that acquires the ability to elicit a conditioned response after being paired with an unconditioned stimulus

Reaction that is automatically produced when an unconditioned stimulus is presented

Response elicited by a conditioned stimulus that has been paired with an unconditioned stimulus; is similar to the unconditioned response

Irrational fear of an activity, object, or situation that is out of proportion to the actual danger

extinction	spontaneous recovery
generalization	discrimination
learned motives	learned goals (learned incentives)
blocking	overshadowing
taste-aversion learning	preparedness

The process of removing reinforcers, which leads to a decrease in
the strength of a CR

Reappearance of an extinguished
CR after the passage of time

Occurrence of responses to stimuli
that are similar to a CS

Occurrence of responses only to a
specific CS

Motives that are learned or acquired through the process of classical conditioning

Goals or incentives that are
learned through the process of
classical conditioning

Situation in which the conditionability of a CS is weakened when it
is paired with a US that has previously been paired with another CS

Situation that occurs when a compound CS is paired with a US and
the more intense (salient) CS elicits
a stronger CR

Development of a dislike or aversion to a flavor or food that has
been paired with illness

Theory that organisms are biologically ready or prepared to associate certain conditioned
stimuli (CSs) with certain unconditioned stimuli (USs)

operant conditioning	reinforcer
primary reinforcer	secondary reinforcer
positive reinforcer	negative reinforcers
cumulative record	schedule of reinforcement
shaping	continuous reinforcement

Learning that occurs when the participant must make a response to produce a change in the environment

Event that increases the frequency of the response that it follows

Stimulus that has innate reinforcing properties

Stimulus that acquires reinforcing properties by being associated with a primary reinforcer

Event presented after the target response that increases the likelihood that this response will occur again

Event removed after the target response, thereby increasing the likelihood that this response will occur again

Results of a series of operant conditioning trials, shown as rate of responding

Preset pattern for delivering reinforcement

A form of operant conditioning in which a desired response is taught by reinforcement of successive responses that more closely resemble the target response

Reinforcement that follows every target response

intermittent, (or partial), reinforcement	ratio schedule
interval schedule	insight learning
latent learning	serial enumeration
punisher	law of effect
punishment	partial reinforcement effect

Reinforcement that does not follow every target response

Reinforcement schedule in which reinforcement is based on the number of responses; number may be set (fixed-ratio [FR] schedule) or may vary from one reinforcement to the next (variable-ratio [VR] schedule)

Reinforcement schedule based on the passage of time and in which a single response at the end of the designated interval is reinforced; intervals may be set (fixed interval [FI] schedule) or may vary from one reinforcement to the next (variable-interval [VI] schedule)

Sudden grasp of a concept or the solution to a problem that results from perceptual restructuring; typically characterized by an immediate change in behavior

Learning that has occurred but is not demonstrated

Ability to remember a series of events

Stimulus that produces a decrease in responding; may take the form of presentation of a stimulus (positive punisher) or termination of a stimulus (negative punisher)

Thorndike's view that reinforcers promote learning, whereas punishers lead to the unlearning of responses

The process of using a punisher to decrease response rate

Phenomenon in which extinction of an operant response following partial or intermittent reinforcement takes longer than extinction following continuous reinforcement

discrimination stimulus

observational learning (social learning theory)

vicarious reinforcement

vicarious punishment

behavior modification

Stimulus or signal telling the participant that responding will be reinforced

Learning that occurs through watching and imitating the behaviors of others

Ability to imagine the effects of a reinforcer

Ability to imagine the effects of a punisher

Using the fundamental principles of learning to change inappropriate behaviors

Textbooks are packed densely with information and can be exhausting to read. Studying your textbook must be an *active* process in order for you to gain the most from it. It is better to study chapters over several study sessions, rather than in a single sitting. Consider the *serial position effect* (see Chapter 7, Memory). According to the serial position effect, you will remember the most from the first and last portions of your study sessions. With this in mind, there are two things to consider when organizing your study sessions: 1) *minimize the middle* portion of your study sessions, and 2) *study actively*.

By minimizing the middle portion, or extending the "ends" of your study session, you will take advantage of the primacy (early part of study session) and recency (last part of study session) components of the serial position effect. By making the process of studying active, you will capitalize on what you will learn about levels of processing in the chapter on memory—in brief, the deeper you process information, the greater your chances are of remembering the information.

In addition to taking full advantage of this study guide, there are two well-known approaches you may wish to consider for studying your textbook. As with discovering which method of *note taking* will work best for you, try different approaches until you find a good fit for your learning style (there is more about understanding your learning style in the *Tip* section at the end of Chapter 8 in this study guide).

What Does Not Work

It is unfortunate that perhaps the most widely used method for studying a textbook is probably the least effective. Look around at your classmates' books and notice of how many people highlight or underline passages of text with fluorescent markers. *Indiscriminate* highlighting is a common practice among students who are at the early stages of learning to study. If you prefer to highlight, that may be just fine; the important thing is to consider carefully what text you will identify, and why.

Material should be highlighted because the reader plans to re-read the passage again later. If each page looks as if it were dipped into a bucket of ink, the notion of re-reading highlighted material can be daunting. As a result, many never re-read that which they took so much time identifying.

What Does Work

A few methods of studying textbook material have been developed through the years. A combination of these may provide you with the best approach. In addition to considering the merits of the following methods, know that the study guide you are reading was organized expressly for facilitating the process of extracting information from your textbook. First, the two main methods for studying text:

1. **SQ3R.** This is an acronym that stands for steps in the process of studying text: Survey, Question, Read, Recall, and Review.

    a. **Survey.** Spend several minutes orienting yourself to the material you are about to study. Knowing where you are headed will make it far easier to recognize the key landmarks along the way. The following sub-steps should be part of the survey step: examine chapter overviews, read summaries at the end of chapters, and read the headings from throughout the chapter. Take time to look at the figures and tables and note how they fit with the sections of the text with which they are associated.

    b. **Question.** As you begin studying either a single paragraph or a larger portion of a chapter, stop first and ask yourself what you are about to learn. Write the questions down. Doing this can be as simple as rephrasing a paragraph heading into a question. Do not rely on your memory—write it down.

c. **Read.** Having surveyed the material and prepared yourself by asking what you expect to learn, you will be well-prepared to read. Read with the questions you posed in mind. Do not bog down and spend your time just staring at words. If you cannot remember what you just read, you are not reading effectively. One way to keep from bogging down is to keep track of how much time you spend reading each page. If you push yourself slightly, you will retain more than if you slow down and relax too much while you read. Summarize the main points from what you read in your notebook. Make sure to do this in your own words. By translating the messages from the text into *your own language,* you are processing it, and thereby improving your chances of remembering it.

d. **Recall.** Look away from your book and notes, even close your eyes if it helps, and use mental imagery to recall what you just read. What words stand out? What was communicated in the tables and figures? If you were to draw a diagram or picture to represent the information, what would it look like?

e. **Review.** Refer to your questions, notes from reading, and textbook to see how well you recalled the information. Take note of any omissions. What needs more attention? Do not go on until you master each page. Generally speaking, it is difficult to benefit from subsequent paragraphs and pages until you understand the ones you have already studied.

This may sound like a time-consuming way to read. In the long run, it is more efficient. Take time to learn the material during your first exposure and you will save yourself from having to re-read later. If you sit down with the idea of finishing a portion of a chapter, rather than trying to study the whole thing, you will find that you can make better use of discrete chunks of time.

What does SQ3R stand for and why does it work so well? _____

_____

_____

The next technique for studying text, the *Notes in the Margin Method,* is used effectively by itself by many students. Consider, however, using it in conjunction with the SQ3R method to improve your potential for learning the material.

2. **Notes in the Margin Method.** Quite literally, this technique involves using the blank space in your textbook to record notes as you read. However, you may wish to record your notes in a notebook. By writing in the notebook, you will preserve the quality of your book and be better able to read your notes without missing some of your comments.

a. **Do Not Mark in Your Text as You Read.** Having identified a reason to read a paragraph (see B, above, for comments on asking questions), you are ready to read. Read with an eye for information that will come up in class lectures and discussions, or on quizzes and exams.

b. **Adopt Your Professor's Perspective.** After reading a section of text, adopt your professor's perspective and write a question or two—record them in your notebook. If you develop your skills at *asking questions,* including multiple-choice items with all the alternatives, you will also develop your skills for *answering questions.*

c. **Refer to the Text.** Next, find the passage in the text that provides the answer to your question. This is the material you could underline or highlight. Better yet, translate the passage into your own words and write it in your notes.

d. **Study Your Notes.** If your goal is to learn course content, study your notes from the textbook and quiz yourself with your own questions. Active note-taking will help you learn; studying your notes compound the effect.

Summarize the steps of the "Notes in the Margins Method": _____

_____

_____

3. **Use of This Study Guide.** The chapters in this study guide were organized to help you benefit the most from your textbook. Attend to the structure of the outline. Which sections are related to which larger topics from the text? How are the vocabulary words related to the material you are studying? The following suggestions may help you combine the methods that were described above and make the best use of this study guide as a learning tool.

  a. **Examine the Outline in the Study Guide.** The outline in the study guide, which always follows the chapter overview, was extracted exactly from the textbook. When surveying the material you are about to study, you may find it convenient to study the outline from the study guide first.

  b. **Learn the Language.** Many students struggle with the language of psychology. The study guide includes each keyword as it appears in the textbook. Take time to record a definition for each word as you progress through the text. Do this *in your own words*, rather than copying verbatim from the text.

  c. **Use the Space.** In addition to providing space for rewriting keyword definitions, you will find space to jot down a few summarizing comments for each section of each chapter. Use this space.

  d. **Destroy This Study Guide!** As you work through the outlines, keyword exercises, and practice tests, tear the pages out and insert them in the proper places in your 3-ring notebook. Also, cut up the keyword 'study cards' at the ends of the chapters. These are to be used as flip cards when learning the terms from the chapters.

How can using this study guide help you get the most from the textbook? _____

_____

_____

You noticed, no doubt, that each of the suggestions for using your textbook involved *active* processing of the text material. If you do not study the material actively, chances are you will not gain as much from it. Also, make sure to study only for reasonable units of time. If you can *minimize the middle* portions of your study sessions, you will retain the most from them.

CHAPTER 7

Memory

OVERVIEW

Use the space provided in this outline to record notes from the textbook as well as from class lectures and discussion. Questions related to the *Psychological Detective* sections in the text have been presented in the outline; use the associated space to respond to the questions and to record your own comments about the issues. *Keywords and terms* from the text have been italicized and inserted in the outline so you can practice writing their definitions. The pages in this study guide are perforated and can be removed for use as study sheets for quizzes and exams.

I. **Initial Studies**

memory—

nonsense syllables—

How many ways could an experimenter measure a participant's memory for nonsense syllables?

serial learning—

paired-associate learning—

free recall—

A. The Curve of Forgetting

B. Recognition and Relearning

recognition test—

relearning test—

savings score—

II. Traditional Models of Memory

A. Human Memory as an Information Processing System

1. Encoding

   encoding—

2. Storage

   storage—

3. Retrieval

   retrieval—

Who was your 4th grade teacher? What process(es) did you use to retrieve the name?

B. The Atkinson-Shiffrin Model

1. Sensory Memory

   sensory memory—

2. Short-Term Memory

   short-term memory (STM)—

Write down the three phone numbers from the *Psychological Detective* section. Why would it be easier to handle two versus three numbers?

 Write down as many of the 15 words as you can. Did you perform better than 7+/-2? If so, why?

    3. Long-Term Memory

        long-term memory (LTM)—

        maintenance rehearsal—

        elaborative rehearsal—

        proactive interference—

        retroactive interference—

III. Other Approaches to Learning and Memory

    A. The Levels-of-Processing Model
        levels-of-processing theory—

    B. Alternate Approaches
      1. Transfer-Appropriate Processing

      2. Parallel Distributed Processing

C. Different Types of Long-Term Memory

    1. Procedural Memory

        procedural memory—

    2. Semantic Memory

        semantic memory—

        tip-of-the-tongue (TOT) phenomenon—

Write the answers to the *Psychological Detective* section questions. How many answers were just "on the tip of your tongue"?

    3. Episodic Memory

        episodic memory—

        flashbulb memory—

    4. Priming or Implicit Memory

        priming or implicit memory—

D. Retrieval

    1. Retrieval from Short-Term Memory

Why is it necessary to *retrieve* information that is in our consciousness?

    2. Retrieval from Long-Term Memory

        semantic network—

        schema—

    3. Encoding Specificity

        encoding specificity—

      a. Eyewitness Testimony

 What are some possible reasons that people give inaccurate eyewitness testimonies?

      b. State-Dependent Learning

        state-dependent learning—

  E. The Repressed-Memory Controversy

  F. Memory Illusions

IV. Techniques for Improving Memory

  A. Influential Factors

      serial position effect—

B. Processing Strategies

   mnemonic devices—

1. Imagery

   imagery—

2. Method of Loci

   method of loci—

How can familiar songs, places on an often-traveled path, or rooms in your childhood home be used to help remember lists of information?

3. Pegword Technique

   pegword technique—

4. Grouping (Chunking)

5. Coding

   a. Acronyms And Acrostics

      acronym—

      acrostic—

V. The Physiological Basis of Learning and Memory

A. Amnesias

amnesia—

1. Anterograde Amnesia and The Hippocampus

anterograde amnesia—

🔍 Why do H.M.'s daily experiences consist exclusively of things he can maintain in STM, except for things he learned prior to 1953?

2. Retrograde Amnesia and the Consolidation Hypothesis

retrograde amnesia—

consolidation hypothesis—

✸ LEARNING OBJECTIVES

After you have studied the chapter, you should be able to respond to the following statements and questions to convey your understanding of the material.

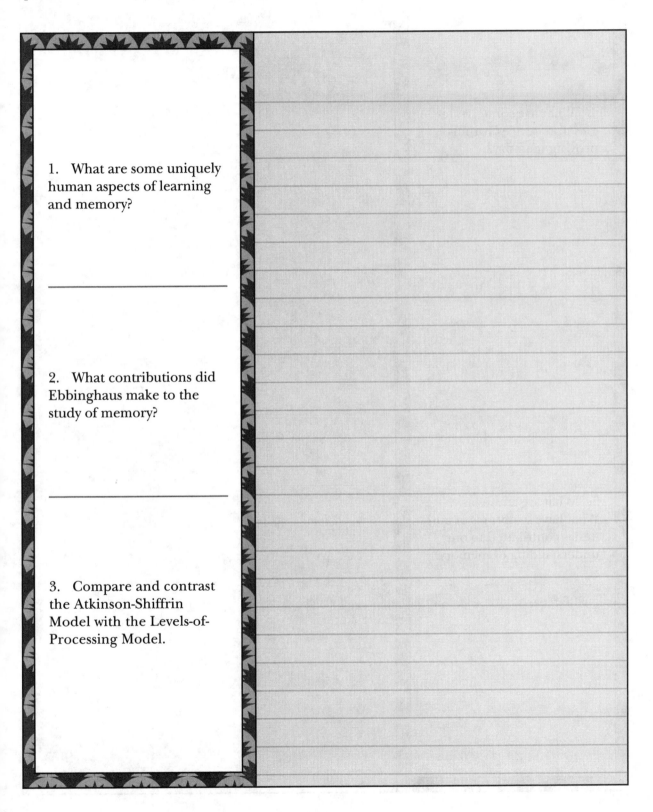

1. What are some uniquely human aspects of learning and memory?

2. What contributions did Ebbinghaus make to the study of memory?

3. Compare and contrast the Atkinson-Shiffrin Model with the Levels-of-Processing Model.

4. What are some strategies and devices for improving memory?

5. What are amnesias? What have symptoms of amnesias contributed to our understanding of memory?

Fill in the blanks in the following statements with key words and terms from the textbook. Answer as many as you can without referring to your notes or to the book. If you have blanks after thinking about each item, try using your book. The answers are presented after the practice test.

1. _____-_____ _____ is a technique that is often used to learn the vocabulary for a foreign language.

2. Identifying a suspect from a police line-up is an example of a _____ _____.

3. Information cannot be retrieved for a test unless it is first _____ and then stored.

4. Sperling elegantly gathered data on the capacity of _____ _____ by assigning tones, to act as signals, to each of three rows in a 12-letter stimulus matrix.

5. _____-_____ _____ is a relatively permanent store that depends on rehearsal or practice.

6. That people do better recalling information from a word list if they are instructed to rate the pleasantness of each word, versus counting the number of letters in each word, is evidence for the _____-____-_____ _____.

7. Remembering how to rollerblade is an example of _____ _____.

8. Psychologists refer to memory of one's personal experiences as _____ _____.

9. People do not always know whether to tip waitstaff when eating out at a pizza place because the context does not exactly match the _____ for either a fast-food joint or for a restaurant.

10. Retrograde amnesia may exist for items that occur just prior to a traumatic event because _____ of the information concerning the items has not taken place yet.

✖ PRACTICE TEST

Circle the letter that corresponds to the *best* alternative for each of the following items. Read each alternative carefully. The answers are presented at the end of this study guide chapter. Be sure to learn *why* each correct alternative is better than the others

1. Ebbinghaus used nonsense syllables in his studies of how associations between stimuli are formed:
   a. because they were short.
   b. because they were supposed to have no meaning.
   c. in order to encourage people from countries that spoke other languages to replicate his work.
   d. because generating the consonant-vowel-consonant sequence was easy to do with a computer.

2. A learning procedure in which material that has been learned may be repeated in any order is called:
   a. the recognition test.
   b. the free recall procedure.
   c. the serial learning procedure.
   d. the randomized recall procedure.

3. One of Ebbinghaus' most important findings was:
   a. the method of loci.
   b. anterograde amnesia.
   c. the curve of forgetting.
   d. the Atkinson-Shiffrin model of memory.

4. The difference between the time it takes to learn material once and the time necessary to learn it a second time is:
   a. called a savings score.
   b. commonly referred to as the difference score.
   c. usually shorter among children than with adults.
   d. long unless the information is particularly salient.

5. The human information processing system has been characterized as having all *but* which of the following stages?
   a. storage
   b. retrieval
   c. encoding
   d. transferring

6. Leonardo da Vinci and Napoleon Bonaparte had in common which of the following:
   a. the capacity for eidetic imagery.
   b. the capacity to form flashbulb memories.
   c. anterograde amnesia due to a closed head injury (e.g., stroke).
   d. retrograde amnesia stemming from an open head injury (e.g., foreign object entering the head.)

7. Which component of the Atkinson-Shiffrin model had the smallest capacity?
   a. sensory memory
   b. long-term memory
   c. short-term memory
   d. the environmental input channel

8. Information in short-term memory is usually lost after:
   a. 20 seconds or so.
   b. about 15 minutes.
   c. a good night's rest.
   d. new information is admitted.

9. The magic number that was proposed by George Miller was:
   a. three: many aspects of memory seem to involve the number three.
   b. not a single number, but span of numbers from about five to about nine.
   c. 8675309: a number that was later treated as a woman's phone number in a pop song.
   d. one. Three Dog Night described *one* as the loneliest number, but Miller thought it was magic.

10. Working memory was proposed:
    a. as a second phase of STM.
    b. as a treatment for broken memory.
    c. as a hypothetical construct to explain processing in LTM.
    d. by Ebbinghaus to explain improved recall for certain items.

11. Saving information for a specified period of time is to ___ as adding to the material to be remembered is to ___.
    a. storage; retrieval
    b. retrieval; encoding
    c. temporal encoding; summation encoding
    d. maintenance rehearsal; elaborative rehearsal

12. With respect to what is recalled (as opposed to what is sought in a memory task), old memories are to new memories as ___ is to ___.
    a. anterograde amnesia; retrograde amnesia
    b. retrograde amnesia; anterograde amnesia
    c. retroactive interference; proactive interference
    d. proactive interference; retroactive interference

13. The levels-of-processing theory states that which of the following relationships exists between processing depth and likelihood of recall?
    a. positive—as processing depth increases, probability of recall increases.
    b. negative—as processing depth increases, probability of recall decreases.
    c. no relationship—the probability of recall is independent of processing depth.
    d. inverse—the probability of recall occurs as a mathematical expression equal to one over the depth of processing.

14. The transfer-appropriate processing model suggests:
    a. we process information in several subsystems simultaneously.
    b. that content is learned best when it is processed at deep versus shallow levels.
    c. we only transfer to memory that which is appropriate, as the model's name implies.
    d. the best learning and memory occur when the encoding and retrieval processes are the same.

15. Which of the following was not discussed in your text as a type of long-term memory?
    a. episodic memory
    b. personal memory
    c. semantic memory
    d. procedural memory

16. The tip-of-the-tongue (TOT) phenomenon is sometimes used to investigate the nature of:
    a. semantic memory.
    b. procedural memory.
    c. flashbulb memories.
    d. none of the above; TOT is strictly a phenomenon and hinders rather than helps investigators.

17. The topic of interest when discussing the role of prior exposure to stimulus items in aiding subsequent learning is:
    a. flashbulb memory.
    b. retrograde amnesia.
    c. anterograde amnesia.
    d. priming or implicit memory.

18. Multiple choice is to essay test as ___ is to ___.
    a. hard; easy
    b. recall; recognition
    c. recognition; recall
    d. semantic memory; episodic memory

19. A network of related concepts that are linked together is called a(n):
    a. schema.
    b. semantic network.
    c. flashbulb memory.
    d. eidetic memorial network.

20. State-dependent learning is closely related to the ___ hypothesis.
    a. flashbulb memory
    b. encoding specificity
    c. eyewitness memory
    d. repression of content

21. A distinction between "memory illusions" and true memories is:
    a. in their relative durations.
    b. in the time it takes to form them.
    c. that memory illusions are usually less detailed.
    d. that memory illusions are usually more detailed.

22. The serial position effect:
    a. is used extensively in determining how to stock shelves in the breakfast aisle in grocery stores.
    b. is most easily demonstrated in experiments that employ tasks including learning word pairs.
    c. refers to the tendency for people to show improved recall for items at the beginning and end of a list in comparison to items in the middle.
    d. refers to the phenomenon whereby participants perform better on recall tests of word lists when the words are from the middle rather than the end of the list.

23. John plays the game *Monopoly* frequently. He recently inferred from studying for his psychology class that he could use his memory for the game's board to his advantage. To his surprise, he finds it easy to recall terms when he associates them with places on the board. He is using a variation on:
    a. imagery.
    b. method of loci.
    c. pegword technique.
    d. flashbulb technique.

24. Acronym is to acrostic as ___ is to ___.
   a. word; saying
   b. saying; word
   c. opposite; same
   d. same; opposite

25. With respect to lost memories, anterograde amnesia is to retrograde amnesia as ___ is to ___.
   a. new; old
   b. old; new
   c. declarative; procedural
   d. procedural; declarative

 ## ANSWERS TO KEY WORD EXERCISE

1. paired-associate learning
2. recognition task
3. encoded
4. sensory memory
5. Long-term memory
6. levels-of-processing theory
7. procedural memory
8. episodic memory
9. schema
10. consolidation

 ## PRACTICE TEST ANSWERS AND EXPLANATIONS

1. b. Ebbinghaus chose to use nonsense syllables because he thought they would have no meaning. It turns out that these syllables sometimes do have meaning, and therefore may confound experiments.

2. b. The *free recall* procedure permits subjects to recollect information in any order they wish.

3. c. Ebbinghaus discovered the curve of forgetting when testing his own memory.

4. a. The savings score is the time saved by having learned the material previously.

5. d. The system involves three steps—encoding, storage, and retrieval—in that sequence.

6. a. Both men were reported to have had the capacities for eidetic imagery (photographic memory).

7. c. The short-term memory component of the model has the smallest capacity.

8. a. Information in STM lasts only 10-20 seconds before being lost from consciousness.

9. b. Miller proposed 7+/-2 (5 to 9) as the limit for normal STM capacity.

10. a. Working memory is considered to be a second component of STM in which attention and conscious effort are used to process material.

11. d. Maintenance rehearsal is used to keep information (e.g., a phone number) for a specified time. Elaborative rehearsal is used when expanding (elaborating) memory.

12. d. Retroactive interference involves new memories being recalled in place of old ones; vice versa for proactive interference.

13. a. The levels-of-processing approach states that greater processing depth results in improved recall.

14. d. The TAP model suggests that the best learning and memory occur when the encoding and retrieval processes are the same. This model, however, has been criticized.

15. b. The other three were discussed as types of LTM, as was *priming or implicit memory.*

16. a. Investigators sometimes use items that evoke TOT to study semantic memory as both TOT and semantic memory involve general knowledge.

17. d. *Priming, or implicit memory,* is unconscious memory processing in which prior exposure to stimulus items may aid in subsequent learning.

18. c. Multiple choice tests are examples of recognition tasks, whereas essay tests examine recall.

19. b. Semantic networks are clusters of related concepts.

20. b. State-dependent learning is an example of learning that supports the encoding specificity hypothesis.

21. c. True memories generally have more detail than memory illusions.

22. c. The serial position effect is the tendency for people to do better when recalling items from the beginning and end of a word list.

23. b. John uses a variation on the method of loci technique, in which familiar places on the game board become associated with items on a wordlist.

24. a. Acronyms are words in which each letter stands for something. Acrostics are verses or sayings in which the first letter of each word is important.

25. a. Anterograde amnesia is an inability to store new memories, while retrograde amnesia is an inability to recall information that was stored prior to a traumatic event.

Key Vocabulary Terms

Cut out and use as study cards; terms appear on
one side and definitions are on the other.

memory

nonsense
syllables

serial learning

paired-associate
learning

free recall

recognition test

relearning test

savings score

Key Vocabulary Terms

Cut out and use as study cards; terms appear on one side and definitions are on the other.

Stimuli used to study memory; typically composed of a consonant-vowel-consonant sequence	System or process by which the products or results of learning are stored for future use
Learning procedure in which items to be recalled are learned in pairs. During recall, one member of the pair is presented and the other is to be recalled	Learning procedure in which material that has been learned must be repeated in the order in which it was presented
Test in which retention is measured by the ability to pick out previously learned items from a list that also contains unfamiliar items	Learning procedure in which material that has been learned may be repeated in any order
Difference between the time or trials originally required to learn material and the time or trials required to relearn the material	Test of retention that compares the time or trials required to learn material a second time with the time or trials required to learn the material the first time

encoding	storage
retrieval	sensory memory
short-term memory	working memory
long-term memory	maintenance rehearsal
elaborative rehearsal	proactive interference

Second stage of the memory process; in it information is placed in the memory system. This stage may involve either brief or long-term storage of memories

First stage of the memory process; in it information is transformed or coded (a transduction process) into a form that can be processed further and stored

Very brief (0.5 to 1.0 second) but extensive memory for sensory events

Third stage of the memory process; in it stored memories are brought into consciousness

Second stage of short-term memory; in it attention and conscious effort are brought to bear on material

Memory stage in which information is held in consciousness for 10 to 20 seconds

Rehearsal used when we want to save or maintain a memory for a specified period of time

Memory stage that has a very large capacity and the capability to store information relatively permanently

Situation in which previously learned information hinders the recall of information learned more recently

Rehearsal in which meaning is added to the material to be remembered

retroactive interference	levels-of-processing
procedural memory	semantic memory
tip-of-the-tongue (TOT) phenomenon	episodic memory
flashbulb memory	priming or implicit memory
semantic network	schema

Theory stating that deeper processing of information increases the
likelihood that the information will
be recalled

Situation in which information
learned more recently hinders
the recall of information
learned previously

Memory for general knowledge

Memory for making responses and
performing skilled actions

Memory of one's
personal experiences

Condition of being almost, but not
quite, able to remember something; used to investigate the nature
of semantic memory

Unconscious memory
processing in which prior
exposure to stimulus items
may aid in subsequent learning

Very detailed memory of an
arousing, surprising, or
emotional situation

Grouping or cluster of
knowledge about an object or
sequence of events

Network of related concepts
that are linked together

encoding specificity	state-dependent learning
serial position effect	mnemonic devices
imagery	method of loci
pegword technique	acronym
acrostic	amnesia

Theory stating that when we learn something while in a specific physiological state, our recall of that information will be better when we are in the same physiological state

Theory stating that the effectiveness of memory retrieval is directly related to the similarity of the cues present when the memory is retrieved

Procedures for associating new information with previously stored memories

Tendency for items at the beginning and end of a list to be learned better than items in the middle

Use of familiar locations as cues to recall items that have been associated with them

Process of visualizing items as they are being learned

A word formed by the initial letter(s) of the items to be remembered

Use of familiar words or names as cues to recall items that have been associated with them

Loss of memory that occurs as a result of physical or psychological trauma

A verse or saying in which the first letter(s) of each word stands for a bit of information

anterograde
amnesia

retrograde
amnesia

consolidation
hypothesis

Loss of memories that were stored before a traumatic event

Inability to store new memories after a traumatic event

Hypothesis that memories must be consolidated or "set" before they can be stored

TIP FOR SUCCESS: PREPARING FOR AND TAKING TESTS

Under the best circumstances, tests are instruments that serve both teachers and students. Teachers rely on them for measuring student progress, and students use them for feedback on the depth and breadth of their understanding. Additionally, students can use tests to demonstrate their enthusiasm for a course. For many students, taking tests is the only way they communicate with their instructors.

Because tests are often closely linked to course grades, it is common for students to become anxious about them. Unfortunately, anxiety sometimes distracts students from focusing entirely on content when preparing for tests, and from performing their very best when taking tests. This section was developed as guide to preparing for and taking exams.

Things to Do Before the Test

1. **Be Prepared.** Preparation for a test can be overwhelming and should be broken into manageable units. Identify test days on your calendar, and set specific preparation goals that maximize your use of available time. By starting early, and proceeding on only after mastering each unit along the way, you will save yourself a great deal of anxiety and frustration as the test day draws closer.

2. **Be Early.** Be early to every class meeting, but be especially early on test days. When you are running late, you will be more anxious. By being early you will be able to make full use of the time available for taking the test. It is unreasonable to ask for additional time on a test if you did not show up on time.

3. **Stake Your Claim.** You learned about state-dependent learning in Chapter 7 of your textbook. State-dependent learning, and a related phenomenon, context-dependent learning, can facilitate recall of information at test time. In general, you want to maintain the same conditions at retrieval time as were in place when information was encoded. Consider the following suggestions:

   a. **Keep Your Physiological State Constant.** Do not drink 19 cups of coffee prior to an exam unless you drink that much coffee before regular class meetings. By changing your physiological state, you disrupt normal functioning, and may not be sensitive to feedback that would normally help cue recall. What is more, you will be distracted by the changes in your bodily activity.

   b. **The Same Goes for Mood.** There are data that indicate that some learning is mood-dependent. Thus, do not show up on test day angry, anxious, or otherwise discombobulated, unless you are that way on regular class days. Maintaining an even temper and stable mood will serve you well in many facets of life.

   c. **Keep Your Seat.** By keeping your normal classroom seat you are holding contextual cues from the environment constant. Since those cues are part of a context where you think and learn about the course material, they may help improve your performance on test day.

4. **Know Your Professor's Style.** Whenever possible, review samples of the questions and other test items your professor has used in the past. Getting these may be as simple as asking her or him if there is a test file you may review, or if he or she would share some samples so you can become better acquainted with their style. Other students who have taken a course from your professor previously may also be of some assistance.

Get as much information as possible that will help you know how to prepare for the test. If there will be multiple choice items, will they focus on definitions, or should you know how to *apply* what you have learned? Will you have to solve analogy problems? In general, your preparations should match the type of text you will take. Learn to anticipate test items, and practice responding to them. Specific ideas for different categories of exam items will be given below.

5. **Recognition is Easier than Comprehension.** Do not convince yourself that you understand material just because you recognize it. This goes for material from textbooks as well as for that which is presented in class. Good books make the most difficult material accessible to a student who is new to the field; good teachers can make challenging concepts seem easy to understand. Beware that even though you may take in material as you read or hear it, additional effort may be required to comprehend it fully. Challenge yourself to recall as much as possible about a given topic without cues from your textbook or notes.

At the Test: Objective Items

There is no substitute for understanding the material. The best thing you can do to improve your score is to study and thoroughly understand the material. Sometimes, though, you will be faced with challenging alternatives, or with an essay question that requires you to think differently than you had anticipated. Learn the following suggestions and use them as appropriate to help you during an exam.

1. **Multiple Choice Questions.** This is a common variety of test item because it allows your instructor to probe your understanding at a variety of depths. The following tips may help:

   a. **Break Each Question into the Stem and the Alternatives.** Study <u>each alternative</u>. Sometimes the wording of alternatives reveals that they are poor fits for the stem. Sometimes there are alternatives that simply do not make sense. After reading each alternative, cross out those that you know are incorrect. If you do not identify a clear best answer, move on to the next item.

   b. **Avoid Absolute Statements and Extremes.** More often than not, answers that are absolutes or extreme statements are decoys, and should be avoided.

   c. **Beware of Jargon.** If an alternative is filled with complicated language, it may not be the right answer.

   d. **Use Your Familiarity with Prefixes, Suffixes, and Root Words.** When you are presented with an unfamiliar word, break the it down and try to discover its meaning *in context.* Also, do not be afraid to ask your professor to define a word for you.

   e. **Study the Grammar.** Sometimes the grammar used in a multiple choice alternative will help give it away as either the correct answer or as a decoy. Pay attention to grammar as it may provide helpful clues.

   f. **If You Must Guess.** Sometimes you simply cannot determine which answer is the best one. If you must guess, do so after eliminating one or two alternatives. Your chances of guessing correctly get significantly better with each alternative you are able to eliminate. If you are not penalized for guessing incorrectly, you should respond to each item.

2. **True-False Items.** Some professors use true-false items to test their students' mastery of detailed information. Consider the following tips for responding to these items.

   a. **Only Two Options.** A statement can be either true or false. If you do not know the answer, guess. With true-false items, you have a 50-50 chance of guessing correctly.

   b. **True Means Always True, False Means Always False.** If a given answer is *true,* it must be true under every circumstance. Test the accuracy of statements by trying to think of examples of when the statement is false.

   c. **Qualifiers.** If a statement is qualified (e.g., some, many, usually, frequently), this may be a cue that it is true.

   d. **Check Names and Dates.** Details such as names and dates can easily be mixed up to test your knowledge of who did what, when.

3. **Matching Sets.** It is important to read directions carefully for matching sets, as the rules sometimes permit re-using alternatives, and sometimes there will be extra items. If you determine that every item will be used once, you have the advantage of being able to use the process of elimination to simplify guessing from among any remaining alternatives.

   a. **Look for Relationships.** Often one column is devoted to terms, and the other to definitions for the terms. Determine whether this or another relationship is present in the set before proceeding as it may help in eliminating alternatives.

   b. **Save Time.** It takes less time to read a long definition and scan a list of short terms for a match, than vice versa. If a matching set has lengthy definitions that are to be paired with short terms, read the longer items first.

   c. **Start with What You Know.** If you are not confident of which alternative should go with a given item, skip it and come back to it later. The process of eliminating alternatives for matches you are confident about may make it easier to decide from among remaining alternatives later.

Comment on Returned Objective Tests

You will need to review your answers to determine which alternatives are correct. While taking an exam, jot notes beside each exam to reflect your decision for an alternative. Make a list of the stems and alternatives that go together. This may require some digging in your notes or in the textbook. If your instructor will not let you take the exam home, ask if you can take notes from it; if so, you will be glad you have developed a shorthand system.

What can you do to improve your preparation for objective exams? How can you use your exams as learning tools after you get them back? _____

_____

_____

_____

Before the Test: Essay Items

Some professors give out a pool of essay questions from which they will choose the one(s) you will write on during an exam; if this is the case in your class, you have no excuse for not preparing thoroughly. Other times you make get some hints about particular content to focus on when preparing for the essay portion of an exam. Take note of these hints. If you have no direction from your professor, there are still some important things you can do to prepare.

As you study your text, you will note that some material seems to lend itself well to objective (i.e., multiple choice, matching) items, while other material does not. If a portion of a chapter contains information that is more easily described in narrative text than in discrete definitions, or if there are important concepts or relationships between and among concepts, these items may be good essay item candidates.

Frequently students are able to anticipate the broad topic that will be addressed in essay questions. Practice reviewing the text and writing essay items of the same format and style that your professor uses. You will get better at this with practice.

Once you have generated a list of potential questions, write outlines for responses to each item. Include in your outline any keywords or examples that would be useful for communicating your understanding of the topic or relationship. It is not necessary to write out your whole answer in longhand if you can include all the topics and elements in your outline. Study the outline to review for the exam.

At the Test: Essay Items

1. **Know the Directions.** Read the directions for the essay section carefully. Sometimes professors will expect grammatically correct answers; sometimes they are merely looking for lists. If you are unsure, ask. Attend to whether you are directed to answer each item, or a subset of the items. How many points are the items worth? It is a good idea to start working on the more valuable items first.

2. **Jot Down Notes.** Take a few minutes to make comments on scratch paper, or in the margins about things to include in each essay. If you observe that there will be overlap in your answers, you may wish to simplify them, and to refer to the content of one while writing the other. This will save you time and energy during the test.

3. **Budget Your Time, and Stick to Your Schedule.** Unless you have been granted unlimited time to work on your exam, you will need to attend to the time that you have available for writing on the essay item(s). If each item you are to answer is of equal length and complexity, distribute your time evenly. You may want to allocate more time to an item if it is weighted more heavily, or if your response to it will have more detailed information. Be sure to allow ample time to re-read your essay. A careful review of your efforts should help minimize grammatical errors and word omissions.

4. **Make an Outline.** Borrowing from the list of things you wish to include, organize a brief outline or diagram that prescribes the flow of your response. Doing this will help keep you from having to erase, cross out, or reorganize major portions of your essay. Your professor will be more favorably impressed by a well-organized, succinctly written essay than one that is wordy and hard to follow.

5. **Write Carefully.** Write legibly and do not rush yourself. The organizational steps you have taken should help the essay flow smoothly onto your paper. Attend to your expression of ideas, keeping in mind who your reader will be. Is your task to write for a well-informed or a naïve audience?

6. **Re-read Your Essay.** When you have finished writing your exam, re-read the essay questions as if you were a journal editor. If you write more than one essay, finish writing each one before moving on to editing your work. As you read, ask yourself the following questions: Are your ideas presented clearly? Did you make good use of transitional sentences? Are there any sentence fragments? Are there subject-verb agreement errors? Is the language gender- or culture-biased? Have you used effective examples to illustrate your points?

How can you improve the quality of your essays through preparation and planning before you begin writing? _____

_____

_____

_____

CHAPTER 8

Thinking and
Intelligence

OVERVIEW

Use the space provided in this outline to record notes from the textbook as well as from class lectures and discussion. Questions related to the *Psychological Detective* sections in the text have been presented in the outline; use the associated space to respond to the questions and to record your own comments about the issues. *Keywords and terms* from the text have been italicized and inserted in the outline so you can practice writing their definitions. The pages in this study guide are perforated and can be removed for use as study sheets for quizzes and exams.

I.   Thinking

    A. Cognitive Psychology

           cognitive psychology—

           thinking—

        1. Images

 What dependent measure(s) could be used in an experiment if you were interested in inferring whether subjects were rotating objects mentally?

        2. Concepts

 What rule(s) define the concept that associates the 1st and 4th examples, but not the 2nd and 3rd from Figure 8-2 in your textbook?

           prototype—

    B. Thinking and Language

        1. Using Language to Limit Thought

    C. Problem Solving

        1. Problem-Solving Methods

           a. Algorithms

algorithm—

🔍 What strategy did you use when solving the anagram? Did you change strategies or stick with just one?

    b. Heuristics

       heuristics—

2. Obstacles and Aids to Problem Solving

3. Setting Subgoals

🔍 How many times will the raft cross the river before all 11 people are on the other side?

4. Approach to Representing Problems

🔍 Use this space to draw the 9-dot matrix and to try to solve the problem.

5. Rigidity

       rigidity—

       functional fixedness—

🔍 What is your solution to the candle problem?

6. The Set Effect

       set effect—

D. Making Decisions

   1. Seeking Information to Confirm a Solution

      confirmation bias—

   2. Representativeness

      representativeness heuristic—

 Will the next toss result in heads or tails (the coin is a fair coin)? Why?

   3. Availability

      availability heuristic—

   4. Comparison

   5. Framing

      framing—

E. Creativity

      creativity—

   1. Defining Creativity

   2. Measuring Creativity

   3. Personal Factors in Creativity

   4. Situational Factors in Creativity

   5. Enhancing Creativity at Work

II. Intelligence

Write down several characteristics and behaviors that are shared by intelligent people.

intelligence—

A. The History of Intelligence Testing

mental age—

1. The Stanford-Binet Intelligence Scale

intelligence quotient—

2. The Wechsler Scales

B. Principles of Psychological Tests
1. Reliability

reliability—

2. Validity

validity—

3. Standardization

standardization—

norms—

normal curve—

C. Extremes of Intelligence
1. Exceptional Children

2. Savant Syndrome

savant syndrome—

D. Kinds of Intelligence

    1. Spearman's Model

    2. Sternberg's Model

    3. Gardner's Multiple Intelligences

E. Misuse of Intelligence Tests

F. Heredity and Environmental Determinants of Intelligence

    1. Hereditary Determinants

heritability—

How could a researcher interested in intelligence determine the contributions of genetic factors (heritability)?

identical twins—

fraternal twins—

    2. Environmental Determinants of Intelligence

What components of Figure 8-15 demonstrate the contributions of environment to intelligence?

    3. Explaining Differences in Intelligence Scores

LEARNING OBJECTIVES

After you have studied the chapter, you should be able to respond to the following statements and questions to convey your understanding of the material.

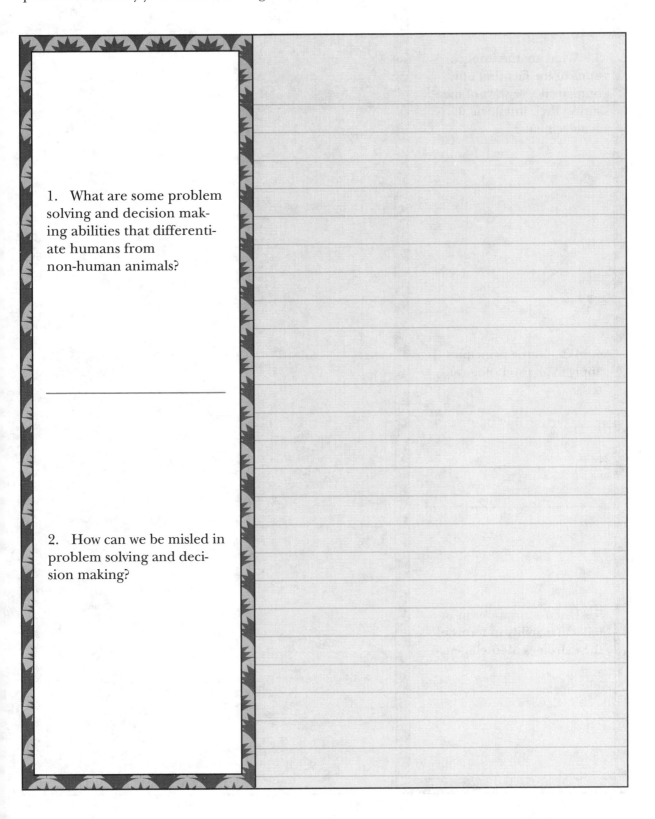

1. What are some problem solving and decision making abilities that differentiate humans from non-human animals?

2. How can we be misled in problem solving and decision making?

3. What are the implications of the fact that only humans devise ways of measuring their intellectual achievements?

4. What three principles apply to all psychological tests?

5. Discuss variations in intellectual ability in terms of the extremes of intelligence.

6. Describe the models of intelligence (Spearman, Sternberg, Gardner).

_____

7. What roles do heredity and environment play in determining one's intelligence?

Fill in the blanks in the following statements with key words and terms from the textbook. Answer as many as you can without referring to your notes or to the book. If you have blanks after thinking about each item, try using your book. The answers are presented after the practice test.

1. _____ involves the manipulation of information in the form of mental images and concepts.

2. If you listed on your resume that you raised grain-consuming animal units, rather than saying you raised farm animals, you would be employing a kind of _____.

3. Chess players do not use _____ because it would take centuries to examine all the possible arrangements of the chess pieces.

4. Sometimes it is helpful when trying to solve a problem to break it into manageable intermediate _____.

5. Functional fixedness is a specific example of _____.

6. The fact that inducing positive feelings can enhance creativity is an example of _____ _____ in creativity.

7. The _____ _____ is calculated by dividing an estimate of one's mental age by one's chronological age and multiplying by 100.

8. The procedures for administering the SAT test are the same no matter where the test is given. This is because the test has undergone _____.

9. Describing a hypothetical experiment in which seeds are planted in different kinds of soil would be analogous to comparing _____ influences on intelligence.

10. _____ _____ was Charles Darwin's cousin, but is best known for his early work in the area of intelligence testing.

PRACTICE TEST

Circle the letter that corresponds to the *best* alternative for each of the following items. Read each alternative carefully. The answers are presented at the end of this study guide chapter. Be sure to learn *why* each correct alternative is better than the others.

1. When Scott Smith injected himself with curare, a poison that causes paralysis, he did so:
    a. because he had done poorly on an intelligence test.
    b. because people had criticized his cognitive abilities.
    c. to test whether he could think in spite of not being able to move.
    d. to test whether his paralysis would be passed on to his offspring.

2. Cognitive psychologists infer mental processes:
    a. from the observable behaviors of the people they study.
    b. based on little or no empirical data to support their inferences.
    c. in spite of the fact that by studying carefully, one can actually observe these processes.
    d. based largely on the reports offered by subjects regarding their notions about problem solving.

3. Interestingly, mental images are not exclusively visual in nature. Which other sensory modalities were presented in the text as being capable of evoking images?
   a. audition
   b. olfaction
   c. both a. and b.
   d. neither a. nor b.

4. High-imagery words are to ___ as low-imagery words are to ___.
   a. smell; hear
   b. nouns; verbs
   c. two pegs; meaning alone
   d. one syllable; multi-syllabic

5. A *prototype* is a specific example of a particular ___.
   a. model
   b. concept
   c. construct
   d. classification

6. "Doublespeak" or *euphemisms* may be cited as:
   a. evidence that our words determine our thoughts.
   b. examples of universal insults to the intelligence of others.
   c. often as necessary when one is describing problem solving abilities.
   d. indices that careful selection of words can be designed to steer our thoughts.

7. Well-defined problems have all but which of the following characteristics?
   a. a clearly specified solution state
   b. a clearly specified beginning state
   c. a clearly specified set of steps for solving the problem
   d. a set of clearly specified tools or techniques for finding the solution

8. Samantha is trying to solve a problem by systematically evaluating all possible solutions until the correct one is found. That is, she is using:
   a. an algorithm.
   b. the availability heuristic.
   c. the trial-and-error procedure.
   d. the representativeness heuristic.

9. The familiar spelling rule, 'i before e except after c', is:
   a. highly overrated.
   b. an example of a heuristic.
   c. effective only with 5-letter words.
   d. more complicated than the algorithm that many use in the same circumstances.

10. Jim just used a dime to open the battery bank on his camera. In doing so he overcame:
   a. frigidity.
   b. poor framing.
   c. confirmation bias.
   d. functional fixedness.

11. The gambler's fallacy is the faulty assumption that independent events are linked: for example believing that four consecutive 'heads' tosses *will be* followed by a 'tails' toss. The gambler's fallacy is an example of:
    a. the law of averages.
    b. the set effect at work.
    c. why gambling is evil.
    d. a representative heuristic.

12. It is safer, in statistical terms, to fly in an airplane than it is to drive to the airport. People who debate this fact often cite a recently publicized plane crash to support their contention. In so doing, they:
    a. use the availability heuristic.
    b. violate the representativeness heuristic.
    c. increase the likelihood of causing a plane crash.
    d. deny the truth about why planes crash in the first place.

13. Terri is trying to talk her dad into taking her fishing tomorrow. After seeing the weather forecast, she realizes she will have to do some fast-talking. When she turned to her father and reported there was a 30% chance of sunshine for tomorrow she:
    a. ignored confirmation bias.
    b. told her father a boldfaced lie.
    c. manipulated the framing of her report.
    d. hoped he would use the representativeness heuristic.

14. Defining *creativity* is not easy. However, one characteristic of creativity is an ability to use ___ thinking.
    a. random
    b. diverging
    c. emerging
    d. converging

15. Tests of intelligence may not be appropriate for use in cultures other than the US because:
    a. only US citizens are intelligent.
    b. the tests cannot be translated into other languages.
    c. intelligence is so hard to manipulate experimentally.
    d. definitions of intelligence appear to vary widely across cultures.

16. Binet and Simon proposed the concept of ___ on the basis of having observed age-related differences in ability levels.
    a. eugenics
    b. mental age
    c. intelligence
    d. chronological age

17. A 9-year-old with a mental age of ___ would have an IQ of 67.
    a. 6
    b. 9
    c. 12
    d. 14

18. Producing consistent scores is to ___ as measuring what is intended is to ___.
    a. reliability; validity
    b. validity; reliability
    c. standardization; validity
    d. reliability; standardization

19. A normal curve is:
    a. a characteristic of the forehead shape of someone with an average IQ.
    b. thrown with the first two fingers in perpendicular orientation to the seams.
    c. a bell-shaped distribution of scores with the majority clustered around the middle.
    d. produced when there is a strong positive relationship (correlation) between variables.

20. A person with mental retardation who manifests at least one remarkable ability:
    a. is said to have a learning disability.
    b. would have the rare savant syndrome.
    c. would be able to use a calculator extremely quickly.
    d. would probably be placed in a gifted and talented curriculum.

21. Which of the following is not part of Sternberg's *triarchic theory of intelligence?*
    a. social intelligence
    b. creative intelligence
    c. practical intelligence
    d. analytical intelligence

22. The proportion of intelligence that is attributable to genetics is called the ___ of intelligence.
    a. biology
    b. heredity
    c. chemistry
    d. heritability

23. If environmental variables were the key determinants of intelligence, which pair of people would score most similarly?
    a. fraternal twins reared apart
    b. identical twins reader apart
    c. adoptive siblings reared together
    d. adoptive siblings reared apart for six years, then reared together for six more years

24. Identical is to Fraternal as ___ is to ___.
    a. one ovum; two ova
    b. two ova; one ovum
    c. x chromosome; y chromosome
    d. y chromosome; x chromosome

25. In Spearman's model of intelligence, *g* refers to:
    a. genetics
    b. general intelligence
    c. the "thousand contributors to intelligence"
    d. the denominator in an equation that is used to predict native ability

ANSWERS TO KEY WORD EXERCISE

1. Thinking
2. doublespeak
3. algorithms
4. subgoals
5. rigidity
6. situational factors
7. intelligence quotient
8. standardization
9. environmental
10. Francis Galton

 PRACTICE TEST ANSWERS AND EXPLANATIONS

1. c. Smith demonstrated that thinking does not require sub-vocal mouth movements as had been thought previously.

2. a. Many believe that the data cognitive psychologists use needs to be public and replicable.

3. c. In addition to visual imagery, people are capable of evoking auditory and olfactory images.

4. c. High-imagery words provide two pegs for hanging memories, whereas low-imagery words require memory for meaning alone.

5. b. A prototype is a special case of a concept. For example, a carrot is a prototypical vegetable.

6. d. Doublespeak is an acceptable or inoffensive term that is used in place of an offensive one.

7. c. Specifying the steps to the solution would be to give away the problem.

8. a. An algorithm is a systematic procedure that involves evaluating all solutions until one is found.

9. b. 'I before e, except after c' is a heuristic (or rule of thumb).

10. d. Functional fixedness is the inability to see new uses for familiar objects (e.g., not recognizing that a dime can be a screwdriver).

11. d. The gambler's fallacy is an example of the representativeness heuristic (a failing problem solving strategy).

12. a. The availability heuristic is a failing problem solving strategy that involves estimating the probability of an event based on how easily it comes to mind (how available it is in one's memory).

13. c. She manipulated the framing, or presentation of negative and positive outcomes.

14. b. Creative solutions tend to be diverging, or moving in search of multiple answers.

15. d. Definitions of intelligence vary widely across cultures.

16. b. Mental age was proposed as a way of assigning people to categories based on test scores.

17. a. IQ = MA/CA x 100; 6/9 x 100 = 67.

18. a. Reliability is the degree to which a test can yield consistent scores over repeated administrations; validity has to do with how well a test measures what it was designed to measure.

19. c. A normal curve is bell-shaped with most scores in the middle of the distribution.

20. b. Persons who have mental retardation, but who possess at least one remarkable ability have *savant syndrome*.

21. a. Social intelligence is not part of Sternberg's model.

22. d. The heritability of intelligence is the proportion that is attributable to genetic factors.

23. c. If environmental conditions were key in determining intelligence, people who were reared most similarly should score most similarly, regardless of parentage. However, it appears that genetics also plays a significant part in determining intelligence.

24. a. Identical twins come from a single egg, or ovum. Fraternal twins come from separate ova.

25. b. The *g factor* in Gardner's theory is generalized intelligence.

Key Vocabulary Terms

Cut out and use as study cards; terms appear on
one side and definitions are on the other.

cognitive psychology	thinking
concepts	prototype
algorithm	heuristics
rigidity	functional fixedness

Key Vocabulary Terms

Cut out and use as study cards; terms appear on one side and definitions are on the other.

Manipulation of information in the form of mental images or concepts

The subfield of psychology concerned with the study of mental processes

A specific example of a particular concept that is readily brought to mind; viewed as the most typical or best example of a particular concept

Mental categories that share common characteristics

Educated guesses or rules of thumb for solving problems

Systematic procedure for solving a problem by evaluating all possible solutions until the correct one is found

Inability to see new uses for familiar objects

Tendency to rely too heavily on past experiences in solving problems

set effect	confirmation bias
representative-ness heuristic	availability heuristic
framing	creativity
intelligence	mental age
intelligence quotient (IQ)	reliability

Committing to one hypothesis without adequately testing other possibilities

Bias toward the use of certain problem-solving approaches because of past experience

Heuristic in which the probability of an event is determined by how readily it comes to mind

Heuristic in which one determines whether a particular instance represents a certain class or category

The ability to produce work that is both novel and appropriate

The tendency for decision making to be influenced by presentation of negative or positive outcomes; our decision making tends to be risk averse

Measure of intelligence derived by comparing an individual's score on an intelligence test with the average performance of individuals of the same age

The ability to excel at a variety of tasks, especially those related to academic success

Degree to which repeated administrations of a psychological test yield consistent scores

Score that indicates how an individual compares with others on an intelligence test

validity

standardization

norms

normal curve

savant syndrome

heritability

identical twins

fraternal twins

The development of procedures for administering psychological tests and the collection of norms that provide a frame of reference for interpreting test scores

Degree to which a psychological test measures what it intends to measure

Symmetrical, bell-shaped distribution of scores or attributes in which the majority of scores are clustered around the middle

Distribution of scores obtained by a large sample of people who have taken a particular psychological test

Percentage of differences among a group of people in a characteristic, such as intelligence, that is believed to be due to inherited factors

Case of a mentally retarded person who displays exceptional ability in a specific area

Twins who develop from two ova fertilized by two different sperm; genetically related as siblings

Twins who develop from one ovum fertilized by one sperm; genetically identical to each other

In Chapter 8, *Thinking and Intelligence,* you learned about theories of intelligence. There are several theories of intelligence, each with different features and emphases. A common theme in them, though, is that intelligence is not a unitary, homogeneous entity. Prevalent theories, for example Gardner's and Sternberg's, propose that there are several types of intelligence.

List the eight kinds of intelligence as proposed by Gardner: _____

_____

_____

_____

What are the components of Sternberg's Triarchic Theory of intelligence? _____

_____

_____

Given the widespread attention these and other theories have received in recent years, it is becoming clear that intelligence is complicated and involved, and is not a homogeneous, unitary entity as has been thought previously. It does not matter whether research supports both of these theories, one at the exclusion of the other, or other ideas altogether. It is important, however, that education and industry take stock of the fact that different people have different intellectual strengths—different intelligences—and that one's ability to excel in a given area will depend in part on her or his native abilities. By logical extension, people should, to some degree, be channeled into curricula in schools, and also into various career tracks, based on their type(s) of intelligence.

More specifically, different people learn and adapt differently, based on their abilities. In order to improve interest and performance in school, and, later on, productivity and satisfaction in a career, it is important that people discover their learning styles.

What is Learning Style?

The term *learning style* means just what its name implies: the way in which one acquires new information, skills, and abilities. As notions regarding intelligence become more complex, definitions of learning style will necessarily become more complicated as well. For example, consider Gardner's concepts of *spatial reasoning intelligence* and *intrapersonal intelligence.* These categories do not fit well with traditional definitions of learning based on the acquisition of knowledge.
Take a few minutes to consider what is involved in developing one's abilities in each of the domains that was proposed by Gardner.

Type of Intelligence	Means of Developing this Category of Intelligence
1. Linguistic:	
2. Musical:	
3. Logical-Mathematical:	
4. Spatial Reasoning:	
5. Movement *or* Bodily Kinesthetic:	
6. Interpersonal Intelligence:	
7. Intrapersonal Intelligence:	
8. Naturalistic:	

What would happen if one were to combine Gardner's and Sternberg's models? For example, if one is strong in Sternberg's *analytical intelligence*, her or his strength is in an ability to break down a problem or situation into its components. This would mean different things for someone learning music than it would for the same person learning a bodily or kinesthetic activity.

What if someone were high in Sternberg's *creative intelligence* and were working to solve a spatial problem or to learn a language? Creative intelligence involves coping with novelty and being able to solve problems in new and unusual ways. It would be beneficial to have creative insight when solving spatial problems or when learning a language, but creativity would mean different things in each circumstance.

The third component in Sternberg's model is *practical intelligence.* This component is akin to what many refer to as "street smarts" or common sense. You probably know people who have practical intelligence, but who do not excel in traditional academic areas. In fact, practical intelligence is not incorporated into most tests of intelligence at all. It takes little imagination to think of how one would benefit from having practical intelligence when attempting any number of endeavors. How would practical intelligence facilitate other domains from Gardner's theory?

How would your teaching strategy change if you were working with someone who was high in practical intelligence as opposed to someone whose strength is not in common sense?

Why Are You in School?

Your answer to this question may vary depending on your learning style. Some people approach their classes with a perspective of finding a purpose for anything they learn. If they cannot find an immediate personal application for information, they would just as soon not learn it. Others are not so concerned with how information can be applied to their personal lives, and want to learn for the sake of learning. Some want to challenge the ideas they are exposed to by testing them in various situations; for them learning is solidified in experience-based activities. Still others are interested in how information can be applied to environments, cultures, and the larger world. It is as though these people view content through a filter that allows them to see how their knowledge can be used to benefit other people and places.

It is helpful to realize the variety of perspectives your classmates use. You may get more from a given class by approaching it from a perspective that is different than your normal one. Sharing perspectives with people who view course content in different ways can make a class more enriching for everyone. There is no best way to learn material. Each approach has its merits; the key is to learn to benefit from as many perspectives as possible.

Learning styles vary by individual. However, teaching styles are fairly consistent from one instructor to another, and do not often reflect the diversity of learning style strengths for a given class.

How can you benefit most from the classes you take in light of your unique learning style?

Things to Consider

1. **Get Out of Your Comfort Zone.** Some of the most valuable experiences you have will result from your willingness to try new things. Humans are creatures of habit, and tend to avoid uncomfortable situations. By trying new things and adopting different perspectives, you will discover exciting things about you and the world. You may even learn that a different career path fits your strengths and abilities better than the one you had been considering.

2. **Adjust Your Learning Style.** Your courses will be far more meaningful if you accept them for what they are. If you are enrolled in a class that has little application to your personal life, try to enjoy it as an opportunity to expand your knowledge base.

3. **Be in Control.** You are ultimately responsible for what you get out of your education. Do not allow yourself to get into a rut of thinking that your professor, the textbook, your classmates, or anything else is stifling your ability to get the most from the class. Nowhere is it stated that you cannot supplement your learning experiences by doing additional reading, or experiments, or by organizing discussion groups or trips to visit people or places that will expand your exposure to material.

4. **Learn from Others.** Often you will have opportunities to work with others in your classes in group projects. More frequently, you will have opportunities to discuss class material with others as you complete assignments and prepare for exams. As often as you can, team up and compare notes with people who take school seriously, but who have a different perspective than you do.

5. **Ask for Guidance.** Think of your professors as learning resources. In addition to preparing for your daily class meetings, you may find it helpful to do additional work in order to gain the most from the class. Your instructor can help you identify interesting topics to explore in the library, resources to consult for further study on a topic of particular interest to you, and may even include you in her or his research if you show some interest and initiative.

CHAPTER 9

Developmental Psychology I

NOTES FROM CLASS AND FROM THE TEXTBOOK

Use the space provided in this outline to record notes from the textbook as well as from class lectures and discussion. Questions related to the *Psychological Detective* sections in the text have been presented in the outline; use the associated space to respond to the questions and to record your own comments about the issues. *Keywords and terms* from the text have been italicized and inserted in the outline so you can practice writing their definitions. The pages in this study guide are perforated and can be removed for use as study sheets for quizzes and exams.

I. **Basic Issues in Developmental Psychology**

   developmental psychology—

   A. Nature and Nurture

   nature—

   nurture—

   behavior genetics—

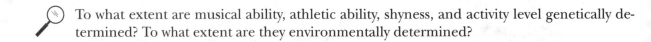
To what extent are musical ability, athletic ability, shyness, and activity level genetically determined? To what extent are they environmentally determined?

   B. Research Methods

   1. Longitudinal Versus Cross-Sectional Studies

   longitudinal study—

   cross-sectional study—

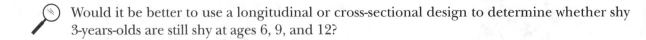
Would it be better to use a longitudinal or cross-sectional design to determine whether shy 3-years-olds are still shy at ages 6, 9, and 12?

Which design, longitudinal or cross-sectional, would be better for determining whether the average 3-year-old is more (or less) shy than the average 6-year-old?

cohort—

II. Development from Conception to Birth

zygote—

mitosis—

embryo—

A. Heredity

chromosomes—

genes—

deoxyribonucleic acid (DNA)—

1. Polygenic Heredity

   polygenic inheritance—

   meiosis—

2. Determination of Sex

3. Sex-Linked Traits

B. Prenatal Development

placenta—

fetus—

1. Barriers to Prenatal Development

a. Teratogens

teratogen—

critical period—

b. Drugs

c. Smoking

d. Alcohol

fetal alcohol syndrome (FAS)—

2. Checking the Health of the Fetus

a. Ultrasound

ultrasound procedure—

sonogram—

b. Amniocentesis

amniocentesis—

c. Additional Genetic Tests

C. Birth

anoxia—

cesarean section—

III. Development in Infancy

rooting reflex—

palmar or grasp reflex—

Moro reflex—

Babinski reflex—

A. Sensory Abilities

  1. Voice Recognition

  2. Vision

  3. Taste and Smell

B. How Newborns Learn

  1. Classical Conditioning

How could you demonstrate classical conditioning in a newborn? Outline a demonstration, naming the components of the conditioning paradigm.

  2. Operant Conditioning

  3. Imitating Others

C. Maturation

  maturation—

  1. Development of the Brain

  2. Physical Development

  precocious—

IV. Psychosocial Development in Childhood

A. Temperament

B. Personality Development
   1. Sigmund Freud

   2. Erik Erikson

      psychosocial crisis—

      basic trust versus basic mistrust—

      autonomy versus shame and doubt—

      autonomy—

      initiative versus guilt—

      industry versus inferiority—

C. Attachment

      attachment—

      contact comfort—

   1. Ethological Theory

      ethological theory of attachment—

   2. The Strange Situation Test

D. The Father's Role
   1. Culture and Fatherhood

E. Day Care
    1. Latchkey Children

        latchkey child—

F. Parenting Styles
    1. Other Influences

        a. The Peer Group

            peer group—

        b. Television

⌕ What steps can parents take to ensure the television programming their children are exposed to is not detrimental?

V. Cognitive Development in Childhood

cognitive development—

A. Piaget's Theory

    assimilation—

    accommodation—

    1. The Sensorimotor Stage

        sensorimotor stage—

        object permanence—

        mental representation—

2. The Preoperational Stage

   preoperational stage—

   symbolic representation—

   egocentrism—

3. The Concrete Operational Stage

   concrete operational stage—

   conservation—

4. Challenges to Piaget's Theory

VI. Language

A. Language Development

   phonemes—

   morpheme—

   syntax—

1. The Acquisition of Language

B. Moral Development

   preconventional level—

   conventional role conformity—

   autonomous moral principles—

❖ LEARNING OBJECTIVES

After you have studied the chapter, you should be able to respond to the following statements and questions to convey your understanding of the material.

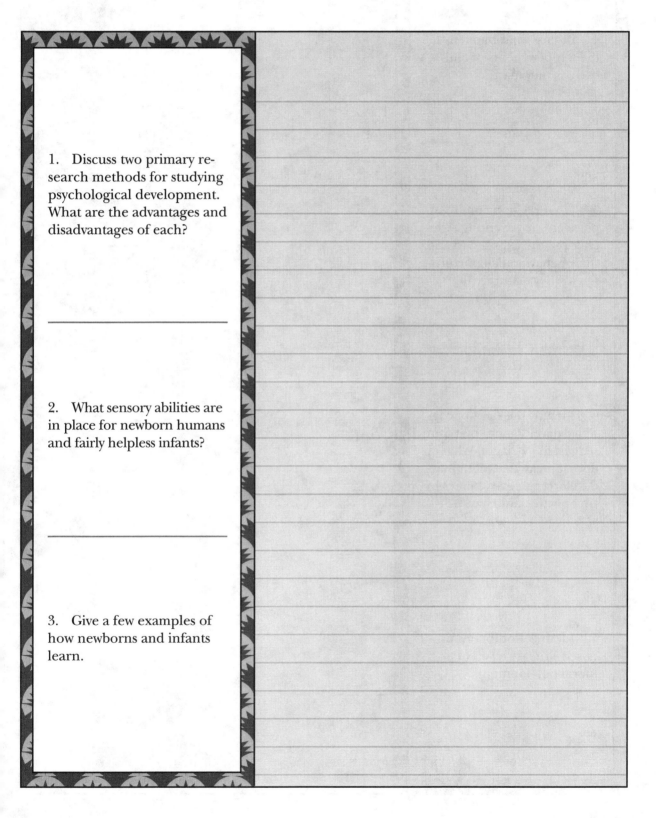

1. Discuss two primary research methods for studying psychological development. What are the advantages and disadvantages of each?

2. What sensory abilities are in place for newborn humans and fairly helpless infants?

3. Give a few examples of how newborns and infants learn.

4. Discuss what happens to the temperaments of children as they mature.

_____

5. What relationships exist between the parenting styles children are exposed to and their behavioral characteristics as they mature?

_____

6. Identify the steps of cognitive development that were suggested by Piaget. What does it mean that all humans develop cognitive abilities in roughly the same way?

_____

7. Identify Kohlberg's proposed primary levels of moral development.

⁑ KEY WORD EXERCISE

Fill in the blanks in the following statements with key words and terms from the textbook. Answer as many as you can without referring to your notes or to the book. If you have blanks after thinking about each item, try using your book. The answers are presented after the practice test.

1. The chemical name for genetic material located in the nucleus of each cell is _____.

2. _____ is a procedure that involves withdrawing fluid from the womb for analyses regarding genetic abnormalities of the fetus.

3. A reduction in or lack of oxygen, such as could occur if the umbilical cord were compressed during delivery, is called _____.

4. Jimmy's mother has a scar on her abdomen that dates to the time of his birth. That is because Jimmy was delivered by _____ _____.

5. Emma, an infant girl, has learned to kick her leg in order to be reinforced by the movement of a mobile. She has demonstrated an ability to learn from _____ conditioning.

6. _____ is the developing of motor and cognitive abilities at an early age.

7. The _____ theory of attachment states that attachment evolved because of its adaptive value to the infant.

8. Children who return home unaccompanied after school are referred to as _____ _____.

9. A form of social influence that usually includes classmates and neighborhood children, and can have both positive and negative influences on the development of a child, is called a _____ _____.

10. To learn to organize words into phrases and sentences is to acquire _____.

⁑ PRACTICE TEST

Circle the letter that corresponds to the *best* alternative for each of the following items. Read each alternative carefully. The answers are presented at the end of this study guide chapter. Be sure to learn *why* each correct alternative is better than the others.

1. Which of the following statements would best characterize John B. Watson's view on the role of heredity in shaping human behaviors?
    a. There is no such thing as an inheritance of capacity, talent, temperament, or mental constitution.
    b. Key human characteristics develop depending mainly on training that goes on in the crib.
    c. It is a unique combination of heredity and environment that permits humans to develop their idiosyncratic abilities and characteristics.
    d. Given the complexities of the human nervous system, coupled with the rich nature of the rearing environment, it is impossible to know which is the greater of environment and heredity.

2. Nature is to nurture as ___ is to ___.
   a. Watson; Piaget
   b. Kohlberg; Erikson
   c. environment; heredity
   d. heredity; environment

3. A research project that involved getting data from people of several different ages at one time to compare some aspect of behavior would be a(n):
   a. nightmare.
   b. longitudinal study.
   c. cross-sectional study.
   d. environmental impact study.

4. It is important to note when studying people from different age groups that while they may share many demographic characteristics, they have not had the same life experiences. That is, they are from different:
   a. cohorts.
   b. cultural strata.
   c. phases and stages.
   d. socioeconomic groups.

5. Which sequence represents the order in which prenatal (before birth) development occurs?
   a. embryo, fetus, zygote
   b. zygote, embryo, fetus
   c. fetus, zygote, embryo
   d. embryo, zygote, fetus

6. Same genetic information is to reduced genetic information as ___ is to ___.
   a. genes; DNA
   b. mitosis; meiosis
   c. DNA; chromosomes
   d. chromosomes; mitosis

7. The principle whereby complex traits are determined by many genes is called:
   a. genetics.
   b. behavior genetics.
   c. polygenic inheritance.
   d. the principle of deoxyribonucleic acid (DNA).

8. Producing a male requires having a Y sex chromosome in the ___ chromosomal pair.
   a. 11th
   b. 21st
   c. 23rd
   d. 31st

9. The placenta is important in prenatal development because it does all but which of the following?
   a. produces hormones
   b. transmits nourishment
   c. filters out certain harmful substances
   d. neutralizes the teratogenic effects of alcohol

10. Babies with low birth weights (under 5.5 pounds) are:
    a. genetically predisposed to have eating disorders.
    b. more likely to pose tremendous risks to their mothers during delivery.
    c. 40 times more likely to die before their 1st birthdays than normal weight babies.
    d. usually from families that characteristically have children with low birth weights.

11. A teratogen:
    a. is any of a number of substances that is thought to promote the "terrible twos".
    b. is any biological, chemical, or physical agent capable of causing birth defects.
    c. should be administered to the mother prior to birth in order to ensure proper delivery.
    d. only causes potential health risks during the embryonic stage of prenatal development.

12. Which of the following is *not* a characteristic of children with *fetal alcohol syndrome (FAS)*?
    a. high birth weight
    b. mental retardation
    c. lower birth weight
    d. small head circumference

13. The outline picture that is produced by projecting sound waves onto the fetus, uterus, and placenta is called a(n):
    a. sonogram.
    b. genetic diagram.
    c. amniocentesis scan.
    d. ultrasound procedure.

14. Which of the following is *not* one of the three stages of birth?
    a. labor
    b. anoxia
    c. delivery
    d. afterbirth

15. Startle reflex is to fanning of the toes as ___ is to ___.
    a. Moro reflex; Babinski reflex
    b. Babinski reflex; Moro reflex
    c. rooting reflex; palmar or grasp reflex
    d. palmar or grasp reflex; rooting reflex

16. While it is initially poor, infant visual acuity improves to about 20/20 by:
    a. 3 weeks of age.
    b. 4 to 10 weeks of age.
    c. 6 to 12 months of age.
    d. the time the child reaches her or his second year.

17. Watson and Rayner demonstrated:
    a. that older infants can be classically conditioned to fear.
    b. the processes of meiosis and mitosis under strict laboratory conditions.
    c. the power of genetic influence in determining whether and what a child can learn.
    d. that "Little Albert" could learn to avoid painful stimuli by operating a manipulandum.

18. Raising rats in enriched environments:
    a. is cruel.
    b. is impractical.
    c. directly influences brain growth.
    d. produces the same results as raising them in impoverished environments.

19. Breast feeding was described in your textbook as a valued way of providing nourishment for children for all *but* which of the following reasons:
    a. mother's milk transfers antibodies.
    b. breast feeding reduces the likelihood of getting pregnant.
    c. mother's milk is more nutritious than milk from other animals.
    d. the diets mothers consume can include things that may harm the developing organism.

20. Erikson's theory of development stresses:
    a. attachment.
    b. psychosocial crises.
    c. psychosexual stages.
    d. the acquisition of morality.

21. Harlow's research with infant monkeys demonstrated:
    a. the role of contact comfort in attachment.
    b. that they all are raised with the same basic parenting style.
    c. the value of attending to the critical window during early development.
    d. little other than that the assumptions about humans generalize well to primates.

22. According to your textbook, delaying having children until the father is older (e.g., 35), results in all but which of the following:
    a. a greater risk for genetic deformity.
    b. the father's spending more time with the child.
    c. parents having higher expectations for the child.
    d. the father being more nurturant toward the child.

23. Which was not identified as one of three common parenting styles?
    a. permissive
    b. dictatorship
    c. authoritarian
    d. authoritative

24. Piaget observed numerous children over many years, and concluded that:
    a. a child's mind is a miniature version of an adult's.
    b. miniature adults are rather like children, but not vice versa.
    c. the children are not like miniature adults; rather they pass through a series of *qualitative* stages.
    d. the children are not like miniature adults; rather they pass through a series of *quantitative* stages.

25. Young Tim and his sister Carrie are having grain burgers for lunch. Each got the same amount, one patty, but when their father cut the patties to make them easier to eat, he cut Carrie's into more pieces than Tim's. Tim whined and complained that he got shorted, thereby demonstrating that:
   a. he had not yet reached the sensorimotor stage of cognitive development.
   b. he had not yet reached the preoperational stage of cognitive development.
   c. he had not yet reached the formal operational stage of cognitive development.
   d. he had not yet reached the concrete operational stage of cognitive development.

 ## ANSWERS TO KEY WORD EXERCISE

1. DNA
2. Amniocentesis
3. anoxia
4. cesarean section

5. operant
6. Precocious
7. ethological

8. latchkey children
9. peer group
10. syntax

 ## PRACTICE TEST ANSWERS AND EXPLANATIONS

1. b. Watson was a strict behaviorist who believed that the only thing that mattered was environment.

2. d. Heredity is associated with natural, or biological issues, while nurture refers to training or upbringing.

3. c. Cross-sectional research involves studying the behavioral characteristics of people from various age groups in order to infer age-related changes.

4. a. A cohort is a group of individuals born in the same period.

5. b. Zygotes are formed by the union of a sperm and an ova; next, the embryo develops, then the fetus.

6. b. Mitosis is a cell division process in which each cell contains the same information as the others. In meiosis, there is a reduction in the amount of genetic material in each of the resulting cells.

7. c. As its name implies, polygenic inheritance involves many genes influencing traits.

8. c. There are 23 pairs of chromosomes in a zygote; it is the 23rd pair that determines the sex.

9. d. The placenta passes alcohol through to the developing baby in the same concentrations that are found in the mother's blood.

10. c. Children born with low birth rates are at much greater risk for early death. Low birth rate often results from poor nourishment during prenatal development.

11. b. Teratogens are agents that are capable of damaging developing organisms severely and irreversibly.

12. a. FAS is associated with all but increased or high birth weight.

13. a. A sonogram is a picture that is produced using the ultrasound procedure.

14. b. Anoxia is a reduction in or lack of oxygen that can cause brain damage during the birthing process.

15. a. The Moro reflex is a startle reflex. The Babinski reflex involves the upward fanning of toes when the foot is stroked.

16. c. Visual acuity usually develops to 20/20 by one year of age.

17. a. They conditioned fear in "Little Albert", who was an older infant at the time.

18. c. Brain development can be influenced significantly by manipulating the quality of the environment.

19. d. No mention of the dietary needs of breast feeding mothers was made in the text.

20. b. Erikson's theory of development focused on a series of psychosocial crises.

21. a. Harlow's work was useful in demonstrating the need for contact comfort during early development. However, other forms of attachment between parent and offspring are important too.

22. a. The other alternatives were cited as advantages to postponing having children.

23. b. Dictatorship was not discussed as a parenting style.

24. c. Piaget believed children to be different than adults, and observed that they pass through qualitative stages of cognitive development.

25. d. During the concrete operational stage children learn the principle of conservation-recognition that a physical change in a substance does not change the amount of that substance. Relax, Tim, most adults get too big a container when putting away leftovers.

Key Vocabulary Terms

Cut out and use as study cards; terms appear on
one side and definitions are on the other.

developmental psychology	nature
nurture	behavior genetics
longitudinal study	cross-sectional study
cohort	zygote

Key Vocabulary Terms

Cut out and use as study cards; terms appear on one side and definitions are on the other.

Theory that holds that physical and cognitive development is genetically determined

Study of physical, cognitive, and psychosocial changes throughout the life span, from conception until death

A new field, combining psychology and biology, that studies the influences of heredity and environment on behavior

Theory that holds that physical and cognitive development is determined by environmental factors

Research technique in which participants, often of different ages, are tested or observed during a limited time span or only once

Research technique in which the same participants are tested or observed repeatedly over a period of time

One-celled organism formed by the union of a sperm and an ovum

Group of individuals born in the same period

mitosis

embryo

chromosomes

genes

deoxyribonucleic
acid (DNA)

polygenic
inheritance

meiosis

placenta

fetus

teratogen

A developing organism during the stage when the major organ systems are formed

Process of cell division in which each cell contains the same genetic information as other cells

Units of hereditary material that line the chromosomes and provide information concerning the form and function of each cell

Segments of genetic material located in the nucleus of each cell; human cells have 23 pairs of chromosomes (numbered according to size), one of each pair being inherited from each parent

Principle of heredity whereby complex traits, such as intelligence and personality, are determined by many genes

Chemical name for the genetic material located in the nucleus of each cell

Organ that develops in the uterus during pregnancy; it produces hormones that maintain pregnancy, transmits nourishment to the fetus, and filters out certain harmful substances

Type of cell division that results in a reduction of the amount of genetic material in each of the resulting cells

Any biological, chemical, or physical agent capable of causing birth defects

The developing baby from about the ninth week after conception until birth

critical period	fetal alcohol syndrome (FAS)
ultrasound procedure	sonogram
amniocentesis	anoxia
cesarean section	rooting reflex
palmar or grasp reflex	Moro reflex

Condition found in some children born to mothers who drank during pregnancy, characterized by lower birth weight, small head circumference, and mental retardation

A specific time during development when damage may occur or certain processes should take place

Outline picture constructed through use of the ultrasound procedure

Projection of sound waves onto the fetus, uterus, and placenta to construct a sonogram

Reduction or lack of oxygen

Withdrawal and analysis of amniotic fluid to detect genetic abnormalities in the fetus

Reflex in which the infant turns its head in the direction of a touch on its face

Procedure in which a baby is surgically removed from the uterus

Startle reflex in response to a loud noise or the sensation of being dropped

Reflex consisting of a very strong hold on any object placed in the palm

Babinski reflex	maturation
precocious	psychosocial crisis
basic trust versus basic mistrust	autonomy versus shame and doubt
autonomy	initiative versus guilt
industry versus inferiority	attachment

Biological unfolding of the genetic plan for an individual's development	Reflex in which the infant's toes fan upward when the bottom of the foot is stroked
Developmental problem or obstacle that is created when a psychological need conflicts with the demands of society	Developing motor and cognitive abilities at an early age
Erikson's second psychosocial crisis (1.5 to 3 years), in which children develop a sense of whether their behavior is under their own control or under the control of external forces	Erikson's first psychosocial crisis (birth to 1.5 years), in which children learn through contact with their primary caregiver whether their environment can be trusted
Erikson's third psychosocial crisis (3-7 years), in which children begin to evaluate the consequences of their behavior	The feeling of being able to act independently and having personal control over one's actions
Intense, reciprocal relationship formed by two people, usually a child and an adult	Erikson's fourth psychosocial crisis (7-10 years), in which children begin to acquire the knowledge and skills that will enable them to become productive members of society

contact comfort	ethological theory of attachment
peer group	cognitive development
assimilation	accommodation
sensorimotor stage	object permanence
mental representation	preoperational stage

Theory stating that attachment evolved because of its adaptive value to the infant

Preference for holding or clinging to objects, such as blankets or teddy bears, that yield physical comfort and warmth

Changes that occur in our thought processes throughout life

Group of neighborhood children, classmates, or selected friends of the same age

Alteration of existing schemas to understand new information

Piaget's term for the process of incorporating information into existing schemas

Recognition that objects continue to exist even though they cannot be directly sense

Piaget's first stage of cognitive development, in which children learn about their environment through direct sensory contact and motor activities

Piaget's second stage of cognitive development, in which the child begins to think about objects that are not physically present

An internal representation of an object or event that is not present

symbolic representation	egocentrism
concrete operational stage	conservation
phonemes	morpheme
syntax	preconventional level
conventional role conformity	autonomous moral principles

Inability to see a situation or event from another person's point of view

Using a mental thought or activity as a substitute for an actual object

Recognition that a physical change in a substance does not change the amount of that substance

Piaget's third stage of cognitive development, in which the child is able to use mental representations to think about current objects and events but is not yet capable of abstract thought

In a language, the smallest unit of sound that conveys meaning

The smallest units of sound understood as part of a language

Kohlberg's first stage of moral development (ages 4 to 10), in which standards set by others are observed in order to receive reinforcement or avoid punishment

The organization of words into phrases and sentences

Kohlberg's third stage of moral development (age 13 or later, if at all), in which control over moral conduct is completely internalized

Kohlberg's second stage of moral development (ages 10 to13), in which rules and standards are internalized and behaviors are performed in order to please others

TIP FOR SUCCESS: STRESS MANAGEMENT

Thus far, the *Tips* sections in this study guide have addressed goal-setting, strategies for making the most of your resources (e.g., time, textbook, classroom experiences, study environment), preparing for and taking exams, and identifying your learning style. Managing all these activities can be both challenging and rewarding. In order to strive for and reach your potential, it is important to think and feel your very best. Sometimes, though, the pressures associated with having a multitude of responsibilities may create stress that will keep you from performing optimally. This tip section was written to help you understand stress, and to learn some ways of keeping stress levels at a minimum.

What is Stress?

Stress refers to that which produces pressure, strain, or tension. Often, stress occurs as a function of perceived or real restraints on time to perform some task or function. However, impending time is not always the source of stress. Think, for example, of the last occasion when you had to speak to a crowd, or perform an attention-demanding task.

Identify several sources of occasional stress in your life:_____

_____

_____

Stress is in the Eye of the Beholder

It is interesting to note that stressful events are different for different people. Sometimes you may find that the relative amount of stress associated with an item in your life changes. You, circumstances, or an interaction between both can cause you to be more (or less) stressed by a task or behavior. Why are things stressful sometimes and not stressful at other times?

An old saying is that *perception is reality*. If that is the case, then it might provide some insight into the reasons why events change with respect to the amount of stress with which they are associated. What is more, if that is the case, it means that you can control the amount of stress you experience at a given moment by learning to alter your perception in order to manage the potentially stressful circumstance.

This idea is probably not new to you, but it is important nonetheless. For example, you may have heard some interesting advice about using imagery to reduce stress while giving a public speech. Some say it is helpful to imagine that your audience is in their underwear. The idea is that they would have more to be embarrassed about than you, and that this should put you at ease. It is important, however, that you imagine that they, and not you, are the ones in underclothes!

The key message here is that your perceptions govern, to a large degree, whether something is associated with stress. Learning to take things in stride, and not to get to worked up about them, will be helpful.

Not All Stress is Bad

The Yerkes-Dodson law of motivation says that optimal levels of performance are associated with moderate levels of stress or anxiety about the event. If stress is too low, one is not sufficiently interested in the event. High levels of stress interfere with one's ability to perform well. You may have had this range of experiences when writing a paper or preparing for an exam. Students sometimes find it difficult to get interested in studying too far in advance. At the other end of the spectrum, they find it difficult to concentrate during the last minutes or hours for a large project that they have put off until it is too late. Somewhere in between is a happy medium: the amount of stress that is necessary to focus your attention without being distracting.

Some people say they work best under pressure. What is the role of stress when this is the case?

_____

_____

High Levels of Stress Can Impair Performance

Chapter 11 in your textbook, *Health Psychology,* covers many facets of the stress response. Please refer to that chapter for a thorough explanation of stress and stress-related issues. In brief, however, you should know that when one experiences stressors (anything that causes an organism to display the nonspecific stress response), a series of responses typically follows. That series of responses, known as the general adaptation syndrome, is associated with changes in vital organ functioning and biochemical activity that can be hard on one's body. Stress can increase one's susceptibility to disease and illness.

Therefore, then, not only do high levels of stress impair the level and quality of behavior, but they take a toll on physiology and physical health as well. Sufficiently high levels of stress suppress immune-system functioning and put one at risk of illness.

Maladaptive Responses to Stress

Imagine someone who has a high-pressure job, such as a salesperson whose income is based on commission. The circumstances of such jobs cause the people who have them to experience tremendous levels of stress. Unfortunately, they often turn to maladaptive behaviors to combat the stress, thereby exacerbating the problem. For example, smoking and consuming large amounts caffeine cause one to become more, not less, restless. After a day of drinking coffee and smoking (both caffeine and nicotine are behavioral stimulants), some will even choose to "relax" with a few alcoholic drinks (alcohol is a central nervous system depressant).

Caffeine, nicotine, and alcohol all impair one's ability to get productive (i.e., REM) sleep. Thus, this pattern of drug use impairs a person's ability to get adequate sleep, which in turn produces feelings of fatigue. Fighting fatigue with caffeine and nicotine is a losing battle. As you can see, using drugs, whether to maintain alertness, or to relax, produces more stress than it alleviates.

Some overeat, or eat unhealthy food instead. Excessive sugar intake will cause wild fluctuations in energy levels. Consuming fats will lead to weight gain, and perhaps to obesity. Over-consumption of either fats or sugars causes people to feel bad about their bodies and about their health. These feelings lead to increased stress. As with the use of drugs, improper diet can have dramatic negative impact on one's health; this will lead to increased health-related stress.

What Can You Do?

Use your critical thinking skills to identify the *causes* that produce the *effect* of stress. Whenever possible, strive to reduce exposure to stimuli and circumstances that produce stress. By eliminating the cause, you will also rid yourself of the effect. For example, if working up to deadlines is highly stressful for you, learn to complete your work earlier so you are not pressured by time.

To do your best, you need to feel your best. This means taking measures to maintain good health, and to eliminate unwanted stressors from your lifestyle. Turn ahead to Chapter 15 in your textbook and look closely at Tables 15-2, 15-8, and 15-9. These tables contain information about behaviors and their effects that will contribute positively to your personal well-being.

List several things you can do to alleviate stress in your life: _____

_____

_____

_____

_____

CHAPTER 10

Developmental Psychology II

Use the space provided in this outline to record notes from the textbook as well as from class lectures and discussion. Questions related to the *Psychological Detective* sections in the text have been presented in the outline; use the associated space to respond to the questions and to record your own comments about the issues. *Keywords and terms* from the text have been italicized and inserted in the outline so you can practice writing their definitions. The pages in this study guide are perforated and can be removed for use as study sheets for quizzes and exams.

I. Physical Changes

   A. Adolescence

      adolescence—

      puberty—

      pubescence—

      secular trend—

      primary sex characteristics—

      menarche—

      secondary sex characteristics—

   B. Early Adulthood

      early adulthood—

   C. Middle Adulthood

      middle adulthood—

presbyopia—

presbycusis—

menopause—

osteoporosis—

D. Late Adulthood

   late adulthood—

Answer the true-false questions in this space. What were the bases for your answers?

   cataracts—

1. Alzheimer's Disease

   dementia—

   Alzheimer's disease—

2. Culture and Life Expectancy

II. Intellectual Changes

A. Adolescence

   formal operational stage—

1. Adolescent Thought Patterns

    imaginary audience—

B. Early Adulthood

Outline a research project that would help determine whether intellectual ability declines with age.

1. Types of Intelligence

    fluid intelligence—

    crystallized intelligence—

2. Nontraditional College Students

C. Middle Adulthood

D. Late Adulthood

    ageism—

E. Schaie's Stages of Thought and Cognition
    1. Acquisition: Childhood and Adolescence

    2. Achievement: Young Adulthood

    3. Responsibility: Middle Adulthood

    4. Reintegration: Late Adulthood

reintegration—

III. Personality and Social Changes

A. Adolescence

identity versus identity confusion—

1. Possible Outcomes of Identity Formation

identity achievement—

foreclosure—

negative identity—

identity diffusion—

moratorium—

2. Adolescent Peer Groups

3. Family Influences

4. Making a Commitment

B. Early Adulthood

1. Intimacy Versus Isolation

intimacy versus isolation—

2. Marriage and Children

What are some advantages of waiting to have children until you are in your late twenties? What are the advantages of having children sooner than that? What about waiting until even later?

3. Career Development

C. Middle Adulthood
   1. Burnout

      burnout—

   2. Midlife Crisis

      midlife crisis—

      generativity versus stagnation—

   3. Other Stresses During Middle Adulthood

      empty nest syndrome—

What are some possible reasons for couples having greater marital satisfaction after their children leave home?

D. Late Adulthood
      integrity versus despair—

1. Retirement

2. The Kansas City Study

IV. Death, Dying, and Bereavement

A. Attitudes toward Death

1. Childhood

2. Adolescence

personal fable—

3. Young Adulthood

4. Middle Adulthood

5. Late Adulthood

B. Confronting Death

C. Bereavement, Grief, and Support

bereavement—

grief—

mourning—

hospice—

V. Highlighting Cultural Views and Practices

A. Birthing and Parenting Practices

B. Intelligence

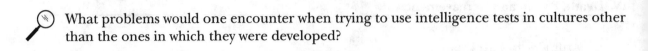 What problems would one encounter when trying to use intelligence tests in cultures other than the ones in which they were developed?

culture-fair intelligence test—

C. Educational Achievement

D. Aging

After you have studied the chapter, you should be able to respond to the following statements and questions to convey your understanding of the material.

1. Discuss significant physical changes that occur as one develops from adolescence through late adulthood.

2. Differentiate between fluid and crystallized intelligences. What is the relationship between these as one develops across the lifespan?

3. What stages of Erikson's theory of psychosocial crises are typically addressed during adolescence, early, middle and late adulthood?

4. Identify and describe the five stages of dealing with death that were offered by Kübler-Ross.

Fill in the blanks in the following statements with key words and terms from the textbook. Answer as many as you can without referring to your notes or to the book. If you have blanks after thinking about each item, try using your book. The answers are presented after the practice test.

1. A _____ ____ _____ is common in some societies and is the key to manhood for boys.

2. _____ is a condition in which the bones become thinner and more prone to fractures and breaks.

3. Tomorrow, Mr. Johnston will have surgery on his eyes. This is because he has _____, a condition whereby his lenses have become clouded.

4. One form of dementia is _____ _____, a degenerative brain disorder that results in progressive loss of intelligence and awareness.

5. As adolescent thought becomes self-centered and self-conscious, adolescents tend to create what some psychologists call a(n) _____ _____.

6. Problem solving and looking for new relationships, such as putting together a jigsaw puzzle, require _____ intelligence.

7. A(n) _____ _____ is developed by some adolescents in response to the expectations their parents have for them.

8. Until yesterday, Jann's life was pretty hum-drum. She is a 47-year-old successful businesswoman who needed a change. She traded in her minivan for a sports car, and bought a new, high-fashion wardrobe. When she pulled in the drive, her husband recognized immediately that she was experiencing a _____ _____.

9. The Kansas City study of aging revealed four personality types among the elderly: integrated, armor-defended, passive-dependent, and _____.

10. Peter is experiencing grief, the emotional changes that are associated with _____ following his mother's death.

Circle the letter that corresponds to the *best* alternative for each of the following items. Read each alternative carefully. The answers are presented at the end of this study guide chapter. Be sure to learn *why* each correct alternative is better than the others.

1. The higher a family's standard of living, the ___ children in succeeding generations will reach puberty.
    a. later
    b. earlier
    c. greater the likelihood
    d. less likely it is that their

2. With respect to the development of full sexual maturity, girls are to boys as ___ is to ___.
   a. menarche; nocturnal emissions
   b. growth of axillary hair; changes in skin
   c. primary sex characteristics; secondary sex characteristics
   d. secondary sex characteristics; primary sex characteristics

3. Presbyopia is to presbycusis as ___ is to ___.
   a. male; female
   b. female; male
   c. hearing; vision
   d. vision; hearing

4. Which of the following does *not* decrease as one develops from middle through late adulthood?
   a. visual acuity
   b. physical strength
   c. susceptibility to disease
   d. ability to hear high frequencies

5. Sarah is beginning to show symptoms of dementia. As a result of dementia, she:
   a. ceases to ovulate and menstruate.
   b. will experience memory loss and disorientation.
   c. may have to have corrective surgery to restore normal vision.
   d. will have to use greater caution in activity as her risk for bone damage will increase.

6. Which is *not* a characteristic that is shared among people who live longer than average?
   a. working throughout life
   b. strong resistance to the use of medication
   c. high content of fruits and vegetables in the diet
   d. relaxation and exercise are part of the daily routine

7. One of the significant indices that one has reached Piaget's formal operational stage is acquisition of:
   a. the Babinski reflex.
   b. the ability to *think abstractly.*
   c. *object permanence,* or knowing things exist when they are out of sight.
   d. *the principle of conservation,* or knowing that changes in shape do not necessarily reflect changes in mass.

8. Ability to see new relationships is to ___ as ability to retrieve and use information is to ___.
   a. middle adulthood; late adulthood
   b. late adulthood; middle adulthood
   c. fluid intelligence; crystallized intelligence
   d. crystallized intelligence; fluid intelligence

9. The expertise that comes with years of experience stems largely from:
   a. good pedagogy.
   b. fluid intelligence.
   c. crystallized intelligence.
   d. knowing how to be in the right place at the right time.

10. It has been estimated that by the year 2030, ___% of Americans will be age 65 or older.
    a. 3
    b. 5
    c. 15
    d. 25

11. K. Warner Schaie's stages of thought and cognition:
    a. pick up where Piaget left off (at *formal operations*).
    b. concern a series of developmental changes that are not experienced until late adulthood.
    c. concern a series of developmental changes that are not experienced until middle adulthood.
    d. were proposed as a way of reconciling the widespread differences among people from different cultural backgrounds and experiences.

12. At 73, Charlie is experiencing reintegration. In other words, he:
    a. is coming to grips with the meaning(s) of his life.
    b. has done what Kübler-Ross calls "completing the cycle".
    c. has started playing checkers and cards with his friends at the old folks' home.
    d. is learning anew how to enter social situations without being embarrassed.

13. Adolescents in what has been called *moratorium:*
    a. have no regard for their lives.
    b. have no regard for others' lives.
    c. sample several different identities without intending to settle on one.
    d. seek the career paths, and associated personal attributes, that will shape their lives forever.

14. According to research involving in-depth interviews with 14-year-old girls who recently gave birth, three key factors in the decision to become sexually active include **all but which** of the following?
    a. the risk of pregnancy was not taken seriously
    b. the partner was someone the young woman trusted
    c. the women's family relationships were less than ideal
    d. the women did not understand that sexual activity could result in pregnancy

15. An interesting characteristic of adolescents in Erikson's *intimacy versus isolation* crisis is that:
    a. the crisis is more common among boys than among girls.
    b. the crisis is more common among girls than among boys.
    c. boys usually develop strong autonomy before becoming intimate, while girls may never have a strong sense of autonomous identity.
    d. girls usually develop strong autonomy before becoming intimate, while boys may never have a strong sense of autonomous identity.

16. The feminization of poverty in the U.S. is ___ it is in other industrialized nations.
    a. less than
    b. greater than
    c. about the same as
    d. a less important issue than

17. Suggestions for decreasing the likelihood that one will experience *burnout* include which of the following?
    a. establishing a social support system
    b. using hobbies to divert focus from work
    c. taking vacations and breaks from the job
    d. all of the above may be effective in reducing the likelihood of experiencing burnout

18. A culture-fair test:
    a. is a test that does not contain culturally loaded items.
    b. would be difficult to design because of translation issues.
    c. does not exist, but data nevertheless suggest that students of Asian descent are stronger in math and science than their American counterparts.
    d. all of the above.

19. The *hospice movement* is:
    a. cruel and inhumane.
    b. essentially an application of humanistic psychology.
    c. an interesting behavior shown by many middle-aged adults.
    d. more a way of using the workforce than providing service to those who need it,

20. The *personal fable:*
    a. includes self-centered ideas and a sense that one is invulnerable.
    b. the term psychologists use to describe the life stories told to them by aging people.
    c. is longer, but not near as loaded with moral messages than the ones recorded by Aesop.
    d. is demonstrated in the young adult woman who thinks she can "solve the world's problems" by becoming a psychologist.

ANSWERS TO KEY WORD EXERCISE

1. rite of passage
2. Osteoporosis
3. cataracts
4. Alzheimer's disease
5. imaginary audience
6. fluid
7. negative identity
8. midlife crisis
9. unintegrated
10. bereavement

PRACTICE TEST ANSWERS AND EXPLANATIONS

1. b. A high standard of living is associated with earlier onset of puberty.
2. a. Menarche (the first menstrual period) marks full sexual maturity for a girl; the ability to ejaculate semen (often in nocturnal emissions) marks sexual maturity for boys.
3. d. Presbyopia is farsightedness that normally develops in middle adulthood; presbycusis is a middle-adulthood related hearing disorder.
4. c. The likelihood that one will contract an illness seems to increase with age; taking multiple medications exacerbates this trend.
5. b. Dementia is a general decline in intellectual ability that is associated with old age.
6. b. As a rule, people who live longer than average do each of those except refusing to take medicine.
7. b. the ability to think abstractly, such as when solving algebra problems, comes with this stage.
8. c. Fluid intelligence concerns the use of new relationships, whereas crystallized intelligence involves the ability to use information that has been learned.
9. c. Crystallized intelligence is related to the knowledge that comes from one's life experiences.
10. d. By 2030, nearly 25% of the population will be 65 or older.

11. a.   Schaie's stages concern changes in adulthood; Piaget's theory ends at adulthood.

12. a.   Reintegration is the final stage in Schaie's model of adult thought and cognition.

13. c.   Moratorium has to do with sampling several different identities without intending to settle on one.

14. d.   The interview research revealed that the key issues were alternatives a. - c. from question 14.

15. c.   Girls are less likely to develop autonomous identities prior to establishing intimate relationships.

16. b.   Because of the high divorce rate, coupled with the fact that children of divorced parents usually stay with their mothers, more women are impoverished in the U.S. than in other countries.

17. d.   All of the above, plus adopting realistic expectations and developing outside interests.

18. d.   It would be difficult, if not impossible to develop a culture-fair test. However, a comparison of American students with students from Hong Kong, Japan, Korea, and Taiwan suggests that Americans are not as strong in math and science.

19. b.   Hospice, which is characterized by a philosophy of treatment for the terminally ill, is an excellent example of the application of (humanistic) psychology.

20. a.   Personal fable is a term used to describe the thoughts and behaviors of adolescents who act as though they do not have to play by the same rules as other members of society.

Key Vocabulary Terms

Cut out and use as study cards; terms appear on
one side and definitions are on the other.

adolescence	puberty
pubescence	secular trend
primary sex characteristics	menarche
secondary sex characteristics	early adulthood

Key Vocabulary Terms

Cut out and use as study cards; terms appear on one side and definitions are on the other.

The time at which an individual achieves full sexual maturity	The years between approximately age 12 and age 20
Tendency of members of one generation to begin puberty at an earlier age than their parents	Period of rapid growth, maturation of sexual organs, and appearance of secondary sex characteristics that precedes puberty
Beginning of menstruation	Characteristics directly related to reproduction
Period from approximately age 20 to age 40	Sex-related characteristics that develop during adolescence and are not directly related to reproduction

middle adulthood	presbyopia
presbycusis	menopause
osteoporosis	late adulthood
cataracts	dementia
Alzheimer's disease	formal operational stage

Farsightedness that normally develops during middle adulthood; stiffening of the lens results in difficulty in focusing on near objects

Period from approximately age 40 to age 65

Cessation of ovulation and menstruation; these changes mark the end of the childbearing years

Middle adulthood hearing disorder involving reduced ability to distinguish sounds at higher frequencies

Period from approximately age 65 until death

Condition in which the bones become thinner and more prone to fractures and breaks; typically appears in postmenopausal women

General intellectual decline associated with old age; may be reversible when caused by medication or blood clots

Clouding of the lens of the eye

Piaget's final stage of intellectual development, characterized by abstract thinking; achieved during adolescence or adulthood

Degenerative brain disorder that results in progressive loss of intelligence and awareness

imaginary audience	fluid intelligence
crystallized intelligence	ageism
reintegration	identity versus identity confusion
identity achievement	foreclosure
negative identity	identity diffusion

Intelligence involving the ability to see new relationships, solve new problems, form new concepts, and use new information

The adolescent's assumption that everyone else is concerned with his or her appearance and behavior

Viewing elderly people in a negative manner

Intelligence that involves the ability to retrieve and use information that has been learned and stored

Erikson's fifth psychosocial crisis, in which the adolescent faces the task of determining his or her identity and role in society

Schaie's fourth stage of cognition and thought, in which individuals in late adulthood come to grips with the meaning of their lives

Uncritical acceptance of parental values and desires; hampers the development of a unique identity

Adoption of a set of well-chosen values and goals

Failure to develop an identity because of lack of goals and general apathy

Adoption of behaviors that are the opposite of what is expected

moratorium	intimacy versus isolation
burnout	midlife crisis
generativity ver-sus stagnation	empty nest syndrome
integrity versus despair	personal fable
bereavement	grief

Erikson's sixth psychosocial crisis, in which the young adult faces the task of establishing a strong commitment to others (intimacy) or having to deal with isolation

Period during which an adolescent may try several identities without intending to settle on a specific one

Potentially stressful period that occurs during the mid-forties and is triggered by reevaluation of one's accomplishments

Emotional and physical exhaustion that interferes with job performance

Period of adjustment for parents after all children have left home

Erikson's seventh psychosocial crisis, which occurs during middle adulthood and reflects concern, or lack thereof, for the next generation

Feeling shared by many adolescents that one is not subject to the same rules as other people

Erikson's eighth psychosocial crisis, which occurs during late adulthood; integrity reflects a feeling that one's life has been worthwhile; despair reflects a desire to relive one's life

The emotional changes associated with bereavement

Emotional and role changes that follow death

mourning

hospice

culture-fair
intelligence test

Institution where terminally ill patients and their families are given warm, friendly, personalized care

The behavioral changes associated with bereavement

An intelligence test that does not contain culturally loaded items

People in and out of academe value *critical thinking*. The scientific method depends on researchers' abilities to think critically about their own work, as well as when they are reviewing others' work. The subject matter of psychology sometimes requires well-honed thinking skills to ensure that causal inferences and conclusions are made only after carefully considering alternative explanations.

What is Critical Thinking?

The term *critical thinking* is so commonplace that it is becoming cliché. It is frequently used because it describes so well a process that is important in innumerable ways. Consider definitions of the two words that comprise the term. Critical means *requiring careful judgment*. Thinking means *to form or have in the mind*. Combined, *critical thinking* means *having careful judgment in the mind*.

Rewrite the definition of critical thinking in your own words: _____

_____

_____

Critical Thinking is Everywhere

Critical thinking is represented in good communication of all forms: reading, listening, speaking, and writing. Part of the active reading process is to consider carefully that which you read. Likewise, a good listener does not merely soak up information like a sponge, but takes it in attending to all the subtleties of meaning in the message. When you communicate with others, whether verbally or in writing, it is important that your message reflects logical reasoning and appropriate expression of your conclusions. Be cautious about making or conveying assumptions.

Why are assumptions not welcome in critical thinking? _____

_____

_____

_____

Seek the Truth

Critical thinking involves concern for that which is accurate. Science in general depends on patterns of research findings that corroborate, or are consistent with one another. Science is based on very carefully calculated inferences; virtually nothing is really known to be true in any scientific discipline. This is certainly true of psychology.

If your mission is to understand the truth, it will be necessary for you to let go of some theories and hypotheses that once seemed plausible. As new theories incorporate the valid aspects of old ones, they simultaneously discard explanations that are rendered invalid in light of new data. As a critical thinker, it is vital that you admit mistakes and recognize flaws in your thinking and the thinking of others. If you strive to improve your understanding of a given phenomenon, you will, at times, be stumped. Do not be afraid to say: *"I do not know."* If you carry this practice into your everyday reasoning and communication, you will feel liberated from having to infer or guess at explanations of things you do not understand fully. That is a mark of a critical thinker.

Critical Thinking in Problem Solving

Problem solving can be both challenging and fun. When you search for solutions to problems, you often find yourself trying approaches until you find one that works. How do you determine that a solution does not work? The answer is simple: you think critically about the problem at hand, the proposed solution, and readily identify the shortcomings of the solution. As you get closer and closer to a solution, you will note that it gets increasingly difficult to find its faults. This circumstance requires that you fine-tune your thinking skills and consider carefully any oversights or shortcomings of the solution.

Qualities of a Critical Thinker

All critical thinkers share many of the same characteristics. Critical thinkers are systematic, open-minded, analytical, patient, curious, informed, and aware. Consider these characteristics:

1. **Systematic.** Adopt a methodical, organized approach to asking and seeking answers to questions. Organization and focus are important components of this quality. As you work through problems, keep track of information and keep sight of your objective.

2. **Open-Minded.** Celebrate differences in opinion and different ways of thinking. By welcoming different approaches to thinking about problems, one often gains valuable insight.

3. **Analytical.** Recognize statements and conclusions that need support. If a claim cannot be substantiated, it is not of value. Similarly, beware of exaggerated claims. A perennial favorite is the famous estimated frequency of occurrence: 99.99 percent of the time.

4. **Patient.** There are many ways of approaching a problem, and many problems have more than one solution. Listen carefully to others and take your time. Wisdom comes from experience, and experience comes from awareness. It takes patience to be aware.

5. **Curious.** Curiosity may have "killed the cat," but it makes critical thinkers. Critical thinkers need to know *why* things occur, and do not accept "just because" as an answer. One can spend a lifetime asking and answering questions and looking for ways of using the information gained.

6. **Informed.** Seek clear answers and definitions. Gather all the facts. Informed judgments are the best ones. Reserve criticism until you have all the relevant information. If you think you have all the information, but do not understand someone's idea or comment, ask good questions. Sometimes it is necessary to adopt a different perspective.

7. **Aware.** Does the person sharing an idea stand to gain from it? Knowing why someone would make a comment can be helpful in understanding the idea. If an idea gets your support, then what? By being aware of the implications of a given idea or solution, people are sometimes better able to evaluate the idea.

Whether you are purchasing products or buying into others' theories and ideas, learning to be a critical consumer will serve you well. How can you use the thinking skills and characteristics that are presented in this section to be a critical consumer? _____

_____

_____

_____

_____

CHAPTER 11

Sex and Gender

Use the space provided in this outline to record notes from the textbook as well as from class lectures and discussion. Questions related to the *Psychological Detective* sections in the text have been presented in the outline; use the associated space to respond to the questions and to record your own comments about the issues. *Keywords and terms* from the text have been italicized and inserted in the outline so you can practice writing their definitions. The pages in this study guide are perforated and can be removed for use as study sheets for quizzes and exams.

I. **Sex and Gender: An Introduction**

> *sex*—

> *gender*—

A. The Biology of Sex

> *hermaphrodite*—

> *pseudohermaphrodite*—

1. The Genetics of Sex

2. Genetic Abnormalities

3. Male Vulnerability

B. The Hormonal Basis of Sex

> *adrenogenital syndrome*—

> *androgen insensitivity syndrome*—

1. Sexual Behavior

How is the sexual behavior of humans different than that of non-humans? What are the consequences of the differences?

sexual orientation—

C. The Development of Gender Roles

gender roles—

1. Psychodynamic Theory

What does learning theory contribute to our understanding of the development of gender roles?

2. Social Learning Theory

3. Cognitive Developmental Theory

cognitive developmental theory—

4. Gender-Schema Theory

gender-schema theory—

D. Gender Stereotyping

stereotype—

How could you study the presence of gender stereotyping in young children who have not acquired the language that would permit simple questioning?

1. Language and Gender

How often are you exposed to language that implies the subject of interest is either female *or* male? List several examples.

2. Components of Gender Stereotypes

3. Mass Media and Gender Stereotypes

II. **Similarities and Differences Between Males and Females**

A. Biological Differences

1. Brain Differences

B. Early Analyses of Sex Differences

C. The Cognitive Realm

1. Verbal Ability

2. Mathematical Abilities

3. Visual-Spatial Abilities

What variable(s), other than those contributed by biology, might be responsible for differences in mathematical or spatial abilities between men and women?

D. The Social Realm

1. Communication

2. Helping Behavior

3. Aggression

III. Social Issues

sexism—

A. Education

1. Elementary School

How could you study whether gender bias is present in elementary school classrooms? What if you were interested in studying gender bias in other locations (list some examples)?

2. High School and Higher Education

B. Work and Careers

1. Sexual Harassment

2. Frequency of Sexual Harassment

3. Perceiving Sexual Harassment

4. Gender Stereotyping on the Job

5. Women as Leaders

C. Family Responsibilities

1. Juggling

After you have studied the chapter, you should be able to respond to the following statements and questions to convey your understanding of the material.

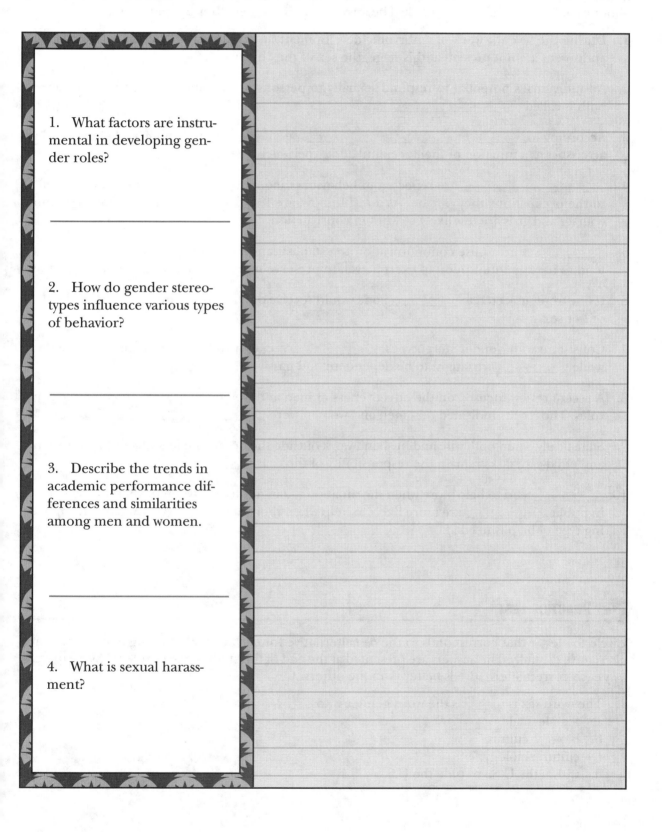

1. What factors are instrumental in developing gender roles?

2. How do gender stereotypes influence various types of behavior?

3. Describe the trends in academic performance differences and similarities among men and women.

4. What is sexual harassment?

⬦ KEY WORD EXERCISE

Fill in the blanks in the following statements with key words and terms from the textbook. Answer as many as you can without referring to your notes or to the book. If you have blanks after thinking about each item, try using your book. The answers are presented after the practice test.

1. During the seventh week of embryonic development, internal reproductive organs develop. If androgens are not present at this stage, the sex of the child will be _____.

2. An individual's potential to respond sexually to persons of the same sex, the opposite sex, or both is called _____ _____.

3. According to _____ _____ _____, people develop masculine and feminine characteristics as a function of their accumulated experiences.

4. _____ _____ are reflected in behaviors ranging from the courses students enroll in to the occupations they pursue. As a result, boys are less likely to enroll in home economics courses and girls are less likely to work in construction.

5. _____ tend to use communication to establish and maintain relationships. _____ tend to use communication to exert power, to preserve independence, and to enhance status.

6. If one were subjected to _____, one would receive differential treatment on the basis of his or her sex.

7. Consistent with gender stereotypes, _____ are taught to be assertive and independent, while _____ are taught to be dependent and passive.

8. A recent review focused on the effectiveness of men and women in leadership and managerial roles. The results indicated that men and women were _____ _____.

9. Statistically, when both wife and husband work outside the home, the majority of the housework and child-care tasks remain the responsibility of the _____.

10. _____ tend to help more when the situation is dangerous and when the helping takes place in public. _____ are more likely to help when there are no observers and when a nurturing type of help is needed.

⬦ PRACTICE TEST

Circle the letter that corresponds to the *best* alternative for each of the following items. Read each alternative carefully. The answers are presented at the end of this study guide chapter. Be sure to learn *why* each correct alternative is better than the others.

1. The word sex is to ___ as the word gender is to ___.
   a. female; male
   b. biology; culture
   c. culture; biology
   d. within the U.S.; outside the U.S.

2. Males and females constitute roughly equal proportions of the population that is up to about 30 years old. After 30,:
   a. that pattern continues.
   b. males begin to outnumber females.
   c. females begin to outnumber males.
   d. it is hard to tell because people tend to stop wearing appropriately colored clothing.

3. *Adrenogenital syndrome* refers to a condition in which:
   a. females develop adrenal glands in place of genitals.
   b. females develop genitals resembling those of males.
   c. people have the functional reproductive anatomy of both genders.
   d. males develop secondary sex characteristics resembling those of females.

4. Researchers have discovered that a nucleus in the hypothalamus (the sexually dimorphic nucleus) is twice as large in men as it is in women. The nucleus is ___ in heterosexual men in comparison to homosexual men.
   a. utterly nonexistent
   b. about the same size
   c. two to three times larger
   d. one to two times smaller

5. The *gender-schema theory* for explaining the development of gender distinctions:
   a. combines elements of social learning theory and cognitive developmental theory.
   b. combines elements of the psychodynamic theory and cognitive developmental theory.
   c. says that people exert control over secondary sex characteristics based on external events.
   d. says that primary sex characteristics develop in response to predictable environmental stimuli.

6. Gender stereotyping
   a. is the exclusive determinant of one's future.
   b. has profound influence over how people shape their lives.
   c. was a serious problem in the 1950's, but thankfully is a thing of the past.
   d. helps boys and girls choose the proper paths when making career and familial decisions.

7. Individuals who have high levels of characteristics associated with both males and females are:
   a. referred to as bisexual.
   b. referred to as androgynous.
   c. most likely to suffer from identity confusion.
   d. usually females with an extra y chromosome.

8. Guidelines for gender-inclusive language include:
   a. using gender-neutral job titles.
   b. avoiding gender-exclusive comments whenever possible.
   c. using plural forms of pronouns whenever possible.
   d. All of the above are guidelines for promoting unbiased language.

9. A woman who experiences a stroke in the left hemisphere is more likely to retain language abilities than a man with the same damage probably because:
   a. the left hemisphere is significantly larger in women.
   b. men have better spatial abilities instead of improved language capacity.
   c. women have proportionately more fibers bridging the two hemispheres (corpus callosum).
   d. None of the above have been offered as explanations for this phenomenon.

10. A *meta-analysis* is:
    a. a procedure for combining the results from several studies.
    b. a means of carefully studying the brain to examine gender differences.
    c. a way of examining metas, or social units that are formed to promote androgyny.
    d. an approach used by developmental psychologists to study gender stereotyping directly.

11. The most consistent finding concerning spatial ability is that:
    a. males and females score alike.
    b. males outperform females on mental rotation tasks.
    c. females outperform males at identifying the direction North.
    d. None of the above are supported in the research on spatial ability.

12. The disappearing of sex differences in cognitive ability may have to do with:
    a. the diversification of sexual preferences.
    b. when the tests are administered rather than the tests themselves.
    c. concerted efforts by classroom teachers to treat everyone the same.
    d. changes that influence gender stereotyping and its effects on education.

13. Imagine that you have just been asked whether males are more aggressive than females. Given what has been presented in your textbook, a good answer would be:
    a. yes, without question.
    b. no, the two genders are strikingly similar.
    c. it depends, the type of aggression under consideration is significant.
    d. how should I know, my psychology book did not mention gender- or sex-based differences in aggression.

14. Pat has just earned a bachelor's degree. With no additional information about Pat, you would predict that Pat is a ___, because since academic year 1984-85 ___ have earned more bachelors degrees than ___ in American undergraduate colleges and universities.
    a. male; men; women
    b. woman; women; men
    c. athlete; athletes; non-athletes
    d. hermaphrodite; hermaphrodites; pseudohermaphrodites

15. Judy has hit a glass ceiling. That is, she:
    a. displayed her strength in an act of aggression directed toward the air.
    b. is facing barriers to getting a job with greater responsibilities and better pay.
    c. is a painter and just whapped her head on the ceiling because she had not noticed how close she was to the ceiling.
    d. none of the above.

16. Incidences of sexual harassment can take which form?
    a. Quid pro quo (Latin for "this for that")
    b. Hostile work environment (degrading, intimidating, or offensive)
    c. Both a. and b.
    d. Neither a. nor b.

17. Which of the following statements is true about sexual harassment?
    a. Every state, and many cities and towns have civil rights laws that deal with sexual harassment.
    b. Sexual harassment is relatively new and laws regarding it are just being developed.
    c. Presently there are no laws (federal, state or civil in nature) that deal with incidences of sexual harassment.
    d. The federal government has issued sexual harassment legislation that supercedes any laws set forth by states and cities.

18. With respect to perceptions of sexual harassment, men and women ___ when the instances are explicitly coercive, and ___ when the instances are less explicit.
    a. agree; agree
    b. disagree; agree
    c. agree; disagree
    d. disagree; disagree

19. Self-reported data on child-care involvement has indicated that:
    a. men and women share child-care involvement roughly equally.
    b. men tend to have far greater levels of involvement in child-care in every category.
    c. women tend to have far greater levels of involvement in child-care in every category.
    d. women tend to more of the child-care related tasks that were rated as unpleasant, while men and women had more comparable involvement in enjoyable tasks.

20. Many women who have careers also do a majority of the house-related work in their homes. Which of the following seems to reflect the impact of juggling multiple (job- and home-related) tasks?
    a. Men seem better equipped to take on a variety of tasks than women.
    b. Women seem better equipped to take on a variety of tasks than men.
    c. Juggling multiple roles seems to insulate women (and men) against depression.
    d. Juggling multiple tasks is the single leading cause of depression in American women.

 ## ANSWERS TO KEY WORD EXERCISE

1. female
2. sexual orientation
3. gender-schema theory
4. Gender stereotypes

5. Females; Males
6. sexism
7. boys; girls

8. equally effective
9. wife
10. Men; Women

 ## PRACTICE TEST ANSWERS AND EXPLANATIONS

1. b. *Sex* refers to one's biological make-up (e.g., anatomy, genetics). *Gender* refers to social and psychological phenomena as defined by a given culture.

2. c. Females make up an increasing percent of the population as age increases.

3. b. Adrenogenital syndrome, which results from excessive exposure to androgens during fetal development, causes females to have genitals resembling those of males.

4. c. The reduced size of the sexually dimorphic nucleus in homosexual men provides some support for theories that sexual preference is determined biologically.

5. a. The gender schema theory combines elements of social learning theory and cognitive developmental theory.

6. b. Gender stereotyping constantly impacts decisions people make, thereby shaping their lives.

7. b. Androgyny is the possession of both male and female behavioral characteristics.

8. d. The American Psychological Association, among other entities recommends a. - c.

9. c. The corpus callosum seems to be larger in women than in men.

10. a. A meta-analysis is a technique that facilitates the combination of data from several research projects for comparison in a single project.

11. b. Males outperform females on mental rotation tasks (spatial ability). However, the similarities of cognitive abilities, including mathematical and language abilities, are far more striking than any small differences between the sexes.

12. d. Societal changes in gender stereotyping and its effects on education seem to be at play.

13. c. Whether a male will react more or less aggressively than a female depends on the type of aggression, and on the context.

14. b. Women have outperformed men at earning bachelor's degrees for the last several years.

15. b. *Glass ceiling* is a term that refers to the differential treatment received by men and women as they pursue the same jobs. It is harder for women to get promoted.

16. c. Incidences of sexual harassment can take two forms: quid pro quo, or hostile work environment.

17. a. Every state, and many cities and towns have civil rights laws that deal with sexual harassment.

18. c. Men and women agree that an incidence constitutes sexual harassment when it is explicit, but disagree when the instance is less explicit.

19. d. Women tend to more of the child-care related tasks that were rated as unpleasant, while men and women had more comparable involvement in enjoyable tasks.

20. c. Juggling multiple roles seems to insulate women (and men) against depression.

Key Vocabulary Terms
Cut out and use as study cards; terms appear on
one side and definitions are on the other.

sex	gender
hermaphrodite	pseudohermaph-rodite
adrenogenital syndrome	androgen insensitivity syndrome
sexual orientation	gender roles

Key Vocabulary Terms

Cut out and use as study cards; terms appear on one side and definitions are on the other.

Social and psychological phenomena associated with being "feminine" or "masculine" as these concepts are defined in a given culture	Category based on biological differences in anatomy, hormones, and genetic composition
Individual who possesses two gonads of the same kind along with the usual male or female chromosomal makeup, but has external genitalia and secondary sex characteristics that do not match his or her chromosomal makeup	Individual who has both ovarian and testicular tissue
Failure by a male embryo to respond to male hormones	Condition caused by exposure to excessive amounts of androgens during the fetal period; can result in a female with genitals resembling those of males
Behaviors considered appropriate for males and females in a given culture	Tendency for a person to be attracted to individuals of the same sex, opposite sex, or both

cognitive
developmental
theory

gender-schema
theory

stereotype

sexism

sexual
harassment

Explanation for the learning of gender roles that suggests that children form schemas of masculine and feminine attributes, which influence memory, perception, and behaviors

Explanation for the learning of gender roles that holds that cognitive factors give rise to gender identity, gender stability, and gender constancy

Differential treatment of an individual on the basis of his or her sex

A set of beliefs about members of a particular group

Under the law, either sexual coercion based on promised rewards or threatened punishments or creation of a hostile workplace environment

At some level, everyone is a leader. By asking or answering a question, or otherwise redirecting the attention of your classmates and teacher, you are an occasional leader in your class. Similarly, when you provide input to project group members, you are assuming a leadership position. When you are a leader, you shape your experience and help determine what your future opportunities will include. Sharing your insights is a sure way to ensure that your needs are understood. Alternatively, if you shy away from sharing your perspective, you may have to live with the consequences of others' interests and motives.

This *Tip* section will focus on ways you can shape your educational and career-related experiences by being a leader. There is no time like the present for you to begin shaping your life by assuming more leadership in your endeavors. The list that follows provides several suggestions for developing and maintaining leadership roles. Your ideas need to be heard. With a little effort, you will set in motion your future as a leader with a range of opportunities.

1. **Be Willing to Make Mistakes.** An old say goes, "nothing ventured, nothing gained." This saying fits a number of topics that involve taking risks. As a leader, you will be constantly making decisions that could result in failure. That is OK. Everyone falls short of her or his expectations from time to time. The hope is that, on balance, your advances will outweigh your setbacks.

Name three things that you avoided doing because you were afraid of making a mistake?_____

_____

_____

What was the worst thing that could have happened if you had made a mistake? What did you stand to gain?_____

_____

_____

2. **Challenge Yourself.** Take a few moments and think of several prominent leaders from history. What set them apart from everyone else? Most likely it was that they made significant contributions or accomplishments in their fields. The only way to make significant accomplishments is to take on challenging tasks. Identify a challenging goal, make a promise to yourself and others about the goal, and go for it! You will keep your interest in your endeavors peaked if you continue to take on meaningful challenges.

What challenging opportunities await you in your near future?_____

_____

_____

3. **Leaders are Role Models.** By assuming leadership positions, you will have unique opportunities to help others and to share your insight into problems and issues. By maintaining your focus, you will encourage others to do the same. When things do not go as planned, keep your focus. Without having to divert energy, everyone will benefit.

4. **Communicate Objective Truths, Make "I" Statements and Be in Control.** Leaders take ownership in their feelings and ideas. A very important leadership skill is to make statements that reflect either objective truths or personalized opinions. If you state something that is *not* an objective truth, preface it with *I think, I feel,* or *I believe.* Always resist passing judgment on others. Pointing fingers and placing blame only makes you feel bad and causes others to harbor resentment.

Only you have the power to decide how you will respond to what others do or say. When you place blame on someone else, you are indicating that you are out of control. If you begin to feel you are losing control, indicate that such is the case by making an *I statement* (e.g., I feel as though I am not in control of what is happening).

Think of three occasions when you have made statements that involved placing blame or pointing your finger at others. Write an *I Statement* that you could have made on each occasion instead.

_____

_____

5. **Focus on the Issue.** By and large, your friends and colleagues are interested in succeeding at the endeavors they take on. If you are working together on something, and meet with frustration, do not blame others. Chances are, they want to succeed too. Focus your attention on aspects of the problem that merit your attention rather than on other people who are also frustrated.

6. **Give Credit to Others.** The most satisfactory feeling that one can experience when something goes well is just that, a feeling. Have you ever noticed that many people like to brag, but that nobody likes hearing someone brag? This has a significant implication for those occasions when you meet with success in your endeavors. Rather than accepting responsibility for your successes, redirect attention to those whose efforts made your success possible. That will make them feel better and have more positive feelings about you.

Identify an accomplishment that you took credit for, even though someone else helped (even if he or she played a minor role that nobody was aware of): _____

_____

7. **Have *Silent Pride*.** Sometimes your successes are well deserved, and are due entirely to your own efforts. When things go your way and you are not able to redirect attention to others who played a role in the success, try being quietly humble. Being quietly humble, or having *silent pride,* will help others to see you more favorably and to wonder why you are not bragging. Since nobody likes to hear someone brag, this behavior will be intriguing. It is better to be intriguing than obnoxious.

Identify an example of someone bragging about her or his success at something. How would that occasion have been different had they adopted the silent pride response?_____

_____

8. **Be Assertive.** To *assert* is to state something positively. Being assertive means making clear statements about your ideas and feelings. Assertive comments and behavior typically come from those who are confident and respectful of others. Aggressive comments and behavior, on the other hand, are divisive and tend to break down relationships. Learn to control your aggression and to assert your position when appropriate.

9. **Listen.** When you adopt a position of leadership, it is important that you listen carefully to what others say. Failure to listen to, and respond to, others' comments reflects poor leadership. If you lead others, it is critical that you understand and represent their interests.

Identify the leadership skills you already practice. Which ones should you attend to?_____

_____

_____

CHAPTER 12

Personality

Use the space provided in this outline to record notes from the textbook as well as from class lectures and discussion. Questions related to the *Psychological Detective* sections in the text have been presented in the outline; use the associated space to respond to the questions and to record your own comments about the issues. *Keywords and terms* from the text have been italicized and inserted in the outline so you can practice writing their definitions. The pages in this study guide are perforated and can be removed for use as study sheets for quizzes and exams.

I. Analyzing Personality

    A. Defining Personality

           personality—

    B. Personality Tests

         1. Self-Report Inventories

              self-report inventory—

         2. The California Psychological Inventory

         3. Projective Tests

              projective test—

         4. Barnum Effect—

 What are the characteristics of statements you are willing to accept about yourself? If they come from someone you know rather than someone you do not know, does that make a difference?

              Barnum effect—

    C. Trait Approaches

           trait—

1. Factors of Personality: Raymond B. Cattell

2. Hans Eysenck

3. The "Big Five" Traits

D. Is Behavior Consistent?

1. Challenges to the Idea of Consistency

2. In Defense of Consistency

List some examples of instances in which people generalize behavioral characteristics based on an isolated incidence of behavior.

3. Evidence of Consistency Based on Multiple Measures

II. Biological Factors in Personality

A. Early Biological Approaches

1. Humors and Bumps

2. Body Types

3. Sensation Seeking

B. Twin Studies

How do you differentiate between a coincidence and an explainable event? Does the distinction change if the event is explained in terms of genetic versus environmental factors?

III. The Psychodynamic Perspective

  A. Basic Concepts

    1. Psychic Determinism

       psychic determinism—

 What, if anything, does it really mean when someone makes a *Freudian slip?*

    2. Instincts

    3. The Unconscious

       unconscious—

  B. The Structure of the Mind

    1. The Id

       id—

    2. The Ego

       ego—

    3. The Superego

       superego—

    4. Interaction of Id, Ego, and Superego

  C. Defense Mechanisms

How could you test the idea that the id, ego, and superego are in conflict?

defense mechanism—

repression—

D. Stages of Psychosexual Development

   1. The Oral Stage

      oral stage—

      fixation—

   2. The Anal Stage

      anal stage—

   3. The Phallic Stage

      phallic stage—

      Oedipal complex—

      Electra complex—

   4. The Latency and Genital Stages

      latency stage—

      genital stage—

E. Freud in Perspective

   1. The Neo-Freudians

   2. Evaluation of Freudian Theory

IV. The Social-Cognitive and Humanistic Perspectives

  A. Learning and Cognitive Perspectives

    1. Rotter's Social Learning Theory

    2. Bandura's Social Cognitive Theory

       reciprocal determinism—

       self-efficacy—

  B. The Humanistic Perspective

     humanistic psychology—

    1. Abraham Maslow

      a. Basic Needs

      b. Self-Actualization

        self-actualization—

    2. Carl Rogers

 How can information from the Q-sort be used to study the relationship between one's real and ideal selves?

After you have studied the chapter, you should be able to respond to the following statements and questions to convey your understanding of the material.

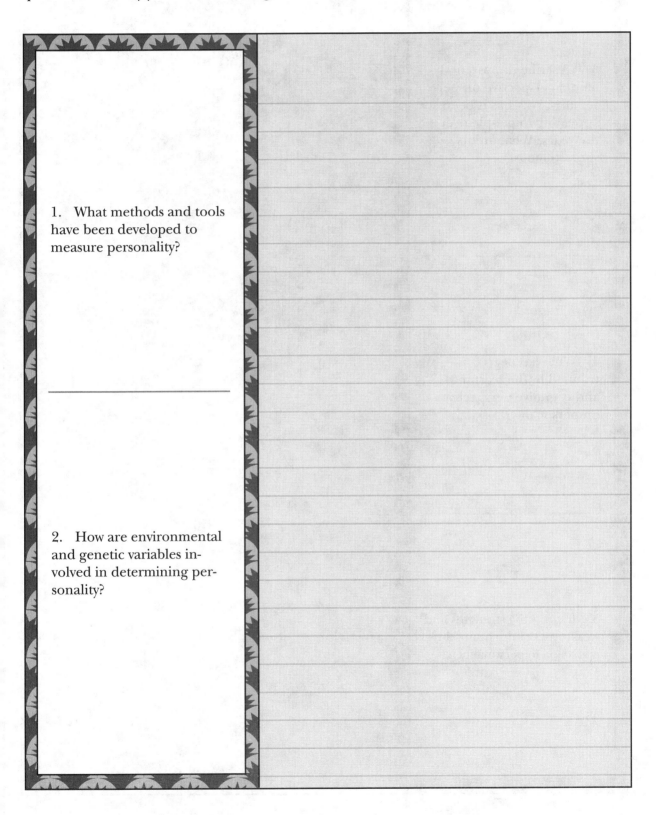

1. What methods and tools have been developed to measure personality?

2. How are environmental and genetic variables involved in determining personality?

3. Describe the psychodynamic perspective on personality. Why has it been so appealing to people over the years? What are its shortcomings?

_____

4. What has been contributed by the learning and cognitive perspectives on personality?

_____

5. Identify the strengths and weaknesses of the humanistic approach to personality.

KEY WORD EXERCISE

Fill in the blanks in the following statements with key words and terms from the textbook. Answer as many as you can without referring to your notes or to the book. If you have blanks after thinking about each item, try using your book. The answers are presented after the practice test.

1. Psychological tests in which individuals answer questions about themselves, usually by responding *yes or no* or *true* or *false* are called _____-_____ _____.

2. The *Thematic Apperception Test* is an example of a(n) _____ _____.

3. _____ is a summary term that describes the tendency to behave, feel, and think in ways that are consistent across situations.

4. Sheldon's terms, *endomorph*, *mesomorph*, and *ectomorph*, came from an early approach to investigating personality based on _____ _____.

5. _____ estimates suggest that genetics are responsible for between 20 and 50 percent of personality characteristics.

6. Freud's model for explaining personality development was based on his idea that people seek to experience pleasure in several parts of the body called _____ _____.

7. _____ complex is to girl are _____ complex is to boy.

8. *Denial, projection, rationalization,* and *repression* are examples of _____ _____.

9. Freud's theory has been highly criticized by psychologists because it is not _____.

10. Bandura labeled one's expectancy about her or his ability to engage in effective behaviors _____-_____ .

PRACTICE TEST

Circle the letter that corresponds to the ***best*** alternative for each of the following items. Read each alternative carefully. The answers are presented at the end of this study guide chapter. Be sure to learn *why* each correct alternative is better than the others.

1. Your friend just took a test with over 500 true-false items on it. Which of the following was it?
   a. The Self-Report Inventory
   b. The Thematic Apperception Test
   c. The Minnesota Multiphasic Personality Inventory
   d. The Generalized Personality Analysis (GPA) Questionnaire

2. A back translation is:
   a. a normal translation that is performed after the fact.
   b. a procedure used to ensure that adaptations of a test in another language are translated appropriately.
   c. a maneuver used by many Olympic platform divers that requires a combination of athletic agility and personality.
   d. done when someone is unsure what a person from another culture has done behaviorally, and describes it to someone back home who can make sense of it.

3. Projective tests involve:
   a. looking into the future.
   b. presentation of unstructured or ambiguous stimuli.
   c. assigning clients to projects and testing their abilities to do the work.
   d. overhead projectors that display images on huge screens for interpretation by subjects.

4. To say that someone has fallen subject to the Barnum effect is to say:
   a. they are depressed.
   b. they just had a good time at the circus.
   c. they actually believe in the work of Sigmund Freud.
   d. they just accepted a generalized description as an accurate statement.

5. Eysenck's theory posits that:
   a. personality consists of three basic traits.
   b. airplane pilots, musicians, and artists are basically the same.
   c. the id, ego, and superego are in constant battle with one another.
   d. that there are 16 personality factors (which may be measured using the 16PF scale)

6. The "big five" traits:
   a. were proposed by Cattell.
   b. were offered by Eysenck.
   c. are really just extensions of the three that Freud originally suggested.
   d. are gaining widespread support, and can be remembered using the acronym OCEAN.

7. Although there is a fair amount of debate about determinants of behavior, it seems clear that:
   a. genetics have insignificant influences on behavior.
   b. situational variables influence behavior in significant ways.
   c. it will always be impossible to know why people do the things they do.
   d. none of the above.

8. Which of the following did Hippocrates not consider as one of the four bodily humors?
   a. blood
   b. phlegm
   c. black bile
   d. vitreous humor

9. You and a friend were strolling through an antiques and curios store when you noticed a porcelain model of a human head with various labels that would have corresponded to parts of the brain that were theorized to control various behaviors. You realized that it was derived from the 1800's idea of ___ that was championed by Franz Joseph Gall.
   a. Oedipus
   b. phrenology
   c. mystic tea vessels
   d. the stream of consciousness

10. Skydivers, race car drivers, SCUBA divers and others who regularly seek stimulation from a variety of sources are known as:
   a. nuts.
   b. riskers.
   c. death wishers.
   d. sensation seekers.

11. The study of identical twins who were separated early in life:
    a. allows researchers to isolate the effects of nature from those of nurture.
    b. has been restricted to the U.S. states of Ohio and Minnesota because it is cruel.
    c. takes relatively little time and effort compared to studying fraternal twins the same way.
    d. is a common practice among developmental psychologists as such separation is commonplace.

12. Research comparing differences between identical twins reared apart, and those reared together,:
    a. has yet to be done in a systematic way.
    b. yielded similar results on many of the MMPI sub-scales.
    c. is by its very nature *longitudinal,* and therefore has not been completed.
    d. helped psychologists realize the greater similarity of fraternal versus identical twins.

13. The size of the genetic effect—estimated by what is called *heritability*—indicates that:
    a. Ohio twins outscore Minnesota twins.
    b. fraternal twins outscore identical twins.
    c. differences among most people are due at least as much to environmental influences.
    d. the parents of fraternal twins are often strikingly similar in comparison to other sets of spouses.

14. Freud's notion of psychic determinism:
    a. assumes that all behaviors result from early childhood experiences.
    b. developed out of the research that was first begun by phrenologist Franz Gall.
    c. is that one's sex determines the varieties of defense mechanisms on which he or she will rely.
    d. assumes that all behaviors result from resonating psychic energy that is in one's home, but cannot be measured.

15. Freud's model for understanding personality can be likened to a(n):
    a. iceberg.
    b. river barge.
    c. enormous cigar.
    d. canyon created by a river.

16. *Id* is to ___ as *ego* is to ___.
    a. Maslow; Freud
    b. identical twin; fraternal twin
    c. steam locomotive; houseboat
    d. pleasure principle; reality principle

17. According to Freud, the *superego:*
    a. is an exceptionally good ego.
    b. is far above the surface of awareness.
    c. incorporates societal and parental standards.
    d. develops out of the ego as one resolves one's innate desire for the opposite sex parent.

18. By and large, the Neo-Freudians:
    a. were Freud's offspring.
    b. found Freud's idea of *ego* to be ridiculous.
    c. disagreed with Freud's focus on the *id* and sexual motives.
    d. All of the above are true about the Neo-Freudians.

19. A widespread criticism of Freudian theory:
    a. has not existed to date.
    b. is that it is largely untestable.
    c. was offered by the man himself at the close of his life.
    d. stemmed from Freud's having an unresolved Oedipal conflict.

20. A significant contribution to personality theory was offered by Julian Rotter who:
    a. developed a scale to measure the *locus of control.*
    b. invented the idea of *sensation seeking* as a way of explaining his own behavior.
    c. was the first name relative of Julian Lennon, son of John Lennon (one of the Beatles).
    d. basically followed in the tradition of the behaviorists in emphasizing non-cognitive factors.

21. *Reciprocal determinism* is an idea that was proposed by Albert Bandura:
    a. to compete with Freud's notion of *psychic determinism.*
    b. to explain the interaction of person variables, situation variables, and behavior.
    c. a psychologist who began his career in the automotive industry—the source of the term.
    d. when he observed that after children hit Bobo dolls the dolls retaliated by kicking the children.

22. Abraham Maslow, who is well known for having developed the *hierarchy of needs,* thought which of the following?
    a. Humanistic psychology was the "third force" in psychology.
    b. Cognitive psychology was the creation science of psychology.
    c. Humanistic psychology would bring the downfall of the discipline.
    d. His idea fit better with traditional Freudian ideology than with Humanistic psychology.

23. Carl Rogers is probably best known for his term:
    a. ego-ideal.
    b. self-actualization.
    c. unconditional positive regard.
    d. conditional reward contingency.

24. Research on the *self* in social contexts has revealed:
    a. that John Watson was right.
    b. that most people are anti-social in nature.
    c. little to nothing of lasting value to psychology.
    d. that there are significant cultural differences with respect to conceptions of the *self.*

ANSWERS TO KEY WORD EXERCISE

1. self-report inventories
2. projective test
3. Trait
4. body type

5. Heritability
6. erogenous zones
7. Electra; Oedipal

8. defense mechanisms
9. testable
10. self-efficacy

PRACTICE TEST ANSWERS AND EXPLANATIONS

1. c. The MMPI is a test that scores people according to 10 different dimensions. It has been adapted for use in at least 22 languages.

2. b. A back translation is performed when testing how well a term or concept from a test translated into another language. The term is translated back into the original language.

3. b. Projective tests involve the presentation of unstructured or ambiguous stimuli and recording peoples' responses to the stimuli.

4. d. The Barnum effect is based on P. T. Barnum's statement about the circus, there is a "little something in it for everybody". Here, it means that a generalized statement is accepted as an accurate description of one's personality.

5. a. Eysenck's model suggests that personality is comprised of three basic traits: extraversion, neuroticism, and psychoticism.

6. d. There is growing agreement about the 5 basic traits, although there is some disagreement about their labels. They are: openness, conscientiousness, extraversion, agreeableness, and neuroticism.

7. b. Among other influences, it is clear that situational variables influence behavior in significant ways.

8. d. The 4 bodily humors Hippocrates championed were black bile, blood, phlegm, and yellow bile.

9. b. The model was based on Gall's idea, *phrenology*, which presumed that a lot could be learned about one's cognitive abilities and behavioral propensities by feeling the bumps on the head.

10. d. *Sensation seeking* is the characteristic of engaging regularly in risky behavior, seeking thrills, and participating in novel experiences through the mind and senses.

11. a. Though it is not easy to find such twins, researchers like to study identical twins that were separated early as it helps separate the environmental influences on development.

12. b. University of Minnesota researchers compared 44 pairs of twins that were separated early in life, and found striking similarities between them in light of their comparability to twins reared together.

13. c. Heritability research, including that done with identical twins reared together and apart, indicates that differences among most people are due at least as much to environmental influences.

14. a. Freud's *psychic determinism* assumes behaviors stem from early experiences, especially conflicts related to sexual instincts.

15. a. Freud's model of personality is often compared to an iceberg. See "The Structure of the Mind" section in your textbook.

16. d. Freud's hypothetical construct (hypothetical construct is a fancy name for idea) *id* operated according to what he called the pleasure principle. The *ego,* he said, was guided by reality.

17. c. The *superego,* according to Freud, is the element that incorporates societal and parental standards in what is commonly referred to as the *conscience* as well as the idealistic *ego ideal.*

18. c. The Neo-Freudians disagreed with Freud's focus on the *id* and sexual motives.

19. b. Freud's theory has received much criticism since it does not lend itself to testing. Even when his ideas do lend themselves to testing, the results are mixed and do not support it well.

20. a. Rotter developed a scale to measure *locus of control.* His research and ideas may be considered extensions of Skinner's, but Rotter's interests include cognitive components such as *expectancies.*

21. b. Reciprocal determinism is Bandura's idea for explaining the interaction of person variables, situation variables, and behavior.

22. a. Maslow thought that Humanistic psychology was the "third force" in psychology because it offered an alternative to psychodynamic theory and behaviorism.

23. c. Rogers, a Humanist and a contemporary of Maslow, coined the term unconditional positive regard. He believed that growing up believing affection is conditional causes one to distort experiences.

24. d. There are significant cultural differences with respect to conceptions of the *self.*

Key Vocabulary Terms

Cut out and use as study cards; terms appear on one side and definitions are on the other.

personality	self-report inventory
projective test	Barnum effect
trait	psychic determinism
unconscious	id

Key Vocabulary Terms

Cut out and use as study cards; terms appear on one side and definitions are on the other.

Psychological tests in which individuals answer questions about themselves, usually by responding yes or no or true or false

A relatively stable pattern of behaving, feeling, and thinking that distinguishes one person from another

The tendency to accept generalized personality descriptions as accurate descriptions of oneself

Psychological test that involves the use of unstructured or ambiguous stimuli in an effort to assess personality

The psychodynamic assumption that all behaviors result from early childhood experiences, especially conflicts related to sexual instincts

A summary term that describes the tendency to behave, feel, and think in ways that are consistent across different situations

In psychodynamic theory, the most basic element of the personality; it is the source of the instincts and operates on the pleasure principle

Part of the personality that lies outside of awareness yet is believed to be a crucial determinant of behavior

ego

superego

defense
mechanism

repression

oral stage

fixation

anal stage

phallic stage

Oedipal complex

Electra complex

In psychodynamic theory, the element of the mind that incorporates parental and societal standards in what is commonly referred to as the conscience as well as the idealistic ego ideal

In psychodynamic theory, the element of the mind that operates according to the reality principle and serves to satisfy the id and the superego

Defense mechanism in which anxiety-arousing ideas are pushed out of consciousness to the unconscious level of the mind

Psychodynamic term used to describe primarily unconscious methods of reducing anxiety or guilt that results from conflicts among the id, ego, and superego

Cessation of further development, resulting in behaviors that are characteristic of the stage of development in which the fixation occurred

The first stage of psychosexual development in which the mouth is the focus of pleasure-seeking activity

The third stage of psychosexual development, in which the genital organs become the focus of pleasure-seeking behavior

Second stage of psychosexual development, during which the focus of pleasure is the anus and conflict often occurs as efforts are made to toilet-train the child

Process that occurs during the phallic stage in which a girl wishes to possess her father sexually

Process that occurs during the phallic stage in which a boy wishes to possess his mother sexually and fears retaliation by his father

latency stage

genital stage

reciprocal
determinism

self-efficacy

humanistic
psychology

self-actualization

Stage of psychosexual development that begins at puberty and usually leads to normal adult sexual development

Stage of psychosexual development that extends from about age 6 until the onset of puberty and is characterized by low levels of sexual interest

A person's expectancy concerning his or her ability to engage in effective behaviors; such expectancies differ from one behavior to another

Contention that person variables, situation variables, and behavior constantly interact

Need to develop one's full potential

General approach to psychology, associated with Abraham Maslow and Carl Rogers, that emphasizes individuals' control of their behavior

Psychology is a popular major at both the undergraduate and graduate levels. The diversity of psychology means that it holds something of interest for many students. Students who take an introductory psychology course are sometimes surprised when they realize that the discipline has implications for so many other academic areas, as well as for a range of career opportunities.

This last *Tip* section addresses some common questions and concerns for students considering a major in psychology. After reviewing this section, you may wish to make an appointment with a professor from your schools' psychology department to pursue additional questions. The career services office, library, and the Internet are other places you can look for answers about the nuts and bolts of a psychology major.

Finally, a new resource has been developed that provides a thorough review of issues surrounding psychology, including academic issues and career possibilities and considerations. The book is called ***The Psychology Major: Career Options and Strategies for Success,*** and was written by R. Eric Landrum, Stephen F. Davis, and Teresa A. Landrum.

The following items may be of interest to you:

1. **Psychology Beyond the Introductory Course.** The psychology curriculum varies from school to school. The courses offered in most psychology departments are extensions of the chapters from your introductory textbook. Here is a list of common courses:

   a. **Methodology:** an introduction to the tools and techniques used by psychologists in their research. This course goes by various names, including Experimental Psychology, Psychological Methods, Principles of Psychological Research, and so on. The methodology course is usually required for majors, and is considered an important part of the curriculum by graduate school admissions committees.

   b. **Statistics:** topics include sampling, distributions, probability, descriptive and inferential statistics. This course may be taught in the psychology department or in the math department at your school. It is usually required as a prerequisite for much of the upper-division psychology curriculum.

   c. **Developmental Psychology:** a study of the physical, cognitive, and psychosocial processes of development. Some schools offer a lifespan development course; others offer separate courses that are based on age ranges.

   d. **Social Psychology:** a study of how people think about, influence, and relate to one another. This class covers a range of interesting topics including altruism, group influences, and prejudice.

   e. **Abnormal Psychology:** a survey of psychological disorders, their characteristics, and their origins. This course represents that aspect of psychology with which lay people are most familiar.

   f. **Cognitive Psychology:** a study of cognitive and memory processes. Topics covered in this course may range from artificial intelligence to biologically based theories of memory formation.

   g. **Learning:** an examination of theories, ranging from the classic to the contemporary, that have been developed to explain learning and related phenomena. The data that support theories in this area are typically from non-human animals.

   h. **Physiological Psychology:** an introduction to the nervous system and its relationship to behavior and experience. Students of biology and physiology often take this course as well.

i. **Psychological Testing:** an introduction to theory underlying test construction, evaluation, and interpretation. This is an important course for those students who may be interested in working in school systems or with clinical populations. This course is sometimes called *Assessment* or *Tests and Measurement*.

j. **Personality:** a survey of psychological theories and research in the study of personality. Some instructors for this course emphasize theoretical issues; others focus more on research.

k. **History and Systems:** a study of the development of psychology. This course usually surveys psychology's historical roots in philosophy and the natural sciences. It is a senior-level, capstone course in many programs.

Compare this list with the course offerings in your school catalog. What additional classes are available at your school? Which courses are you interested in taking?_____

_____

_____

_____

2. **Getting Involved in Research.** Most academic psychologists have research interests that are accessible to undergraduate students. If you convey your interest in helping with research, you may get an opportunity to become involved. Participating in research is arguably the best way for you to demonstrate initiative and commitment to your career. Establish a goal of presenting findings from a research project at a psychology convention. Attending and presenting data at conventions is a great way to meet others who share an interest in psychology, to get research ideas, and to learn about the latest developments in the field.

What topic(s) are you most interested in researching?_____

_____

3. **Getting an Internship.** In addition to participating in research, you may want to do a psychology internship at a clinic, school, or business in your town. Internships can be helpful in determining whether you should pursue a given line of study in psychology, and may even open up job opportunities if you decide to seek employment after graduation. If you are interested in doing an internship, consult a professor from your psychology department who can share with you the department's policies and procedures regarding student internships.

What careers in psychology would you like to learn more about?_____

_____

4. **Careers with a Bachelor's Degree in Psychology.** People with academic training in psychology hold a wide variety of positions. Often, psychology-related careers require some level of graduate training, but there are many jobs that one can get with bachelor's level training in psychology. The following list indicates areas in which people who studied psychology at the bachelor's level have found meaningful employment.

a. **Education and Teaching**

b. **Consulting and Statistics**

c. **Administration/Clerical**

d. **Professional Services**

e. **Sales**

f. **Health and Related Services**

g. **Research and Development**

5. **Careers with Graduate Degrees in Psychology.** After completing your bachelor's degree, you may choose to pursue graduate education in psychology. There are a several options to consider if you are interested in graduate training. Are your interests in applied careers (e.g., industrial and organizational psychology, school psychology, counseling)? Are you interested in doing basic research in psychology or a related discipline (e.g., neuroscience)? Would you enjoy teaching as part of your career? The answers to these questions will have some bearing on your decision.

Depending on which career(s) you are interested in, you may plan to complete a master's degree or a doctorate degree. Some undergraduate psychology majors attend professional schools (e.g., medical school, law school) after finishing their undergraduate work. Master's degrees and professional degrees are usually preparation for applied work, whereas a doctorate is required if one is interested in teaching at the college level and in some career fields (e.g., clinical psychology).

Will additional schooling be required for you given your present career interests? If so, how will you begin learning about graduate programs to suit your needs? If not, what can you do as an undergraduate student to improve your chances of getting the job you are interested in?_____

_____

_____

_____

6. **Identifying a Role Model or Mentor.** Many of the most successful people gained their success by working with, or otherwise modeling themselves after, other successful people. Find someone who has the career in which you are interested. Ask that person if you can make an appointment to interview her or him in order that you can learn more about everything the job entails. Assuming you are able to get an appointment, plan your questions ahead of time and take notes during the meeting. The following are some items you may wish to address:

a. **Educational Background.** Where did the person attend school? What subject(s) did he or she study? What were critical steps and turning points that helped her or him get the job? How long has he or she been in the position?

b. **Job Characteristics.** What kinds of things constitute the person's daily responsibilities and activities? How much time does the person spend on career-related work each week? What are the advantages and disadvantages of that career as that person perceives them?

c. **Is There Anything You Can Do?** Make certain to communicate your interest in learning outside the classroom. Indicate that you would like to participate in research, read and discuss journal articles, help out with filing, or anything else the person might suggest. Initially you may have less than glamorous responsibilities, but if you do good work and are reliable, you will gain greater opportunities. This may be the beginning of an instructive and mutually beneficial relationship.

CHAPTER 13

Psychological Disorders

Use the space provided in this outline to record notes from the textbook as well as from class lectures and discussion. Questions related to the *Psychological Detective* sections in the text have been presented in the outline; use the associated space to respond to the questions and to record your own comments about the issues. *Keywords and terms* from the text have been italicized and inserted in the outline so you can practice writing their definitions. The pages in this study guide are perforated and can be removed for use as study sheets for quizzes and exams.

I. Abnormal Behavior

    A. Criteria of Abnormality

        1. Statistical Rarity

        2. Interference with Normal Functioning

            dysfunctional—

        3. Personal Distress

        4. Deviance from Social Norms

            social norms—

    B. A Working Definition

        abnormal—

    C. The Concept of Insanity

        insanity—

🔍   How often is the insanity plea used? How often does it result in acquittal?

    D. Models of Abnormal Behavior

1. The Medical Model

    medical model—

2. The Psychological Models

    psychodynamic model—

    behavioral model—

    cognitive model—

    sociocultural model—

II. Classifying and Counting Psychological Disorders

diagnosis—

A. DSM-IV

B. The Labeling Issue

C. The Prevalence of Psychological Disorders

epidemiologist—

prevalence—

incidence—

III. Anxiety, Somatoform, and Dissociative Disorders

A. Anxiety Disorders

anxiety—

1. Phobias

phobia—

agoraphobia—

social phobia—

specific phobia—

2. Panic Disorder

panic disorder—

Why do only some of the 15 to 30 percent of people that have experienced at least one panic attack develop chronic disorder? What role might cognitive interpretation of symptoms contribute to the likelihood that one will develop the disorder?

3. Generalized Anxiety Disorder

generalized anxiety disorder (GAD)—

4. Obsessive-Compulsive Disorder

obsessive-compulsive disorder (OCD)—

🔍 What behavior is being reinforced, and what is the reinforcer, when one feels less anxious after taking a shower? What principle of operant conditioning is in effect when each shower reduces anxiety?

B. Somatoform Disorders

> *somatoform disorders—*

   1. Hypochondriasis

> *hypochondriasis—*

   2. Somatization Disorder

> *somatization disorder—*

   3. Conversion Disorder

> *conversion disorder—*

C. Dissociative Disorders

> *dissociative disorders—*

   1. Dissociative Amnesia and Dissociative Fugue

> *dissociative amnesia—*

🔍 How would the medical model view Ed's amnesia for the accident? How would that explanation differ from one from the psychodynamic model?

dissociative fugue—

2. Dissociative Identity Disorder

dissociative identity disorder—

IV. MOOD DISORDERS

A. Depression
   1. Symptoms

   depression—

   2. Prevalence and Course

   3. Suicide

B. Bipolar Disorder

   mania—

   bipolar disorder—

C. Causes of Mood Disorders
   1. Biological Explanations

   concordance rate—

   2. The Psychodynamic Explanation

   3. Cognitive and Behavioral Explanations

   learned helplessness—

🔍 Use the three dimensions of explanatory style to anticipate how you would respond to a grade of F on an exam. How would a person who is prone to depression respond?

       arbitrary inference—

4. Multiple Causes

V. Schizophrenia

       schizophrenia—

       psychosis—

A. Symptoms of Schizophrenia
 1. Positive Symptoms

       delusion—

       hallucinations—

 2. Negative Symptoms

B. Subtypes of Schizophrenia

C. Causes of Schizophrenia
 1. Genetic Factors

🔍 What can research with groups of twins, some reared together and some reared apart, tell researchers about the causes of schizophrenia?

 2. Brain Abnormalities

3. Neurotransmitters

4. Environmental Causes

5. Multiple Causes

VI. Personality and Sexual Disorders

A. Personality Disorders

personality disorders—

antisocial personality disorder—

How could a researcher measure physiological arousal? Design an experiment to study whether low levels of physiological arousal are related to antisocial behavior.

B. Sexual Disorders

1. Gender Identity Disorder

gender identity disorder—

2. Paraphilias

paraphilias—

3. Fetishism

fetishism—

After you have studied the chapter, you should be able to respond to the following statements and questions to convey your understanding of the material.

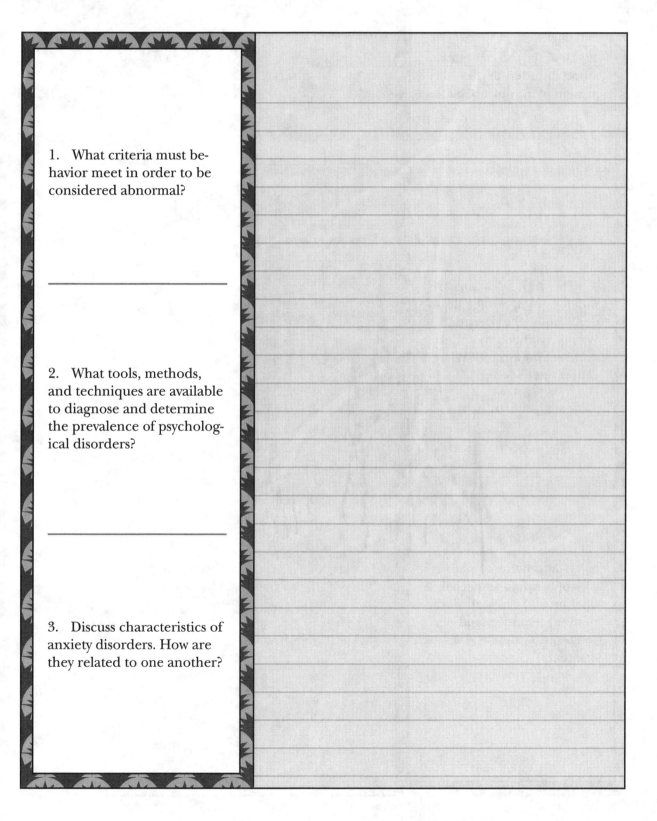

1. What criteria must behavior meet in order to be considered abnormal?

2. What tools, methods, and techniques are available to diagnose and determine the prevalence of psychological disorders?

3. Discuss characteristics of anxiety disorders. How are they related to one another?

4. Describe the causes of mood disorders as they were presented in your textbook.

5. The word *schizophrenia* is widely known, but the disorder is not well understood. Why is it difficult to understand schizophrenia? What causes this disorder?

6. How can one use principles of learning (especially operant and classical conditioning) to understand personality disorders and sexual disorders?

Fill in the blanks in the following statements with key words and terms from the textbook. Answer as many as you can without referring to your notes or to the book. If you have blanks after thinking about each item, try using your book. The answers are presented after the practice test.

1. The _____ _____ criterion for determining whether behavior is abnormal involves determining whether the peoples' behaviors are upsetting, distracting, or confusing to themselves.

2. According to the _____ _____, psychological disorders are learned and follow the principles of classical and operant conditioning.

3. _____ _____ _____ involves a chronically high level of anxiety that is not associated with a particular stimulus.

4. _____ is the number or percentage of newly diagnosed cases of a particular disorder in a given population.

5. In some cases major depression and _____ _____ occur together in a condition that is referred to as double depression.

6. What was once called multiple personality disorder is now known as _____ _____ _____.

7. _____ _____ is the belief that one cannot control outcomes through one's actions.

8. A(n) _____ _____ is a conclusion that is drawn in the absence of supporting information.

9. Believing you are Santa Claus would be an example of a(n) _____.

10. An experiment involved MRI scanning of the brains of 'normal' people and persons with schizophrenia. Results indicated that the *thalamus* and surrounding regions in schizophrenic patients were significantly _____ than the same regions in 'normal' brains.

Circle the letter that corresponds to the **best** alternative for each of the following items. Read each alternative carefully. The answers are presented at the end of this study guide chapter. Be sure to learn *why* each correct alternative is better than the others.

1. The criteria for abnormality, as presented in your textbook, include all but which of the following?
   a. statistical rarity
   b. deviance from social norms
   c. interference with normal functioning
   d. adherence to rules for alternative fashion

2. Which example fits best the description of a *dysfunctional* family?
   a. The head of the household rarely functions before noon.
   b. Maids, gardeners, and cooks do all the work for the family.
   c. Typical familial interactions adversely affect the family's functioning.
   d. Both husband and wife get along well, but there are no children or pets.

3. Social norms are:
   a. guys named Normal that like to go to parties.
   b. behaviors such as keeping one's house well organized.
   c. difficult to follow for most people because of their elusive nature.
   d. guidelines (that are usually unwritten) that define the acceptability of behavior.

4. The U.S. public believes felony indictments involve the insanity plea ___ % of the time, and that ___ % of those pleas result in acquittal. Actually only about 1% of cases involve the plea, and less than 1/4 of 1% are successful.
   a. 10; 80
   b. 50; 75
   c. 37; 44
   d. 89; 14

5. Psychological models for explaining abnormal behavior emphasize:
   a. the probability that underlying organic causes are at play.
   b. the likelihood that mental illness results from possession by demons.
   c. mental functioning, social experiences, and learning histories as having important causal links.
   d. all of the above.

6. Sociocultural variables apparently influence the likelihood that one will have a psychological disorder. For example, poverty is related to the prevalence of psychological disorders, and rates of psychological disorders are influenced by socioeconomic status. Another (category of) disorder that seems related to cultural variables is:
   a. bipolar disorder.
   b. phobic disorders.
   c. anorexia nervosa.
   d. obsessive-compulsive disorder.

7. A major reason people are diagnosed is:
   a. to be able to make predictions.
   b. so labels can be assigned to them.
   c. so that insurance companies can reimburse diagnosticians.
   d. to determine whether they were insane when they committed their crimes.

8. In the Rosenhan study in which 'normal' people entered hospitals and reported hearing voices:
   a. the people were admitted for an average of 19 days and were administered over 2,000 pills.
   b. while the people were taken seriously, they were not diagnosed as having any type of illness.
   c. the people were referred to a hearing specialist as it was determined their problem was not psychologically based.
   d. it was determined that the diagnostic criteria were very effective at discriminating 'normal' from those with mental illness.

9. The most frequently used diagnostic system for classifying mental disorders was developed by:
   a. Rosenhan and his colleagues.
   b. the American Psychiatric Association.
   c. the American Psychological Association.
   d. members of the American Psychiatric Association and members of the American Psychological association, under the leadership of Rosenhan.

10. An epidemiologist:
    a. is someone who study the bugs that cause mental disorders.
    b. is handy to have around if one experiences an epidemio infestation.
    c. studies the distribution and causes of accidents, diseases and psychological disorders.
    d. has to have several years of training in brain scanning (e.g., MRI) in order to work effectively.

11. A *comorbid* psychological disorder is:
    a. one that develops initially with symptoms that one has died.
    b. a disorder that co-occurs with one or more other psychological disorders.
    c. a disorder that develops just as the symptoms of another disorder come under control.
    d. all of the above.

12. Phobias are:
    a. innate fears (not related to environment or experience).
    b. excessive fears that are categorized under anxiety disorders.
    c. more prevalent in third world than in highly industrialized countries.
    d. fears that develop as a result of eating diets that are proportionately high in saturated fats.

13. The most severe anxiety disorder(s) is (are):
    a. panic disorder.
    b. simple phobias.
    c. generalized anxiety disorder.
    d. obsessive-compulsive disorder.

14. Obsessions are to ___ as compulsions are to ___.
    a. OCD; GAD
    b. acts; thoughts
    c. thoughts; acts
    d. early onset; chronic syndromes

15. Somatoform disorders involve:
    a. physical symptoms with no known medical cause.
    b. the irrational repetitive creation (forming) of somas (bodies).
    c. medical symptoms that are known to result from psychological issues.
    d. peculiar behaviors that are targeted at reducing anxiety about repetitive thoughts.

16. Sally is forever going to the doctor and consulting pharmacists about what she can do to address a constellation of symptoms that most people would ignore. Sally probably has:
    a. OCD.
    b. cancer.
    c. hypochondriasis.
    d. anterior-lateral sclerosis.

17. A truck driver recently picked up Hans while he was walking toward town after crashing his car. Hans had absolutely no idea where he was, or for that matter where he had come from. After some careful investigative work, officials were able to determine that Hans had rented a car after flying to the U.S. from Europe. However, Hans could recall nothing of his adventure or the events leading up to it. Hans is likely suffering from:
    a. dissociative fugue.
    b. retrograde amnesia.
    c. conversion disorder.
    d. comorbid hypochondriasis.

18. Surveys of people in the U.S., Western Europe, the Middle East, Asia, and the Pacific Rim regarding depression have revealed which of the following?
    a. Depression is beginning at an earlier age with each successive generation.
    b. Rates of depression have risen steadily for each successive generation since 1915.
    c. Both a. and b., above, are true.
    d. Neither a. nor b. is true; depression is becoming decidedly less common world-wide.

19. The most serious complication of severe depression is:
    a. comorbidity.
    b. the possibility of suicide.
    c. that slowed heart rate can least to cardiac rest.
    d. that people with substance abuse disorders often also are depressed.

20. Bipolar disorder involves alternating cycles of ___ and ___.
    a. OCD; GAD
    b. wash and rinse
    c. depression; mania
    d. somatoform disorder; conversion disorder

21. The *concordance rate* is:
    a. a measure of treatment efficacy for mental disorders.
    b. the percentage of twin pairs in which both twins have a disorder.
    c. an index of the proportion of the population that has a given disorder.
    d. usually 7/10s of a percentage point behind the 30-year mortgage rate.

22. Schizophrenia is a psychotic disorder. That is, it:
    a. involves the symptom of the afflicted person losing contact with reality.
    b. is most effectively treated with psychotherapies rather than drug therapies.
    c. inevitably results in a slow, painful death in which the individual is tormented by peers.
    d. is a violent disorder. As a result many people with schizophrenia have to be incarcerated.

23. Flattened affect is to hallucination as ___ is to ___.
    a. neurosis; psychosis
    b. psychosis; neurosis
    c. positive symptom; negative symptom
    d. negative symptom; positive symptom

24. Someone with antisocial personality disorder is:
    a. outcast, and transforms feelings of rejection into positive feedback.
    b. typically in late adulthood before symptoms develop sufficiently for diagnosis.
    c. characterized as deceitful, impulsive, and reckless and feels no remorse for her or his behavior.
    d. fun to be with at parties because even though others do not treat them well, they have what Freud referred to as strong unconscious needs to enrich the lives of others.

25. Transsexualism:
    a. is a particular form of paraphilia.
    b. is another name for homosexuality.
    c. is approximately three times more common in males than females.
    d. involves thinking like one gender, and acting like the other gender.

 ## ANSWERS TO KEY WORD EXERCISE

1. personal distress
2. behavioral model
3. generalized anxiety disorder
4. Incidence
5. dysthymic disorder
6. dissociative identity disorder
7. Learned helplessness
8. arbitrary inference
9. delusion
10. smaller

 ## PRACTICE TEST ANSWERS AND EXPLANATIONS

1. d. Adherence to rules for alternative fashion is not a criterion for abnormality.
2. c. *Dysfunctional* is a term used to describe behaviors that adversely affect functioning.
3. d. *Social norms* are guidelines for what is acceptable and what is unacceptable for a particular group.
4. c. Surveys have demonstrated that people grossly overestimate the frequency with which the insanity plea is used, and the likelihood that people who use it will be successful.
5. c. Psychological models reflect perspectives on behavioral issues. Medical models focus on organic causes (as they do with physical illnesses).
6. c. Anorexia nervosa occurs mainly in Western cultures where thinness is considered a sign of beauty.
7. a. Diagnosis is used primarily to make predictions about patterns in people's behaviors.
8. a. People acting as if they had experienced hallucinations were diagnosed and treated as if they had mental illness.
9. b. The American *Psychiatric* Association developed the Diagnostic and Statistical Manual of Mental Disorders (DSM). The DSM is in its 4th edition (DSM-IV).
10. c. Epidemiologists estimate the distributions and causes of maladies, accidents, and problems.
11. b. Comorbid disorders are disorders that co-occur; often people who experience symptoms of one disorder also experience symptoms of additional disorders.
12. b. Phobias are fears, often stemming from experiences that comprise a specific category of anxiety disorder.
13. a. Panic disorder is considered the most severe anxiety disorder.
14. c. Obsessions are repetitive thoughts; compulsions are acts (often targeted at allaying obsessions).
15. a. Somatoform disorders involve physical symptoms with no known medical cause.
16. c. Hypochondriasis involves the interpretation of normal bodily symptoms as indices that one is contracting dreaded disease.
17. a. The symptoms of dissociative fugue include amnesia, flight from the workplace or home, and establishing a new identity.

18. c. More people seem to be developing depression at earlier ages.

19. b. People with severe depression are at great risk for suicide.

20. c. People with bipolar disorder show symptoms of depression and mania, in alternation.

21. b. Concordance refers to the percentage of twin pairs in which both twins have a disorder.

22. a. Psychosis is any disorder in which a severely disturbed individual loses contact with reality.

23. d. Negative symptoms are reductions in functioning, such as failing to show appropriate emotional responses. Positive symptoms are excesses or distortions in normal functioning, as with hallucinations.

24. c. Antisocial personality disorder is characterized by deceitful, impulsive, and reckless activity for which one feels no remorse.

25. c. Transsexualism is approximately three times more common in males than females.

Key Vocabulary Terms

Cut out and use as study cards; terms appear on
one side and definitions are on the other.

dysfunctional

social norms

abnormal

insanity

medical model

psychodynamic
model

behavioral
model

cognitive model

Key Vocabulary Terms

Cut out and use as study cards; terms appear on one side and definitions are on the other.

Guidelines, usually unwritten, that define behavior that is acceptable or unacceptable within a particular group

Term used to describe behaviors that adversely affect an individual's functioning

Legal ruling that a person accused of a crime is not held responsible for that act; defined in most states as the inability to tell the difference between right and wrong at the time the crime is committed

Term used to describe behavior that is rare or dysfunctional, causes personal distress, or deviates from social norms

The view that psychological disorders result from unconscious conflicts related to sex or aggression

The view that mental disorders are like physical illnesses and have underlying organic causes

A view that emphasizes thinking as the key element in causing psychological disorders

The view that psychological disorders are learned behaviors that follow the principles of classical and operant conditioning or modeling

sociocultural model	diagnosis
epidemiologist	prevalence
incidence	anxiety
phobia	agoraphobia
social phobia	specific phobia

The process of deciding whether a person has symptoms that meet established criteria of an existing classification system

A view that emphasizes the importance of society and culture in causing psychological disorders

Number or percentage of people in a population that ever had a particular disorder during a specified period

Scientist who studies the distribution and causes of accidents, diseases, and psychological disorders in a given population

General feeling of apprehension characterized by behavioral, cognitive, or physiological symptoms

Number or percentage of newly diagnosed cases of a particular disorder in a given population

Avoidance of public places or situations in which escape may be difficult should the individual develop incapacitating or embarrassing symptoms of panic

Irrational fear of an activity, object, or situation that is out of proportion to the actual danger

Any phobia other than agoraphobia or the social phobias, including the fear of specific animals, of elements of the natural environment, and of such things as blood, injections, or injury

A fear related to being seen or observed by others

panic disorder	generalized anxiety disorder (GAD)
obsessive-com- pulsive disorder (OCD)	somatoform dis- orders
hypochondriasis	somatization disorder
conversion disorder	dissociative disorders
dissociative amnesia	dissociative fugue

Chronically high level of
anxiety that is not attached
to a specific stimulus

The most severe anxiety disorder,
characterized by intense physiological arousal not related to a
specific stimulus

Disorders involving physical complaints that do not have a known
medical cause but are related to
psychological factors

An anxiety disorder characterized
by repetitive, irrational, intrusive
thoughts, impulses, or images
(obsessions) and irresistible,
repetitive acts (compulsions) such
as checking that doors are locked
or washing hands

Somatoform disorder involving
multiple physical complaints that
do not have a medical explanation
and do not suggest a specific
known disease

Somatoform disorder in which a
person believes that he or she has
a serious disease despite repeated
medical findings to the contrary

Disorders affecting a function of
the mind, such as memory for
events, knowledge of one's identity,
or consciousness

Somatoform disorder in which a
person presents sensory or motor
symptoms that do not have a
medical explanation

Dissociative disorder involving amnesia and flight from the workplace or home; may involve
establishing a new identity in a
new location

Dissociative disorder that involves
a sudden inability to recall important personal information; often
occurs in response to trauma or
extreme stress

depression	mania
bipolar disorder	concordance rate
learned helplessness	arbitrary inference
schizophrenia	psychosis
delusion	hallucinations

Excessive activity, accelerated speech, poor judgment, elevated self-esteem, and euphoria that occur in bipolar disorder

Mood disorder characterized by sadness; feelings of guilt; changes in sleep, appetite, and motor behavior; and sometimes thoughts of suicide

Percentage of twin pairs in which both twins have a disorder that is of interest to an investigator

Mood disorder in which a person experiences episodes of mania and depression, which usually alternate

Conclusion drawn in the absence of supporting information

Belief that one cannot control outcomes through one's actions; usually leads to passivity and reduced motivation and may cause depression

Any disorder in which a severely disturbed individual loses contact with reality

Psychotic disorder characterized by positive symptoms (excesses) such as delusions, hallucinations, and fluent but disorganized speech or negative symptoms (deficits) such as flat or blunted affect

Sensory experiences that are not caused by stimulation of the relevant sensory organ

An obviously false belief that is difficult to change

personality disorders	antisocial personality disorder
gender identity disorder (transsexualism)	paraphilia
fetishism	

Personality disorder characterized by deceitful, impulsive, reckless actions for which the individual feels no remorse

Disorders characterized by long-standing, difficult-to-treat, dysfunctional behaviors that are typically first observed in adolescence

Sexual arousal by objects or situations not considered sexual by most people

Sexual disorder characterized by a person's belief that he or she was born with the wrong biological sex organs

Paraphilia involving sexual arousal by unusual objects or body parts

C H A P T E R 1 4

Therapy

Use the space provided in this outline to record notes from the textbook as well as from class lectures and discussion. Questions related to the *Psychological Detective* sections in the text have been presented in the outline; use the associated space to respond to the questions and to record your own comments about the issues. *Keywords and terms* from the text have been italicized and inserted in the outline so you can practice writing their definitions. The pages in this study guide are perforated and can be removed for use as study sheets for quizzes and exams.

I. **Therapy Through the Ages**

    A. The History of Therapy

        1. Asylums and Hospitals

        2. Moral Therapy

        3. State Mental Hospitals

        4. New Forms of Treatment

        5. Deinstitutionalization

            deinstitutionalization—

        6. The Community Mental Health Movement

    B. Therapy and Therapists

        biomedical therapies—

        psychological therapies—

        psychotherapy—

II. Psychologically Based Therapies

A. Psychoanalytic Therapy

psychoanalytic therapy—

1. Free Association

free association—

2. Dream Interpretation

3. Resistance

resistance—

4. Transference

transference—

5. Evaluation of Psychoanalysis

B. Humanistic Therapies

humanistic therapies—

1. Client-Centered Therapy

client-centered therapy—

2. Gestalt Therapy

Gestalt therapy—

C. Cognitive Therapies

   cognitive therapies—

   1. Rational-Emotive Behavior Therapy

      rational-emotive behavior therapy (REBT)—

   2. Beck's Cognitive Therapy

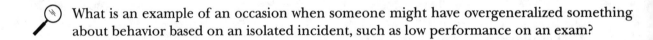 What is an example of an occasion when someone might have overgeneralized something about behavior based on an isolated incident, such as low performance on an exam?

   3. Stress Inoculation Training

      stress inoculation training—

D. Behavior Therapies
   1. Systematic Desensitization

      systematic desensitization—

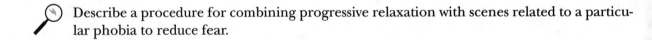 Describe a procedure for combining progressive relaxation with scenes related to a particular phobia to reduce fear.

   2. Aversion Therapy

      aversion therapy—

   3. Modeling

   4. Extinction

What can one do to extinguish inappropriate behavior? What can one anticipate to happen to the frequency of the behavior during the early stages of extinction?

    5. Punishment

    6. Token Economy

        token economy—

 What are some advantages of using tokens to reward behavior? What steps can one take to ensure that tokens have value?

    7. Combining Behavior Therapy Techniques

  E. Group Therapies
        group therapy—

    1. Marital and Family Therapy

  F. Self-Help

III. The Effectiveness of Psychotherapy

  A. Eysenck's Challenge
     1. Meta-Analysis

  B. Characteristics of Effective Psychotherapy

  C. Changing Psychotherapy to Meet the Needs of Diversity

  D. When to Begin Psychotherapy and What to Expect

IV. Biomedical Therapies

A. Drug Therapy

1. Antianxiety Drugs

   antianxiety drugs—

2. Antidepressant Drugs

3. Mood Stabilizers

4. Antipsychotic Drugs

   antipsychotic drugs—

   tardive dyskinesia—

5. Evaluating Drug Therapy

B. Electroconvulsive Therapy

electroconvulsive therapy (ECT)—

What effect would ECT have on a patient immediately after treatment? What psychological processes would be affected?

C. Psychosurgery

psychosurgery—

After you have studied the chapter, you should be able to respond to the following statements and questions to convey your understanding of the material.

1. Discuss the history of treatment approaches for the mentally ill.

2. What are key differentiating elements of psychoanalytic therapy, humanistic therapy, cognitive therapy, behavior therapy, and group therapy?

3. What are some important considerations when evaluating the effectiveness of psychotherapy?

4. Compare and contrast the biomedical therapies (drug therapy, ECT, and psychosurgery).

Fill in the blanks in the following statements with key words and terms from the textbook. Answer as many as you can without referring to your notes or to the book. If you have blanks after thinking about each item, try using your book. The answers are presented after the practice test.

1. _____ _____ convinced many states to build institutions to treat people suffering from mental disorders.

2. The policy of discharging mentally ill patients from institutions on the assumption that they can be cared for in their communities is called _____.

3. A feature of *extinction* as a form of therapy is that the frequency of the undesirable response often _____ initially.

4. Andy gets a coin for every nice thing he says or does during a day, and loses four coins every time he is mean. Andy is on a _____ _____.

5. Jayme is suffering from _____ _____ as a result of taking antipsychotic drugs. Her symptoms include involuntary motor symptoms.

6. Research with people from different cultures who have various disorders has revealed that Asians require _____ doses of some drugs (e.g., tricyclic antidepressants, lithium) than Caucasians.

7. Freud called _____ "the royal road to the unconscious". They presumably consist of manifest and latent content.

8. A form of therapy in which therapists may frustrate and challenge clients to lead them toward self-acceptance is called _____ _____.

9. One of the most effective techniques for treating phobias is _____.

10. A guiding principle for _____-_____ groups is that compassion and understanding do not require advanced degrees.

Circle the letter that corresponds to the **best** alternative for each of the following items. Read each alternative carefully. The answers are presented at the end of this study guide chapter. Be sure to learn *why* each correct alternative is better than the others.

1. *Bedlam* is a term used to describe disorganized, unorganized conditions. The term came from:
   a. the Greek word for chaos.
   b. a contraction of Bethlehem.
   c. the first letters in each ancient, pre-Hippocrates form of psychological treatment.
   d. the mid-1950s when psychotherapeutic drugs were first being administered to patients.

2. Philippe Pinel, Jean-Baptiste Pussin, and Benjamin Rush had in common:
   a. that they all recovered from mental illness.
   b. that they all advocated moral/humane treatment of mental patients.
   c. ancestry in Dorothea Dix, a leader in the mental health movement.
   d. a view that people with psychological disorders were possessed by demons.

3. The first antipsychotic drug was available in:
   a. 1945.
   b. 1950.
   c. 1955.
   d. 1960.

4. ___ prevention is designed to reduce the damage caused by disorders for both the patients and society.
   a. Drug
   b. Primary
   c. Tertiary
   d. Secondary

5. Biomedical therapies include all but which of the following?
   a. drug therapy
   b. psychotherapy
   c. psychosurgery
   d. electroconvulsive therapy

6. People with master's degrees who have job titles such as *psychotherapist* and *counselor* are accountable to licensing boards,:
   a. but are not necessarily regulated by state or federal agencies.
   b. but are called *psychologists* by the American Psychological Association.
   c. and are therefore to be trusted with one's problems and confidential concerns.
   d. ironing boards, surf boards, pegboards, running boards, and many other types of boards.

7. Free Association is:
   a. the original name for state-supported in-patient mental institutions.
   b. the name for reinforced trials in a classical conditioning experiment.
   c. a psychoanalytic technique in which the patient reports whatever comes to mind.
   d. far more expensive than the name implies because of taxes imposed by federal legislation.

8. Researchers of psychoanalytic therapy face all but which of the following:
   a. hypothetical constructs that are hard to define and measure
   b. knowing when the essential elements of treatment are present
   c. the difficulty of defining the essential elements of the treatment
   d. Sigmund Freud as they lie on his couch and report on their experiences

9. Carl Rogers is to ___ as Aaron Beck is to ___.
   a. humanistic therapy; cognitive therapy
   b. cognitive therapy; humanistic therapy
   c. behavior therapy; Gestalt therapy
   d. Gestalt therapy; behavior therapy

10. Stress inoculation training:
   a. is required of all emergency room physicians for licensure.
   b. helps clients interpret events and develop self-talk that reduces stress levels.
   c. involves learning to give one's self shots to combat the stresses of daily living.
   d. all of the above

11. Hank employed *systematic desensitization* to overcome his fear of entering libraries. This technique:
    a. probably involved a good deal of reading.
    b. is based on principles from classical conditioning.
    c. was pioneered by Freud as a means of dealing with repression.
    d. was developed by cognitive therapists in response to symptoms that eventually led to depression.

12. Some alcoholics have used a drug called Antabuse (disulfiram) when trying to stop drinking. This approach to therapy fits with which of the following categories?
    a. aversion therapy
    b. inoculation training
    c. maltreatment of insects
    d. systematic desensitization

13. Which of the following was not identified in the textbook as an advantage of group therapy?
    a. anonymity
    b. social support
    c. opportunities to receive feedback
    d. opportunities to practice coping skills

14. *Spontaneous remission* is:
    a. analogous to psychological recidivism.
    b. a term used to describe improvement without treatment.
    c. an index of severe psychosis, usually undifferentiated type.
    d. an early symptom of depression and can be treated successfully with psychotherapy.

15. Antianxiety drugs:
    a. are also known as minor tranquilizers.
    b. can reduce the severity of physiological symptoms (e.g., heart rate).
    c. increase the ability of GABA to bind to receptor sites at synapses in the brain.
    d. all of the above.

16. Which is not one of the three major classes of antidepressant drugs?
    a. major tranquilizers
    b. tricyclic antidepressants
    c. monoamine oxidase inhibitors
    d. selective serotonin reuptake inhibitors

17. A therapeutic technique that involves inducing seizures and has been effective with some depressed patients is:
    a. ECT.
    b. drug therapy.
    c. psychosurgery.
    d. all of the above

18. When patients have received ECT as a treatment for a psychological illness, they often report confusion and a lack of memory for the experience. This is because:
    a. they are administered drugs that block their memories.
    b. they are hypnotized prior to undergoing the therapy session.
    c. people with psychological illnesses have impaired memories.
    d. electric shock seems to disrupt the memory consolidation process.

19. Today, psychosurgery is:
    a. less common than it was in the 1930s.
    b. more common than it was in the 1930s.
    c. limited to an experimental procedure for treating schizophrenia.
    d. being studied in 100s of labs as people strive for the ultimate treatment for anxiety.

20. The natural mineral salt *lithium* is used:
    a. to treat tardive dyskinesia.
    b. to treat symptoms of bipolar disorder.
    c. recreationally by many substance abusers.
    d. in place of sodium chloride for people who use psychotherapeutic drugs.

 ## ANSWERS TO KEY WORD EXERCISE

1. Dorothea Dix
2. deinstitutionalization
3. increases
4. token economy
5. tardive dyskinesia
6. lower
7. dreams
8. Gestalt therapy
9. modeling
10. self-help

 ## PRACTICE TEST ANSWERS AND EXPLANATIONS

1. b. Bedlam is a contraction of Bethlehem, as in the St. Mary of Bethlehem Hospital in London.

2. b. Though they worked on different continents, and with different interpretations of what is humane, all three were interested in employing therapeutic techniques that were morally based.

3. c. The first antipsychotic drug was available for use in 1955.

4. c. An example of tertiary prevention is an after-care program for patients living in a mental hospital.

5. b. Psychotherapy is an example of a psychological, rather than a biomedical, therapy.

6. a. It is important to choose mental health professionals carefully as many are not regulated by government agencies.

7. c. Free association is a psychoanalytic technique in which the patient reports whatever comes to mind.

8. d. Sigmund Freud is dead. The problems with researching psychoanalytic therapy have to do with the nature of the definitions and the fact that psychoanalytic theory does not lend itself to testing.

9. a. Rogers was a humanistic psychologist who practiced *client-centered* therapy; Beck is a cognitive therapist and has focused much of his work on depression.

10. b. Stress inoculation training helps clients learn to interpret and respond to stress differently.

11. b. Systematic desensitization is a technique that represents an application of classical conditioning.

12. a. Inasmuch as Antabuse causes one to become nauseous when it is present in the body with alcohol, this is a form of aversion therapy.

13. a. Anonymity is not a feature of group therapy as comments are shared with everyone present.
14. b. Spontaneous remission is a term used to describe improvement without treatment.
15. d. All of these are true of antianxiety drugs.
16. a. Major tranquilizers are used to treat psychoses, not depression.
17. a. ECT is effective, for reasons that are not well understood, in treating some people with depression.
18. d. ECT disrupts memory consolidation.
19. a. Psychosurgery was performed on untold numbers of people in the 1930s. Today, psychosurgery is rare and only considered as a last resort.
20. b. Lithium is used to stabilize the moods of people suffering from bipolar disorder.

Key Vocabulary Terms

Cut out and use as study cards; terms appear on
one side and definitions are on the other.

deinstitutional-
ization

biomedical
therapies

psychological
therapies

psychotherapy

psychoanalytic
therapy

free association

resistance

transference

Key Vocabulary Terms

Cut out and use as study cards; terms appear on one side and definitions are on the other.

A set of treatments for mental illness that includes drugs, psychosurgery, and electroconvulsive therapy

The policy of discharging mentally ill patients from institutions on the assumption that they can be cared for in their communities; the policy also led to the closing of part or all of these institutions

A special relationship between a distressed person and a trained therapist in which the therapist aids the client in developing awareness and changing his or her thinking, feeling, and behavior

Treatments for psychological disorders such as psychotherapy or therapies based on classical or operant conditioning principles

A psychoanalytic technique in which the patient is asked to say whatever comes to mind without censoring anything

Treatment of maladaptive behavior developed by Sigmund Freud; its goal is to uncover unconscious conflicts and feelings and bring them to the conscious level

In psychoanalysis, the patient's positive or negative reaction to the therapist, which is believed to reflect the patient's relationship to a significant person outside of therapy

A stage of psychoanalysis in which blocking of free association occurs because critical unconscious material is close to conscious awareness

humanistic therapies	client-centered therapy
Gestalt therapy	cognitive therapies
rational-emotive behavior therapy (REBT)	stress inoculation training
systematic desensitization	aversion therapy
token economy	group therapy

Therapy designed to create an environment in which the client is able to find solutions to his or her problems

Therapies that emphasize the present and the ability of clients to solve their own problems once they are able to accept themselves

Therapies designed to change cognitions in order to eliminate maladaptive behaviors

A humanistic form of therapy developed by Fritz Perls in which therapists may frustrate and challenge clients to lead them toward self-acceptance

A cognitive therapy that helps clients learn ways to interpret stressful events and develop self-talk that reduces stress levels

A cognitive therapy in which the therapist challenges and questions the client's irrational ideas

Classical conditioning technique for reducing or eliminating behavior by pairing the behavior with an unpleasant (aversive) stimulus

A behavioral technique, based on classical conditioning, that is used to treat phobias; the technique usually combines training in relaxation with exposure to imagined scenes related to a phobia

Therapy in which clients discuss problems in groups that may include individuals with similar problems

A technique that reinforces desirable behaviors with tokens (secondary reinforcers), which can be redeemed for other reinforcers, especially primary reinforcers

antianxiety drugs	antipsychotic drugs
tardive dyskinesia	electroconvulsive therapy (ECT)
psychotherapy	

Drugs that reduce the symptoms of schizophrenia by blocking dopamine receptors in the brain; the typical antipsychotic drugs work by blocking dopamine, whereas the atypical drugs (such as Clozapine) also block serotonin

Minor tranquilizers, such as the benzodiazepines, used to reduce anxiety, usually by increasing the ability of the neurotransmitter GABA to bind at synapses

A biomedical treatment in which an electric current is passed through the brain to induce a seizure; most often used to treat severe depression

A serious adverse effect of antipsychotic drugs characterized by involuntary motor symptoms such as lip smacking

The alternation of brain tissue in an attempt to alleviate psychological disorders

CHAPTER 15

Health Psychology

OVERVIEW

Use the space provided in this outline to record notes from the textbook as well as from class lectures and discussion. Questions related to the *Psychological Detective* sections in the text have been presented in the outline; use the associated space to respond to the questions and to record your own comments about the issues. *Keywords and terms* from the text have been italicized and inserted in the outline so you can practice writing their definitions. The pages in this study guide are perforated and can be removed for use as study sheets for quizzes and exams.

I. **Health Psychology: An Overview**

        health psychology—

II. **Stress And Illness**

        stress—

        stressor—

    A. The General Adaptation Syndrome

        general adaptation syndrome (GAS)—

      1. Alarm Stage

      2. Resistance Stage

      3. Exhaustion Stage

        psychophysiological disorders—

    B. Sources of Stress

      1. Catastrophes

      2. Major Life Events

Why is there variation among people with respect to the physical and psychological symptoms they develop in response to stress?

    3. Posttraumatic Stress Disorder

        posttraumatic stress disorder (PTSD)—

    4. Everyday Hassles

        conflict—

C. What Makes Events Stressful?

        primary appraisal—

        secondary appraisal—

D. How Stress and Disease May Be Related

        immune system—

        antigens—

    1. Psychoneuroimmunology

III. Lifestyle Influences On Disease Risk

A. Smoking

    1. Who Smokes and Why?

 What factors can account for the trend that the number of smokers has declined over the past decade?

2. Quitting the Smoking Habit

B. Heart Disease

    Type A behavior—

    3. The Toxic Component of Type A Behavior

    4. Reducing the Risk of Heart Disease

C. Acquired Immunodeficiency Syndrome (AIDS)

    human immunodeficiency virus (HIV)—

    acquired immunodeficiency syndrome (AIDS)—

    1. HIV: A Global Perspective

D. Nutrition and Eating

    obesity—

    1. How Does My Weight Compare?

 How could you go about getting meaningful information to use in comparing your weight to others?

    2. The Body Mass Index (BMI)

        body mass index (BMI)—

Calculate your body mass using this formula: BMI = 703 x (weight in pounds) / (height in inches)^2.

3. The Biology of Obesity

According to setpoint theory predict what would happen if you were to reduce daily caloric intake.

4. Social Factors and Weight

5. Dieting

6. Eating Disorders

   anorexia nervosa—

   bulimia nervosa—

IV. Coping with Stress

   coping—

A. Psychological Moderators of Stress
   1. Hardiness

      hardiness—

   2. Explanatory Style

   3. Distraction

4. Social Support

    social support—

5. Sense of Humor

B. Ways of Reducing Arousal: Relaxation and Physical Activity
    1. Relaxation Techniques

        progressive relaxation—

        relaxation response—

        biofeedback—

    2. Physical Activity

    3. Does Physical Activity Reduce Stress?

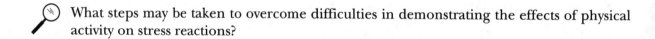 What steps may be taken to overcome difficulties in demonstrating the effects of physical activity on stress reactions?

After you have studied the chapter, you should be able to respond to the following statements and questions to convey your understanding of the material.

1. Describe the General Adaptation Syndrome (GAS).

2. Identify several common sources of stress.

3. Differentiate between risk factors for heart disease that can and cannot be modified.

4. What is the role of nutrition and eating in stress and stress-related issues?

5. What are several steps one can take to cope effectively with stress?

KEY WORD EXERCISE

Fill in the blanks in the following statements with key words and terms from the textbook. Answer as many as you can without referring to your notes or to the book. If you have blanks after thinking about each item, try using your book. The answers are presented after the practice test.

1. A(n) _____ is anything that causes one to adjust and display the nonspecific stress response.

2. When a stressful situation continues beyond the alarm stage, the body moves into the second stage of the general adaptation syndrome, known as the _____ stage.

3. Unpredictable catastrophes, such as fires and hurricanes, are _____ ____ _____.

4. In an _____-_____ conflict, the goal's positive values attract us while its negative features repulse us.

5. _____ is the study of how psychological and physical factors interact to influence the immune system.

6. Reductions in recurring heart attacks are more likely with counseling to reduce _____ ____ behavior or personality in comparison to counseling related to heart disease only.

7. _____ _____ _____ is a numerical index calculated from a person's height and weight that is used to indicate health status and disease risk.

8. Fat cells expand rather easily and are _____ for the body to maintain.

9. The three Cs—commitment, control, and challenge—seem to make the _____ individuals more resistant to the negative effects of stressors.

10. _____ support can play a role in reducing the possible negative side-effects of major life events.

PRACTICE TEST

Circle the letter that corresponds to the *best* alternative for each of the following items. Read each alternative carefully. The answers are presented at the end of this study guide chapter. Be sure to learn *why* each correct alternative is better than the others.

1. Deaths owing to infectious diseases have increased 58% from 1980 to 1992. Much of that increase was the result of:
   a. AIDS.
   b. glucocorticoids.
   c. general adaptation syndrome (GAS).
   d. posttraumatic stress disorder (PTSD).

2. Another name for the well-known fight-or-flight response is:
   a. anxiety.
   b. alarm stage.
   c. resistance stage.
   d. primitive fear response.

3. When demands for adjustment exceed the body's ability to respond, the body enters the:
   a. twilight zone.
   b. posttraumatic syndrome.
   c. exhaustion stage of the GAS.
   d. fight-or-flight response stage.

4. A set of symptoms that may follow deeply disturbing events is called:
   a. nerve-wracking.
   b. adaptation stage.
   c. psychophysiological fear.
   d. posttraumatic stress disorder.

5. Slow-moving traffic, long lines at the supermarket, and lost keys are examples of:
   a. hassles.
   b. annoying habits.
   c. newsworthy events.
   d. symptoms of stress.

6. Determining whether an event is a threat is to ___ as deciding how to deal with the stress-producing situation is to ___.
   a. primary appraisal; secondary appraisal
   b. secondary appraisal; primary appraisal
   c. implementation stage; evaluation stage
   d. decision-action stage; recuperation stage

7. The substances that trigger an immune response are:
   a. illegal.
   b. called antigens.
   c. released by the stressor(s).
   d. hard to identify, but easy to deal with.

8. About ___ percent of smokers smoked their first cigarette before the age of 18.
   a. 13
   b. 50
   c. 76
   d. 90

9. Although someone in the U.S. dies of heart disease about every 34 seconds, many of those deaths can be prevented. Which of the following risk factors **cannot** be modified?
   a. stress
   b. obesity
   c. hypertension
   d. increasing age

10. Hypertension varies as a function of one's:
    a. race.
    b. gender.
    c. lifestyle.
    d. all of the above

11. HDL is to LDL as ___ is to ___.
    a. hypertension; hypothermia
    b. hypothermia; Harpo Marx
    c. "good cholesterol"; "bad cholesterol"
    d. risk for hypertension; risk for glucocorticoids

12. Type A behavior is:
    a. healthy for promoting HDL.
    b. negatively correlated with risk of heart disease.
    c. associated with competitiveness, aggressiveness, and achievement drive.
    d. the first behavior that is shown by humans; by adulthood, humans usually exhibit Type R
       (R is for risk) behavior.

13. ___ accounts for most of the cases of HIV in sub-Sahara Africa.
    a. Incest
    b. Homosexual sex
    c. Intravenous drug use
    d. Unprotected heterosexual sex

14. Obesity is:
    a. having body weight of 20 percent greater than desirable body weight.
    b. often attributed to the prevalence of overweight models for textile goods.
    c. more common in third-world countries than in industrialized Western countries.
    d. the result of genetic programming that can in no way be modified by afflicted individuals.

15. Research findings on environmental and heredity influences on obesity include **all but** which of
    the following?
    a. There was no correlation between the weights of adoptive siblings who share the same en-
       vironment but share no genes.
    b. The correlation between the weights of identical twins varied little whether they were
       raised together or were separated and raised in different environments.
    c. Spouses who lived together did not show increased resemblance in weight as compared
       with engaged couples who had not yet lived together.
    d. All of the above were conclusions of the literature review on influences on obesity.

16. Weight loss early in any diet:
    a. is due almost entirely to loss of water.
    b. is nearly impossible relative to that which occurs later.
    c. is ill-advised; people should put off weight loss until later in a diet.
    d. None of the above are true about weight loss early in a diet.

17. Men comprise ___ of all the cases of *anorexia nervosa.*
    a. 1/10 of 1%
    b. less than 10%
    c. approximately 35%
    d. approximately 60%

18. Which group of subjects experienced the least pain while submerging their arms in a tank of ice-cold water?
    a. the group that imagined scenes such as riding on a merry-go-round at a carnival (distraction group)
    b. the group that imagined they were in a hot desert on a very hot day (reinterpretation group)
    c. the group that reinterpreted the sensation as refreshing by imagining they were hot and tired
    d. All groups showed comparable reduction in pain.

19. Which of the following statements is **true?**
    a. While a sense of humor can be fun it does not seem to buffer stress.
    b. Even a little sense of humor can be helpful in buffering the effects of stressors.
    c. These was a significant difference between people with "average" and "high" senses of humor with respect to incidence of depression as a function of *average* levels of negative life stressors.
    d. These was a significant difference between people with "average" and "high" senses of humor with respect to incidence of depression as a function of *high* levels of negative life stressors.

20. There is converging evidence from correlational and experimental research to indicate that:
    a. exercise aids in dealing with stress.
    b. anaerobic and aerobic exercise are equally helpful in dealing with stress.
    c. exercise is negatively correlated with stress reduction, as was indicated in experimental research.
    d. one must dedicate time exclusively for exercising in order to reap any benefits with respect to stress reduction through exercise.

 ## ANSWERS TO KEY WORD EXERCISE

1. stressor	2. resistance	3. sources of stress
4. approach-avoidance	5. Psychoneuroimmunology	6. Type A
7. Body mass index (BMI)	8. easy	9. hardy
10. Social		

PRACTICE TEST ANSWERS AND EXPLANATIONS

1. a. Acquired immunodeficiency syndrome was responsible for much of the increase.
2. b. The alarm stage of the general adaptation syndrome is the same as the fight-or-flight response.
3. c. The exhaustion stage of the GAS is the third phase of the typical biological response to stressors.

4. d. Posttraumatic stress disorder is characterized by a set of symptoms that may follow deeply disturbing events.

5. a. Hassles are minor everyday occurrences that are distressing, frustrating, and irritating.

6. a. One has to determine whether something is a stress before deciding what to do about it.

7. b. Antigens (e.g., bacteria, fungi, parasites, viruses) are the substances that trigger immune responses.

8. d. About 90% of smokers began smoking by 18. Consequently, more effort is directed toward preventing smoking by people in this age group.

9. d. Age, gender, and heredity cannot be modified. However many of the significant risk factors for heart disease can be modified.

10. d. All of the above are related differentially to hypertension.

11. c. High levels of HDL (high-density lipoprotein) cholesterol are desirable, whereas one does not want high levels of LDL (low-density lipoprotein) cholesterol.

12. c. Type A behavior is associated with competitiveness, aggressiveness, and achievement drive.

13. d. Unprotected heterosexual sex is most closely linked with HIV in sub-Sahara Africa.

14. a. Obesity is having body weight in excess of 20 percent greater than desirable body weight.

15. d. Alternatives a. - c. were all conclusions from the Grilo and Pogue-Geile (1991) study.

16. a. Weight loss early in a diet is due primarily to loss of water.

17. b. Men comprise less than 10% of the cases of anorexia nervosa.

18. d. The three groups (imagination, reinterpretation, and distraction) responded comparably.

19. b. Even a little sense of humor can be helpful in buffering the effects of stressors.

20. a. Exercise aids in dealing with stress.

Key Vocabulary Terms

Cut out and use as study cards; terms appear on
one side and definitions are on the other.

health
psychology

stress

stressor

general
adaptation
syndrome (GAS)

posttraumatic
stress disorder
(PTSD)

conflict

primary
appraisal

secondary
appraisal

Key Vocabulary Terms

Cut out and use as study cards; terms appear on one side and definitions are on the other.

Nonspecific response of the body to any demand made on it	Subfield of psychology that is concerned with how psychological and social variables affect health and illness
Typical series of responses to stressful situations that includes the alarm, resistance, and exhaustion stages	Anything that causes an organism to adjust and display the nonspecific stress response
A state that occurs when an individual must choose between two or more competing goals	Set of symptoms that may follow deeply disturbing events; symptoms include reliving the event, difficulty in concentrating, sleep disturbances, anxiety, and guilt
The second step in coping with stress; consists of deciding how to deal with the stress-producing situation	The first step in coping with stress; consists of determining whether an event is a threat

immune system	antigens
Type A behavior	human immuno-deficiency virus (HIV)
acquired immun-odeficiency syn-drome (AIDS)	obesity
body mass index (BMI)	anorexia nervosa
bulimia nervosa	coping

Foreign substances such as bacteria that trigger an immune response

System that protects the body against foreign substances such as viruses and bacteria

A virus that is usually contracted through the transfer of semen, blood, or vaginal secretions and is the cause of AIDS

Behavioral and personality characteristics that include competitiveness, aggressiveness, achievement drive, and inability to relax

Body weight of 20 percent or more in excess of desirable body weight

Viral disease transmitted via bodily fluids such as blood and semen usually during sexual relations or by sharing needles used by a person infected with the human immunodeficiency virus (HIV); the virus attacks the body's immune system, resulting in vulnerability to infections and diseases, which eventually cause death

A potentially life-threatening eating disorder occurring primarily in adolescent and young adult females; an intense fear of becoming fat leads to self-starvation and weight loss; accompanied by a strong belief that one is fat despite objective evidence to the contrary

A numerical index calculated from a person's height and weight that is used to indicate health status and disease risk

Cognitive and behavioral efforts that are used to reduce the effects of stress

Eating disorder in which a victim alternately consumes large amounts of food (gorging) and then empties the stomach (purging), usually by inducing vomiting

hardiness

social support

progressive
relaxation

relaxation
response

Availability of comfort, recognition, approval, advice, money, or encouragement from others

A psychological characteristic that can reduce the impact of stressors; it consists of commitment, belief in a sense of control, and viewing change as a challenge

Relaxation technique that involves the use of a mental device

Series of exercises consisting of alternately tightening and relaxing major muscle groups

CHAPTER 16

Social Psychology:
The Individual
in Society

Use the space provided in this outline to record notes from the textbook as well as from class lectures and discussion. Questions related to the *Psychological Detective* sections in the text have been presented in the outline; use the associated space to respond to the questions and to record your own comments about the issues. *Keywords and terms* from the text have been italicized and inserted in the outline so you can practice writing their definitions. The pages in this study guide are perforated and can be removed for use as study sheets for quizzes and exams.

I. **Social Psychology and Culture**

        social psychology—

        ethnocentrism—

        individualism—

        collectivism—

II. **How We View Others and Their Behavior**

        impression formation—

    A. Impression Formation

        1. Aspects of the Perceiver

            stereotype—

        Why do stereotypes persist in spite of the fact that individuals in a given category do not share the same personality traits?

            self-fulfilling prophecy—

        2. Aspects of the Actor

a. Appearance

b. Speech

self-disclosure—

c. Nonverbal Communication

d. Prior Information

B. Social Judgments: Attributing Causes to Behavior

attribution—

1. Internal Versus External Causes

Write the attributions you assign to the three events in this space.

a. Distinctiveness

b. Consistency

c. Consensus

d. Attributional Biases

e. The Fundamental Attribution Error

fundamental attribution error—

Identify two circumstances in which internal attributions about someone's behavior were probably incorrect.

f.   The Actor-Perceiver Bias

g.   Self-Serving Bias

How do the attributions made by an actor change as a function of successes and failures at tasks and behaviors?

self-serving bias—

C. Attitudes

   attitudes—

   1.   Components of Attitudes: Affect, Cognition, and Behavior

   2.   Functions of Attitudes

      a.   Ego Defense

      b.   Adjustment

      c.   Knowledge

   3.   Measuring Attitudes

      a.   Likert Scales

         Likert scale—

      b.   Behavioral Measures

   4.   How Are Attitudes Formed?

a. Learning

b. Cognitive Dissonance

cognitive dissonance—

III. Interpersonal Relations

A. Attraction

attraction—

1. Proximity

2. Affect and Emotions

3. Reinforcement

4. Similarity

B. Friendship

friendship—

1. Self-disclosure

C. Love

passionate love—

companionate love—

1. Sex Roles

2. Marital Satisfaction and Dissatisfaction

What are some reasons that abused women (or men) stay in relationships with their abusive spouses?

interdependence theory—

comparison level—

D. Prosocial Behavior: Helping Others
    prosocial behavior—

    altruism—

1. Situational and Personal Influences on Helping Behavior

    bystander effect—

E. Aggression
    aggression—

    hostile aggression—

    instrumental aggression—

1. Biological Views of Aggression

2. Environmental Conditions and Aggression

    frustration-aggression hypothesis—

How do situational variables impact the likelihood that a given experience will be frustrating?

   3. Additional Environmental Cues

   4. Sexual Aggression

IV. Social Influences on Behavior

A. Persuasion

   persuasion—

   1. Source Factors

      a. Expertise

      b. Attractiveness

 Design an experiment to evaluate the role of attractiveness in persuasion. How is the experimental design similar to or different from one that looks into the role of expertise in persuasion?

      c. Trustworthiness

         sleeper effect—

   2. Message Factors

      a. Attention

      b. Drawing Conclusions

      c. Message Acceptance

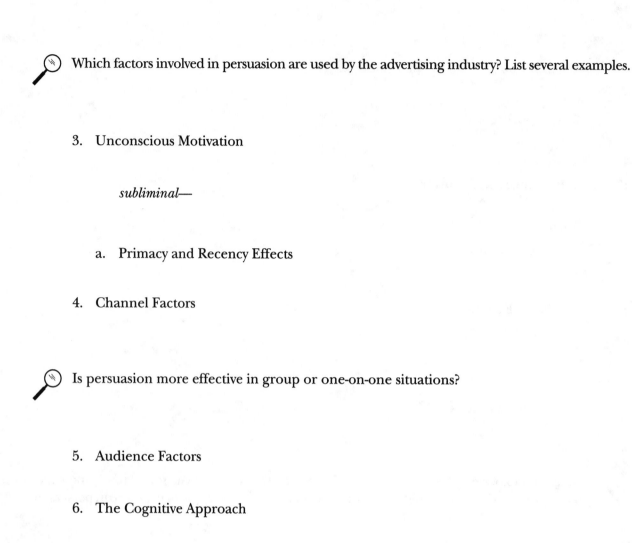

reactance—

Which factors involved in persuasion are used by the advertising industry? List several examples.

3. Unconscious Motivation

    subliminal—

    a. Primacy and Recency Effects

4. Channel Factors

Is persuasion more effective in group or one-on-one situations?

5. Audience Factors

6. The Cognitive Approach

B. Obedience

    obedience—

C. Conformity and Compliance

    conformity—

What experimental control condition(s) were necessary for Asch to support his claim about conformity in the line experiment?

risky-shift phenomenon—

group polarization—

compliance—

foot-in-the-door effect—

reciprocity—

V. The Individual as Part of a Social Group

A. Social Facilitation

    social facilitation—

B. Social Loafing

    social loafing—

C. Audiences and Coactors

    coactors—

    1. Deindividuation

        deindividuation—

D. Group Interactions and Group Decisions

    1. Group Formation and Effectiveness

    2. Brain Storming

brainstorming—

🔍 Why are fewer ideas generated in group brainstorming sessions than when people work alone?

3. Groupthink

    groupthink—

E. Prejudice and Discrimination
    1. Prejudice

        prejudice—

🔍 Where, given that most prejudices are general, do specific prejudice-related comments and behaviors come from?

    2. Discrimination

        discrimination—

    3. Sources and Functions of Prejudice

        a. Social Function

        b. Emotional Function

    4. How to Reduce Prejudice

After you have studied the chapter, you should be able to respond to the following statements and questions to convey your understanding of the material.

1. How does the presence of others, or being part of a group, influence individuals' behavior?

2. Discuss several factors contributing to patterns of social judgment or attributions.

3. What variables are important in developing and maintaining interpersonal relationships?

4. Differentiate between *persuasion, obedience,* and *conformity and compliance* as social influences on behavior.

5. Compare and contrast social facilitation and social loafing.

6. How do groups influence decision-making?

7. Discuss the development and maintenance of prejudice and discrimination as a social psychologist.

✳ KEY WORD EXERCISE

Fill in the blanks in the following statements with key words and terms from the textbook. Answer as many as you can without referring to your notes or to the book. If you have blanks after thinking about each item, try using your book. The answers are presented after the practice test.

1. Research on _____-_____, the amount of personal information a person is willing to share with others, indicates that the more a person reveals, the more positive others' impressions are.

2. The internal attribution bias that involves attending more closely to a behavior than the context in which it occurs is called the _____ _____ _____.

3. Psychologists define _____ as a form of interpersonal attraction that is governed by an implicit set of rules.

4. _____ _____ stresses the costs and rewards involved in interpersonal relationships.

5. Suzy becomes more aggressive when she is frustrated than when she is not frustrated. This trend supports the _____-_____ _____.

6. _____ is the use of social influence to cause people to change attitudes or behavior.

7. Milgram's experiment, the Jonestown massacre, and the behaviors of Nazis in Germany all provide examples of people initiating or changing behavior in response to direct commands. This change in behavior is called _____.

8. A mechanic has offered to provide several checks on your vehicle free of charge while it is in the shop for an oil change. This is done in hopes that in exchange for this added service you will _____ and will have anything that shows up from the checks repaired at that shop.

9. The blindfolded tug-of-war experiment revealed what students who have worked on class projects with other students already knew. Both the experiment and real-life experiences reveal that _____ _____ occurs when groups work on a task for which there is no individual evaluation.

10. Scott and Meri tried giving candy to trick-or-treaters last Halloween on the honor system. They put a few bowls of candy on their porch, and went to a friend's house for a party. Much to their chagrin, when they returned the candy and the bowls were gone. The likelihood the bowls were stolen was probably increased as a function of the _____ that occurred when the trick-or-treaters donned their costumes.

✳ PRACTICE TEST

Circle the letter that corresponds to the *best* alternative for each of the following items. Read each alternative carefully. The answers are presented at the end of this study guide chapter. Be sure to learn *why* each correct alternative is better than the others.

1. Jean studies *impression formation*. In other words, she is interested in:
   a. how people present themselves.
   b. how people form impressions about others.
   c. various techniques that are used in embossing paper.
   d. why people resist forming impressions on their first exposure to others.

2. A stereotype is:
   a. a brand of hi-fidelity equipment.
   b. a set of beliefs about members of a particular group.
   c. an individual's decision to share personal information.
   d. a bias toward members of one's group (i.e., the ingroup).

3. Carl and his friends went to watch the comedian-hypnotist at a local theater. The entertainer selected Carl as an "assistant". Soon, Carl was clucking like a chicken on stage, playing the role "the human plank", and being generally entertaining. He had not planned to participate, but when asked to, played the part well. Which of the following was at work in influencing his behavior?
   a. self-disclosure
   b. attribution theory
   c. the self-fulfilling prophecy
   d. the fundamental attribution of hypnotists error

4. In an experiment on ___, students in a class were given descriptions of a visiting lecturer that portrayed him as either *warm* or *cold*. After the lecture, those who had been told he was warm rated his presentation more favorably than those who were told he was cold.
   a. the self-serving bias
   b. cognitive dissonance
   c. the effects of prior information
   d. the fundamental attribution error

5. The tendency to make internal attributions when we are successful and external attributions when we fail is called the:
   a. self-serving bias.
   b. cognitive dissonance.
   c. unconscious motivation.
   d. fundamental attribution error.

6. Which of the following was **not** identified in your textbook as a component of *attitude?*
   a. affect
   b. behavior
   c. cognition
   d. environment

7. You just filled out a questionnaire on which you to rated the degree to which you agreed or disagreed with a variety of statements. The questionnaire employed:
   a. Likert scales.
   b. behavioral measures.
   c. minimum wage workers.
   d. the yes-no response scale.

8. An aversive state produced when an individual has two incompatible thoughts simultaneously is called:
   a. confusion.
   b. attitude clash.
   c. thought distraction.
   d. cognitive dissonance.

9. Proximity to others is ___ to the establishment of friendships.
   a. not related
   b. positively related
   c. negatively related
   d. all of the above

10. Which of the following was **not** identified as a contributing factor in attraction?
    a. IQ
    b. similarity
    c. reinforcement
    d. affect and emotions

11. Strong emotional reactions are to ___ as commitment is to ___.
    a. friendship; love
    b. passionate love; companionate love
    c. companionate love; passionate love
    d. compassionate love; dispassionate love

12. Altruism is one of the most widely studied forms of ___.
    a. prosocial behavior
    b. cognitive dissonance
    c. interpersonal attraction
    d. social influence on behavior

13. The tendency for a group of people to be less likely than an individual to provide assistance to a person in trouble is called:
    a. the bystander effect.
    b. the individual effect.
    c. the bystander intervention effect.
    d. the individual intervention effect.

14. ___ aggression is to the specific intent of harming another as ___ aggression is to harming others in the process of achieving another goal.
    a. Implicit; explicit
    b. Outright; concealed
    c. Instrumental; hostile
    d. Hostile; instrumental

15. Source factors that contribute to one's persuasiveness include **all but** which of the following?
    a. expertise
    b. attractiveness
    c. trustworthiness
    d. all of the above

16. ___ is another name for what is popularly known as "reverse psychology."
    a. Reactance
    b. Unconscious reversing
    c. Subliminal transference
    d. None of the above; psychologists do not describe the constellation of phenomena popularly described as "reverse psychology."

17. The *foot-in-the-door* technique is a good example of persuasion that:
    a. backfires when persuaders say things they should not say.
    b. gets cut off by the audience before the persuader's message has been heard entirely.
    c. is more effective in a face-to-face situation than with one person addressing many people.
    d. is based on another persuasion technique that involves telling lies in order to maintain audience attention.

18. In psychology, the term *confederate* refers to someone:
    a. acting for the experimenter.
    b. who fought for the South in the Civil War.
    c. who attempts to block the federation by subjects in an experiment.
    d. who realizes the goal of an experiment and produces meaningless data.

19. Asch's "line experiment" was designed to provide insight into:
    a. the phenomenon of conformity.
    b. factors contributing to one's persuasiveness.
    c. why subjects in Milgram's experiment acted as they did.
    d. a perceptual phenomenon that was originally studied by Gestalt psychologists.

20. ___ is a phenomenon in which group decision making enhances or amplifies the original opinions of the group's members.
    a. Reciprocity
    b. Risk taking
    c. Deindividuation
    d. Group polarization

21. People will wind fishing line more quickly when they are competing against others at the same task than when they are racing against the clock. This is an illustration of:
    a. social conformity.
    b. social facilitation.
    c. bystander intervention.
    d. a hypothetical construct.

22. The activities of the Ku Klux Klan and lynch mobs reflect ___ in action.
    a. groupthink
    b. social loafing
    c. outgroup bias
    d. none of the above

23. The free expression of ideas by members of a group to solve a problem is called:
    a. risky-shift.
    b. expressionism.
    c. brainstorming.
    d. free determinism.

24. ___ frequently results in behaviors that adversely affect members of a targeted group.
    a. Altruism
    b. Prejudice
    c. Groupthink
    d. Brainstorming

25. Because the majority of psychological research is conducted in the U.S., many of the results have been seen through ___ eyes.
    a. angry
    b. naked
    c. geocentric
    d. ethnocentric

 ## ANSWERS TO KEY WORD EXERCISE

1. self-disclosure
2. fundamental attribution error
3. friendship
4. Interdependence theory
5. frustration-aggression hypothesis
6. Persuasion
7. obedience
8. reciprocate
9. social loafing
10. deindividuation

 ## PRACTICE TEST ANSWERS AND EXPLANATIONS

1. b. Impression formation is the process of forming an opinion about another person.

2. b. Stereotypes are beliefs about members of particular groups.

3. c. The self-fulfilling prophecy is a phenomenon whereby expectations elicit behaviors in others that confirm those expectations.

4. c. The classic experiment was designed to study the effects of prior information about others.

5. a. The self-serving bias involves crediting one's self for one's successes and blaming circumstances for one's failures.

6. d. Environment was not identified as a component of attitude.

7. a. Likert scales are tools for measuring extent of agreement (e.g., 1 = strongly disagree...7 = strongly agree).

8. d. *Cognitive dissonance* involves two simultaneous, incompatible thoughts or cognitions.

9. b. Mere proximity to others increases the likelihood that people will become friends.

10. a. Age was not listed among the variables that contribute to interpersonal attraction.

11. b. Passionate love involves strong emotional reactions; companionate love involves lasting commitment.

12. a. Prosocial behavior is that which benefits society or helps others; altruism is prosocial behavior that is done voluntarily with no anticipation of reward.

13. a. The *bystander effect* describes the decreased likelihood of people who are part of groups (as compared to individuals) to come to the assistance others.

14. d. Hostile aggression involves harming others as the primary goal. Instrumental aggression involves harming others when striving to reach a primary goal.

15. d. Each of the items in the list play a role in determining one's persuasiveness.

16. a. *Reactance* is the tendency to react in the opposite direction to a persuasive message.

17. c. Most forms of persuasion are more effective in face-to-face situations; this is true with the foot-in-the-door technique.

18. a. A confederate is someone who, unbeknownst to the subject(s), acts as a subject in an experiment.

19. a. Asch's experiment provided surprising results regarding conformity.

20. d. Group polarization involves the enhancement or amplification of the original opinions of the group's members.

21. b. Social facilitation involves improved performance in the presence of others.

22. a. The activities of these groups reflect groupthink. Groupthink is also thought to have been involved in decisions to initiate or escalate wartime strategies (including some well-known poor decisions).

23. c. Brainstorming is the free expression of ideas in a group. However, it is noteworthy that many people are more creative when brainstorming alone.

24. b. Prejudice most frequently involves judging others on the basis of negative stereotypes.

25. d. Ethnocentrism is the belief that one's own country or culture is superior to all other countries or cultures. Failure to consider other cultures when designing research studies is an extension of this.

Key Vocabulary Terms

Cut out and use as study cards; terms appear on
one side and definitions are on the other.

social psychology	ethnocentrism
individualism	collectivism
impression formation	stereotype
self-fulfilling prophecy	self-disclosure

Key Vocabulary Terms

Cut out and use as study cards; terms appear on one side and definitions are on the other.

Belief that one's own country or culture is superior to all other countries and cultures	Study of the causes, types, and consequences of human interaction
Placing group goals above individual goals	Placing one's own goals above those of the group
Set of beliefs about members of a particular group	The process of forming an opinion about another person
An individual's decision to share personal information	Phenomenon whereby our expectations elicit behaviors in others that confirm those expectations

attribution	fundamental attribution error
self-serving bias	attitudes
Likert scale	cognitive dissonance
attraction	friendship
passionate love	compassionate love

The tendency to attribute behaviors to internal causes	The process of assigning causes to events and behaviors
Evaluative judgments about objects, people, and thoughts that include affective, knowledge, and behavioral components	The tendency to make internal attributions when we are successful and external attributions when we fail
Aversive state produced when an individual has two incompatible thoughts or cognitions simultaneously	Questionnaire that requires individuals to indicate their degree of agreement or disagreement with a set of statements
Form of interpersonal attraction that is governed by an implicit set of rules	The extent to which we like or dislike other people
Long-lasting form of love that involves commitment	Transitory form of love that involves strong emotional reactions, sexual desires, and fantasies

interdependence theory	comparison level
prosocial behavior	altruism
bystander effect	aggression
hostile aggression	instrumental aggression
frustration-aggression hypothesis	persuasion

General outcome expected from a particular relationship

Theory of interpersonal relationships that stresses the costs and rewards involved

Helping behavior performed voluntarily with no anticipation of reward

Behavior that benefits society or helps others

Physical or psychological behavior that is performed with the intent of doing harm

The tendency for a group of bystanders to be less likely than an individual to provide assistance to a person in trouble

Aggression that causes harm in the process of achieving another goal

Aggressive behavior that is performed with the specific intent of harming another person

The use of social influences to cause people to change attitudes or behavior

The hypothesis that aggression is likely to occur when a person is frustrated

sleeper effect	reactance
subliminal	obedience
conformity	risky-shift phenomenon
group polarization	compliance
foot-in-the-door effect	reciprocity

The tendency to react in the opposite direction to a persuasive message when compliance might place limits on personal freedom

Occurs when the message and its source become detached; messages from sources low in expertise, attractiveness, and trustworthiness may increase in effectiveness

Initiating or changing a behavior in response to a direct command of an authority

Below the level of conscious awareness

The finding that groups make riskier decisions than individuals

Initiating or changing a behavior in response to indirect social pressures

Initiating or changing a behavior in response to a request

Phenomenon in which group decision making enhances or amplifies the original opinions of the group's members

Tactic for increasing compliance that involves doing something for others to create a feeling of obligation on their part

Phenomenon in which a person who has agreed to a small request is more likely to comply with a subsequent larger request

social facilitation	social loafing
coactors	deindividuation
brainstorming	groupthink
prejudice	discrimination

The tendency to exert less effort when working on a group task that does not involve evaluation of individual participants

An increase in performance that occurs when other people are present

Phenomenon in which the presence of a group results in a loss of personal identity and a decrease in responsibility

Other people who are present and are engaging in the same behaviors as an individual at the same time

The tendency to make decisions intended primarily to promote the harmony of the group

Free expression of ideas by members of a group to solve a problem

Behaviors that adversely affect members of a particular group

Judging a person on the basis of stereotypes about the group to which the person belongs

CHAPTER 17

Industrial and Organizational Psychology

Use the space provided in this outline to record notes from the textbook as well as from class lectures and discussion. Questions related to the *Psychological Detective* sections in the text have been presented in the outline; use the associated space to respond to the questions and to record your own comments about the issues. *Keywords and terms* from the text have been italicized and inserted in the outline so you can practice writing their definitions. The pages in this study guide are perforated and can be removed for use as study sheets for quizzes and exams.

I. **Industrial/Organizational Psychology**

industrial/organizational psychology—

II. **Personnel Psychology**

personnel psychology—

 Interviews have poor validity for determining which applicants for a position will work well. Nevertheless, employers continue to use this selection technique. Identify a few causes for continued use of interviews, given how poorly interviewing works.

A. Using Personality Tests in Selecting Police Officers

B. Training

training—

C. Performance Appraisal

performance appraisal—

III. **Organizational Psychology**

organizational psychology—

A. Motivation

B. Job Satisfaction

IV. Human-Factors Psychology

human-factors psychology—

A. Human-Machine System

B. Workplace Design

engineering anthropometry—

C. Safety

After you have studied the chapter, you should be able to respond to the following statements and questions to convey your understanding of the material.

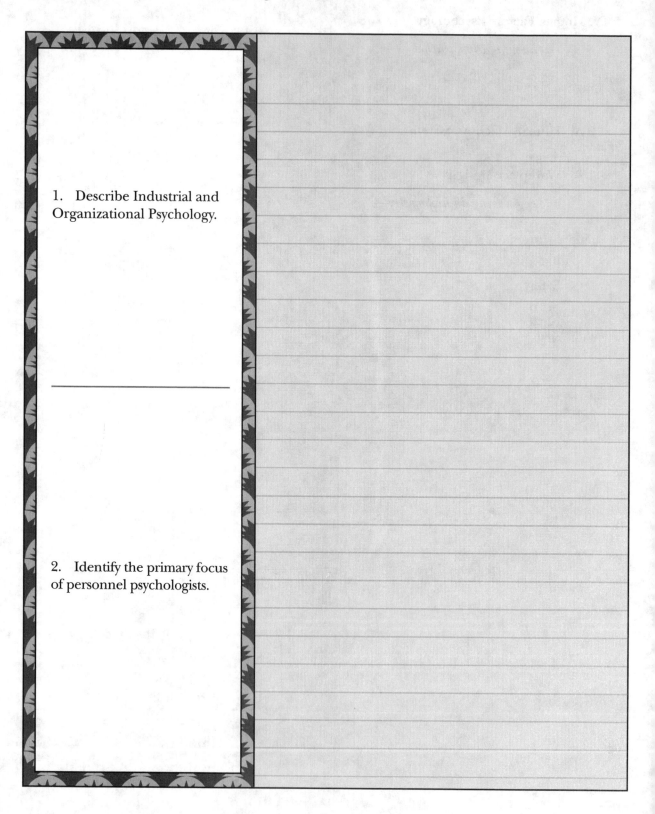

1. Describe Industrial and Organizational Psychology.

2. Identify the primary focus of personnel psychologists.

3. How are training and performance appraisal used in employment settings to assure worker efficiency and productivity?

4. What factors contribute to the likelihood that one will be satisfied with one's job?

5. Discuss the variety of topics human-factors psychologists study.

✹ KEY WORD EXERCISE

Fill in the blanks in the following statements with key words and terms from the textbook. Answer as many as you can without referring to your notes or to the book. If you have blanks after thinking about each item, try using your book. The answers are presented after the practice test.

1. _____ _____ involves measurement of human physical characteristics and development of machines to fit those characteristics.

2. The _____ _____ _____ is used in U.S., Canada, and Australia in selecting police officers.

3. The deliberate and planned process by which employees are exposed to learning experiences designed to teach new skills and improve job performance is called _____.

4. Using a red light on a machine to indicate that one should stop doing something is an example of good use of the _____ ___ _____.

5. The U.S. Army's M-1 Abrams tank was used to illustrate poor _____ _____.

✹ PRACTICE TEST

Circle the letter that corresponds to the *best* alternative for each of the following items. Read each alternative carefully. The answers are presented at the end of this study guide chapter. Be sure to learn *why* each correct alternative is better than the others.

1. *Army Alpha* is to *Army Beta* as ___ is to ___.
   a. soldier; officer
   b. literate; illiterate
   c. boot camp; retirement
   d. 1st Battalion; 2nd Battalion

2. A key responsibility of personnel psychologists is to determine which of the following?
   a. skills
   b. abilities
   c. knowledge
   d. all of the above

3. The best interviews are:
   a. structured.
   b. situational.
   c. both a. and b.
   d. neither a. nor b.

4. Employers screen prospective employees for drug use because:
   a. drug use correlates with absenteeism and turnover.
   b. most state governments mandate that the employers do so.
   c. the federal government mandates that all employers do so.
   d. None of the above are true.

5. According to the textbook, which of the following types of measures is not used in evaluating a training program?
   a. Reaction Measures
   b. Learning Measures
   c. Behavior Measures
   d. Perception Measures

6. Samantha has been with her employer for six months. She has just been handed feedback ratings from her boss on a series of criteria. This is part of the process of:
   a. training.
   b. applicant screening.
   c. performance appraisal.
   d. a formal exit interview.

7. Clive studies labor unions, including rules and benefits of membership, as well as the social dynamics of them. Clive is a(n):
   a. personnel psychologist
   b. industrial psychologist.
   c. organizational psychologist.
   d. human-factors psychologist.

8. Expectancy suggests employees are concerned with *valance, instrumentality, and expectancy.* This combination means:
   a. the average employee is not smart enough to know what they want.
   b. workers will be motivated if they believe they have the means and opportunity to succeed.
   c. that employees are bound to be dissatisfied with their jobs because one cannot have all three.
   d. that worker motivation is equivalent to a given employee's desirability by another employer.

9. The most widely researched work attitude in organizational psychology is:
   a. job satisfaction.
   b. employer loyalty.
   c. employee benefits appreciation.
   d. worker efficiency (expressed as a ratio of worker cost to worker productivity).

10. Greg's patio door baffles most of his houseguests. For some reason, everyone tries to get it to open out, when actually it was made to open into his house. The designers of the door should:
    a. consult human-factors psychologists.
    b. carefully consider using a more effective training program.
    c. go to Greg's house and see whether it was installed properly.
    d. approach the labor union for the company that made the door and consult about plant conditions.

11. Some psychologists are concerned with distinguishing workplace accidents that occur as the result of unsafe conditions from those that occur as the result of unsafe acts. Reducing the likelihood of accidents by modifying some aspects of work conditions, by redesigning tools and machines is:
    a. the ergonomic approach.
    b. more effective than prohibiting unsafe acts.
    c. not worth the trade-off when one considers efficiency.
    d. usually done at the expense of workers' wages and benefits.

ANSWERS TO KEY WORD EXERCISE

1. Engineering anthropometry
2. California Psychological Inventory (CPI)
3. training
4. principle of compatibility
5. workplace design

 PRACTICE TEST ANSWERS AND EXPLANATIONS

1. b. The *Army Alpha* was the first large-scale group intelligence test; the *Army Beta* was developed subsequently for testing illiterate and non-English-speaking soldiers.

2. d. Personnel psychologists try to determine the knowledge, skills, and abilities of job applicants.

3. c. To be effective interviews should be structured (every candidate gets asked the same questions) and situational (providing job-related questions that require candidates to "think on their feet").

4. a. Though it is controversial many employers screen applicants for drug use because it is useful in predicting absenteeism and employee turnover.

5. d. The fourth type of measure of training programs is *results measures*.

6. c. Performance appraisal involves evaluation of a person's functioning on job-related tasks.

7. c. Organizational psychology is a blend of work-related psychology, social psychology, human relations, and business.

8. b. Workers need to have the means and opportunities to succeed in pursuit of a desired outcome.

9. a. Job satisfaction is the most widely studied attitude in organizational psychology.

10. a. Human-factors psychologists focus on the designing of equipment and machines for human use.

11. a. The ergonomic approach involves focusing on the fit and design of tools, machines, and instruments with which humans interact.

Key Vocabulary Terms

Cut out and use as study cards; terms appear on
one side and definitions are on the other.

industrial/
organizational
(I/O) psychology

personnel
psychology

training

performance
appraisal

organizational
psychology

human-factors
psychology

engineering
anthropometry

Key Vocabulary Terms

Cut out and use as study cards; terms appear on one side and definitions are on the other.

The study and analysis of individual differences in relation to jobs and the development and maintenance of an organization's human resources (its workers)

The scientific study and application of psychology to the work place

The evaluation of a person's functioning on job-related tasks; this usually includes some formal assessment and feedback

The deliberate and planned process by which employees are exposed to learning experiences designed to teach new skills and improve job performance

The science of engineering and designing equipment and machines for human use and modifying human behavior so that workers can operate machines more efficiently (also known as engineering psychology and ergonomics)

The scientific study of organizations and their social processes

The measurement of human physical characteristics and development of machines and equipment to fit those characteristics